An Advaitic Modernity?

An Advaitic Modernity?

Raimon Panikkar and Philosophical Theology

Andrew D. Thrasher

LEXINGTON BOOKS/FORTRESS ACADEMIC
Lanham • Boulder • New York • London

Published by Lexington Books/Fortress Academic
Lexington Books is an imprint of The Rowman & Littlefield Publishing Group, Inc.
4501 Forbes Boulevard, Suite 200, Lanham, Maryland 20706
www.rowman.com

86-90 Paul Street, London EC2A 4NE, United Kingdom

Copyright © 2024 by The Rowman & Littlefield Publishing Group, Inc.

All rights reserved. No part of this book may be reproduced in any form or by any electronic or mechanical means, including information storage and retrieval systems, without written permission from the publisher, except by a reviewer who may quote passages in a review.

British Library Cataloguing in Publication Information Available

Library of Congress Cataloging-in-Publication Data Available
ISBN 9781978716261 (cloth) | ISBN 9781978716278 (electronic)

♾️ The paper used in this publication meets the minimum requirements of American National Standard for Information Sciences—Permanence of Paper for Printed Library Materials, ANSI/NISO Z39.48-1992.

Contents

Acknowledgments and Dedication	vii
Introduction: Raimon Panikkar as Philosophical Theologian	1
Chapter 1: The Cosmotheandric Intuition: From Metaphysics to Theology	9
Chapter 2: Panikkar's Relational Ontology: Being, Relation, and Ontonomy	25
Chapter 3: Heidegger's Ontology, Panikkar's Advaita: Ontology, Metaphysics, and Tempiternity	45
Chapter 4: Desmond's Metaxu, Panikkar's Advaita: Opening to Transcendence	67
Chapter 5: The Problems and Promises of a Postmodern Ontology: Theological Critiques of Modernity	89
Chapter 6: Postmodern Ontology at the Limits of Modernity: Three Genealogies of Modernity	111
Chapter 7: Panikkar's Postsecular Vision: A Panikkarean Reading of Charles Taylor	141
Conclusion: An Advaitic Modernity?	159
Bibliography	167
Index	177
About the Author	181

Acknowledgments and Dedication

"Andy, *is Panikkar your God?*" Such were the offensively and cynically intended, yet insightful words of a close friend in 2014 when I was deep in my idolatry of Raimon Panikkar. While my ultimate concern has shifted, this book reflects an enduring engagement with the thought and work of Raimon Panikkar that, even with the publication of this book, has not ended—I plan to write two more books on Panikkar, one dialoguing Panikkar with Christian theology and the other with continental philosophy. These projects will take several more years to come, but I hope that this book instigates the legitimacy of Raimon Panikkar for Western philosophy and theology.

This book benefited from several academic mentors, friends, and conferences where I have been invited and warmly received into Panikkarean scholarship and friendship. Joseph Prabhu, Fred Dallmayr, and Abraham Velez de Cea each motivated me in the pursuit of connections between Heidegger and Panikkar. Young-chan Ro and Anthony Savari Raj (my first two mentors in Panikkar) have been immensely supportive of my pursuits of Panikkar. Peter Phan, Michiko Yusa, Gerard Hall, and Amos Yong have been especially supportive of a junior scholar of Panikkar. I am especially thankful to Milena Carrara Pavan and the Vivarium foundation for an honorable mention and a memorable trip to Catalonia with several other young Panikkar scholars. The honor shown to me and the trip were life changing. The friendships cultivated and experiences shared with my fellow Panikkar scholars in Spain are treasured memories of life and belonging. The cover art is of the church in Tavertet, Spain, where Panikkar's spent the latter part of his life.

Many of the chapters in this book saw light at various conferences and by and large appeared in the (longer) manuscript that won an honorable mention in the International Panikkar Prize of 2022. Parts of chapters one, two, five, and seven were presented at various conferences in meetings of the Society of Asian and Comparative Philosophy at Bath Spa University, UK, in 2019, and at the American Academy of Religion in San Antonio, TX, in 2021, and at the tenth annual meeting of the Polish Philosophical Congress in Poznan, viii *Acknowledgments and Dedication*

Poland, in 2015. Parts of various chapters were adapted from my two master's theses on Panikkar, written at George Mason University in 2014 and Regent University in 2017. I only wish the late Michael D. Palmer were alive to celebrate this book with me.

Thanks also goes to my doctoral supervisors David Cheetham and Nicholas Adams who have become supportive friends and mentors in all of my academic endeavors. Thank you for silently acknowledging my pursuits, even while I labored under your guidance. Your shepherding has made me a better writer and I have often applied what we did with my dissertation on Charles Taylor to this book. The reader has much to thank them for, even while its errors are still my own. Thanks also to my cousin, Allen Wright Thrasher, who is an expert on Advaita Vedānta, who copyedited early versions of this book. I hope there will be another academic in the family that I may pay it forward to in the next generation.

This book is dedicated to Henry T. Thrasher and Young-chan Ro, a father and a mentor who have become friends that I love and trust most dearly. Thank you both. Finally, I would like to acknowledge the permissions of the following publishers for quoted materials:

Hall, Gerard Vincent. "Raimon Panikkar's Hermeneutics of Religious Pluralism." Catholic University of America. Ann Arbor, MI: UMI Dissertation Services, 1994.

Introduction

Raimon Panikkar as Philosophical Theologian

What does Raimon Panikkar have to do with contemporary postmodern philosophical theology? This question should cause us to pause. Was not Raimon Panikkar the pioneer in inter-religious dialogue? If so, what would he have to offer to postmodern philosophical theology? Indeed, what do we mean by postmodern philosophical theology? This book understands postmodern philosophical theology to include in particular the writings and work of those found within, alongside, and/or sympathetic to those sensibilities found among the Radical Orthodoxy Movement. In particular, this book engages primarily with the work of John Milbank and Catherine Pickstock, as well as the work of Charles Taylor, William Desmond, and to a lesser extent David Bentley Hart. Furthermore, each of these theological and philosophical voices are indebted to the continental tradition of twentieth century philosophy. In light of the indebtedness of postmodern philosophical theology to this continental tradition, this book will utilize at least three figures (Martin Heidegger, Jean-Luc Nancy, and Emmanuel Levinas) in this tradition that offer important background frameworks, insights, and/or dialogues with both Panikkar and postmodern philosophical theology.

And yet, why Panikkar? What does he have to do with this tradition? Many know of Panikkar as a unique religious pluralist who offered important catalysts into inter-religious dialogue in his personal heritage as a meeting place between East and West. Born to a Hindu Father and Catalonian Catholic mother, Panikkar embodied two religious sensibilities in his blood. He mediated between Catholic theology of the mid-twentieth century, Continental philosophy (especially Heidegger), and Hindu and Buddhist philosophy and theology. Arguably, Panikkar's works in inter-religious dialogue are his most well-known, stemming from his deep engagement in Hindu philosophy,

2   *Introduction*

scripture, and theology, as well as his inclusivistic-turned-pluralistic under-standings of Christ. To a lesser extent his resourcement of Hindu and Buddhist thought reflect an early and similar sensibility to that found in the discipline of Comparative Theology associated with Francis Clooney. But what is often overlooked in scholarly engagements with Raimon Panikkar are his philosophical and theological contributions. Throughout his *Opera Omnia*, his work on religious philosophy and theology makes up some of the most substantial portions of his corpus. Arguably, these are some of the more underdeveloped aspects of his work.

With this in mind, this book addresses the dialogical intersection between Raimon Panikkar, Martin Heidegger, and contemporary postmodern philo-sophical theology. But this book analyzes and appraises Raimon Panikkar's contributions to Western philosophy as an Indian postmodern philosophical theologian. That is, while Panikkar was trained in Western philosophy and Catholic theology, the distinctive flavor of his contributions to philosophi-cal theology finds its resources in his Indian heritage. At the crossroads of Panikkar's Indian and European heritage are important insights into Western philosophical theology. These insights are developed throughout this book as an advaitic interpretation of contemporary philosophical theology. It posits the possibility of an advaitic modernity—a mutual fecundation and dialogical reformation between Panikkar and Western philosophical theology. It does so by articulating the central contributions of his cosmotheandric understand-ing of reality, dialoguing and contextualizing Panikkar with contemporary Western phenomenology and metaphysics (Martin Heidegger and William Desmond), and creatively articulating his (unlikely) confluences in late mod-ern philosophy and theology (the Radical Orthodoxy Movement, Jean-Luc Nancy, David Bentley Hart, Emmanuel Levinas, and Charles Taylor).

Raimon Panikkar offers rich resources in rethinking the intersections of theology, metaphysics, and philosophy in late modernity. Within Panikkar's philosophical and theological vision, it is worth examining how he fits into late modernity as a dialogical reformer who offers an Indian spin upon Western thought. This advaitic spin addresses how, through confluences and dialogues, Panikkar's thought applies to the problem of modernity. The problem of modernity is precisely the eclipse of religion and transcendence in the Western historical processes of secularization and the rejection of divine immanence. The problem for Panikkar is the modern overemphasis on divine transcendence which eclipses the possibility of divine immanence—the latter of which is posed throughout this book as Panikkar's answer to the problem of modernity.

This book poses the question of how non-dualism, or *advaita*, offers answers to the theological problems of modernity and how it offers a critique of modernity. Central to the question of an advaitic modernity is the emphasis on divine immanence and the collapse or removal of the ontological distinction between God and creation. This book argues that Panikkar's advaitic modernity envisions a cosmotheandric vision of reality that challenges modernity in its eclipse of divine transcendence through his emphasis on the ontological participation of finite being in the infinitude of divine immanence. Tied to the argument for an advaitic modernity are several themes and questions that circulate throughout this book. In particular are Panikkar's notions of cosmotheandric ontonomy, sacred secularity, and a relational ontology.

Whereas cosmotheandric ontonomy refers to the inter-in-dependency of reality as co-constitutively cosmic/material, human, and divine, it also entails the irreducibility of reality to one dimension of reality. Cosmotheandric ontonomy implies the harmony, co-constitution, inter-relationality, and co-participation of each dimension of reality with one another as well as within one another—without reducing reality to one dimension. As chapters one and two argue, Panikkar's cosmotheandric ontonomy entails a trinitarian logic and structure that is applied to his understanding of reality. Panikkar's notion of sacred secularity entails the idea that humans are liturgical, ritual beings, and that secular action may be sacralized through faith into worship, just as religious worship finds its secularization in and through human action and work. Sacred secularity entails the religious sacralization of the secular as well as the secularization of the religious in and through human action. Finally, this book develops Panikkar's relational ontology as a hermeneutical key to understanding Panikkar's cosmotheandric understanding of reality, as well as what may be called Panikkar's advaitic understanding of Being. A major question of this book is centered around Heidegger's ontological question—"what is the meaning of Being?"—and develops Panikkar's appropriation of Heidegger's ontology, like several of the philosophers and theologians addressed in this book, and uses it as a catalyst for theological and/or philosophical engagement.

But key to Panikkar's ontology is the centrality of relationality and the question of how to understand the relationship between transcendence and immanence when the ontological distinction between God and creation, transcendence and immanence, is rejected. Indeed, Panikkar fits squarely in the sensibilities of the *Nouvelle Theologie* tradition's argument that the problem of modernity is a theological problem that rejects transcendence and/or over-infinitizes transcendence to the point that God becomes so transcendent that God is no longer accessible to or in the immanence of creation.[1] While Henri de Lubac's insights into the eclipse of transcendence in modern Catholic theology are presupposed here, this book assumes that Panikkar also assumes this position as central to his critique of modernity—all the while positing a recovery of divine immanence and rejection of the ontological distinction

4   *Introduction*

between God and creation (both of which are influenced by Panikkar's deep dwelling in South Asian traditions).

Western philosophy and theology can learn much from Panikkar. This book argues in chapter one that Panikkar's cosmotheandric metaphysics poses particular insights into his theology of religions in ways that metaphysics serves as a foil for particular cosmotheandric theologies found among religious traditions. Furthermore, chapter two argues that Panikkar's cosmotheandric ontonomy offers religious innovations to both Martin Heidegger and Jean-Luc Nancy's fundamental ontology and Charles Taylor's moral ontology in ways that takes the notion of a relational ontology beyond the questions of the meaning of being and the good life into a participatory ontology that is ontologically constituted by a cosmotheandric experience of reality. Chapter three argues that Panikkar resolves problems in Martin Heidegger's onto-theology by offering an understanding of the relationship between eternity, Being, and time through his idea of tempiternity. Chapter four argues for an analogous confluence between Panikkar and the work of William Desmond around an understanding of immanence as open to transcendence, but from an advaitic perspective where divine immanence proposes a way of participating in the divine. Furthermore, chapter five and six argue that Panikkar's advaitic critique of modernity problematizes the problems, promises, and limits of a postmodern ontology in ways that articulates agonistic and unlikely confluences between Panikkar, Charles Taylor, and those found among or alongside the Radical Orthodoxy Movement. Finally, chapter seven argues that Panikkar resolves problems in Charles Taylor's accounts of the secularization of ordinary life through a development of his idea of sacred secularity and the re-mythologization of ordinary life. As such, the reader should read chapters one and two together to understand Panikkar's cosmotheandric understanding of reality. Chapters three and four ought to be read together to understand Panikkar's advaitic metaphysical vision. Chapters five and six ought to be read together to understand his advaitic critique of modernity through an analysis of the problems and promises of a postmodern ontology. Chapter seven, however, stands alone through a close engagement between Panikkar and the postsecular.[2]

Thus, this book offers a mutual fecundation of what Panikkar offers to Western philosophical theology in ways that dialogues Panikkar with Western philosophical theology. As such, this book is not so much trying to argue that Panikkar offers better answers than Western philosophical theology. Rather it is merely opening up a dialogue between Panikkar and Western philosophical theology to generate further dialogue and problematizations of how to make sense of transcendence when traditional Western notions of God have relegated God out of the picture. This means that this book is offering an advaitic or Indic understanding via interpretations of Panikkar that address theological

Introduction 5

and philosophical issues found among contemporary Western philosophical and theological traditions.

The dialogical approach of this book will emphasize not only an interpretation of what Panikkar has to offer postmodern philosophical theology, but also that while Panikkar offers an advaitic, Indic reading of modernity, his insights can offer catalysts for thinking through these issues with Western philosophers and theologians. The point of this book is not so much to argue as if Panikkar's answers are better than those offered by the interlocutors engaged with throughout this book. Rather the emphasis is to engage in a generative dialogue between these philosophers and theologians to see what answers Panikkar offers, even if his positions are theologically problematic or heterodox. This book is an intellectual exercise intended to broaden the scope of contemporary postmodern philosophical theology and take into account what Panikkar has to offer to the discourse. And what Panikkar has to offer is a distinctly advaitic or non-dual critique of modernity—but what do we mean by advaita and how is it used throughout this book?

WHICH NON-DUALITY, WHOSE ADVAITA?

Theoretically, non-dualism is neither monistic nor dualistic. In its variegated forms found across religious traditions, it implies the sense of harmony and an intuitive insight into the ultimate and relative nature of reality. Non-dualism typically argues against the idea of reality as two separate entities in which no relations exist and against the idea of a plurality of entities in which there is no *unitive* factor. Non-dualism is a subject of study that states that we are not just a single monism, nor are we a plurality of independent entities unconnected from one another. Non-dualism is a combination of the two, a harmony or complementarity between the one and the many. It incorporates diversity-in-unity to show the inter-relational character of the "not-two-ness" of reality. It is the many in the one, but each form in which it comes is a complete unity related to and in itself.

Panikkar typically understands advaita as "a-duality," or the absence of duality. In particular he applies this to his cosmotheandric understanding of reality. Panikkar's cosmotheandrism understands reality as triadic or even trinitarian. It is marked by the co-constitutive experience and participation in reality as cosmic (material), human, and divine. For Panikkar, what it means to be is to be constituted by each dimension of reality without reducing reality to one dimension—it emphasizes the inter-relatedness of material, human, and divine realities as co-constitutive of the real. It is to be experienced as a wholistic and harmonious reality of the unity-and-diversity of what it means to be real.

6   *Introduction*

From this it is also worth conceptually defining how Panikkar understands and uses "advaita." Anthony Savari Raj argues that for Panikkar, "advaita" is the intuition that opens the confidence in polarities in the context of a worldview to diversities that are neither absolutized, nor ignored, neither idolized, nor reduced to mere illusions of reality.[3] From this it is clear that Panikkar did not use "advaita" as Śaṅkara or the Vedāntic tradition did. (Nor is it used in such a way throughout this book). Rather, Panikkar used advaita in a variety of ways to highlight his nuance of the idea as a way of phenomenologically pointing out the plurivocal harmony that holds in tension similarities and differences in his cross-cultural hermeneutics.

Building on this, for Panikkar uses "advaita" in a variety of ways, leading to a level of seeming ambiguity as to how he uses it. However, his use of advaita is extremely nuanced and is plurivocal: it can be used in a variety of ways to emphasize new ways of thinking the harmony between differences. Like cosmotheandrism, for Panikkar, advaita is a cluster of ideas. First, it must be differentiated from the Vedāntic tradition rooted in the thought of Śaṅkara—it does not refer to reality as a creative illusion of a cosmic essence (it is not fundamentally monistic). Second it is not primarily, though can be, used to mean a-dual or the absence of duality, similar to but not exactly like the Buddhist *advāya* or "not-two-ness." Rather, Panikkar's understanding of advaita primarily refers not to monism, but rather to a constitutive holism where parts are constitutive of the whole and it refers to the notion of relativity, not relativism, where the "relation" is primary over against the substance. Furthermore, it refers to truth not as found from binary perspectives, but rather from the dialogical synthesis and harmony between perspectives. This implies that it refers to pluralism as recognizing the incommensurability of truth and the harmony of truths as co-existing, appealing to the mystery of truth where both identity and difference are held in tension.

This refers to what Panikkar calls a radical relativity, meaning the inter-in-dependency of reality, implying a both a relational, causal, and constitutive inter-dependence between a cosmotheandric reality as well as a relational *in*-dependency of beings in relation to one another for them to exist. More ambiguously, Panikkar also uses advaita somewhat interchangeably with his understanding of Karma, when referring to the law of causality governing the structure of reality. Likewise, advaita for Panikkar is used somewhat interchangeably with the Buddhist notion of *shunyata*, to characterize a broadly Indian phenomena of a-duality rather than simply emptiness (which implies via Buddhist two-tiered metaphysics an a-dual view of reality). Finally, advaita when combined with variations of "Trinity" refers to a heterodox Christian understanding of the Trinity that nonetheless remains distinctively Panikkarean insofar as it focuses on the relational holism of the

Introduction 7

Trinity and the radical kenosis of the substantiality of God the Father into and as the Son and mediated between the two by relationality of the Holy Spirit.[4]

Variously used throughout Panikkar's corpus, *pars pro toto* is also used to describe the relation between the part and the whole. Again, *pars pro toto* is a cluster of ideas. It refers to the part as a particular manifestation of the whole while also manifested in the whole; that the part is constitutive of the whole without exhausting it; that the whole is in the part, in the sense that the whole is microcosmically present within the part as a particular manifestation of the macrocosmic whole; that the part is a concrete manifestation of the whole; and finally that the part or whole do not refer to abstract realities, but rather to particular manifestations or representations of a concrete reality that can be experienced.

For the purposes of his book, advaita is understood in terms of the inter-in-dependency of reality; where the infinitude of the sacred and the finite meet; where transcendence and immanence meet. Furthermore, advaita in this book implies an understanding of the harmony and inter-relatedness between infinitude and finitude. Advaita, then, implies that beings are constituted ontologically in and as a cosmotheandric reality where the relationship between our own ontological finitude and infinitude constitutes one another in terms of both transcendence and immanence as well as cosmotheandrically in terms of being human, cosmic, and divine. It implies that human beings are ontologically constituted by the radical relativity or inter-in-dependency as cosmotheandric persons as well as by the harmonious co-participation between transcendence and immanence, finitude and infinitude.

NOTES ON THE TEXT

First, throughout this book, the reader may note that the writing in some places is better written than others. This is because this book was written over a twelve-year span. The earliest writings date to 2012–2015, and they will be found in chapters two and five. Parts of chapters one, two, and three date to the years 2015–2017. By contrast the reader will note a level of sophistication and maturity in the writing found among chapters four, parts of five, and especially six and seven. This is because they are the latest chapters to be written and reflect a more mature writing style that was cultivated during my doctoral research and writing (2019–2023). Throughout the compilation of this book, an attempt was made to smooth out the wrinkles of the older material, but in distinct places it still remains because of the value still seen in the earliest material and its distinctly rhetorical writing style. Whereas the oldest material reflects my then dwelling in continental philosophy, the middle material reflects the compilation and organization of various research material, and the latter material reflects the clarity of argument and thinking that particularly developed through the rigorous processes of my doctoral research at the University of Birmingham.

Second, a note on spelling and capitalization. Where relevant, when using Sanskrit terms, the transliteration of these terms is offered with their relevant accent marks instead of spelling out long vowels. Furthermore, when Being and Reality are capitalized, this is when they have ultimate connotations. When they are not capitalized, they are referring to non-ultimate understandings and usages of the terms. Finally, when the text states "be-*ing*" it is referring to an action and is being used as a verb rather than a noun. Furthermore, the use of "-" throughout the text is used intentionally to refer to puns or non-traditional pronunciations of terms to emphasize alternate ways of saying the word that includes both traditional and alternate meanings and usages of the word.

NOTES

1. C.f. Henri De Lubac, *The Mystery of the Supernatural*, trans. Rosemary Sheed (New York: Herder and Herder, 2022); Henri De Lubac, *Augustinianism and Modern Theology*, trans. Lancelot Sheppard (New York: Herder and Herder, 2000).

2. My work on postsecularism is further developed in my doctoral dissertation at the University of Birmingham. While chapter seven here focuses on Panikkar's answers to postsecularism in dialogue with Charles Taylor, my doctoral dissertation focuses on the sociological and theological implications Charles Taylor's postsecular contributions.

3. Anthony Savari Raj, *A New Hermeneutic of Reality: Raimon Panikkar's Cosmotheandric Vision* (New York: Peter Lang, 1998), 38.

4. Raimon Panikkar, *Trinity and the Religious Experience of Man* (Maryknoll, NY: Orbis Books, 1973), 41–69.

Chapter 1

The Cosmotheandric Intuition

From Metaphysics to Theology

This chapter argues that Raimon Panikkar's notion of cosmotheandrism is characterized by a movement from a metaphysical intuition into the mystery of reality into the particular expressions of cosmotheandric theologies enpresented in human religious experience, that is, a cosmotheandric intuition into reality.[1] It is an intuition into the triadic structure of reality that is tripartite, relational, wholistic, and interconnected while at the same time non-reductive and characterized by a level of harmony between unity and difference. It tells us that reality is constituted by the inter-constitutiveness between divinity, materiality, and humanity. But to understand this metaphysical vision of reality we must also understand the theoretical frameworks that shape Panikkar's cosmotheandric vision of reality. The following illustrates these theoretical frameworks by defining cosmotheandrism and its structural frameworks of advaitic trinitarianism and radical relativity. Then it describes a framework for understanding Panikkar's plurivocal metaphysics and how it can be concretized and articulated through two examples of cosmotheandric theologies via Christian and Hindu traditions. The chapter closes with an emphasis on the importance of the cosmotheandric experience as a central component of the cosmotheandric intuition. Furthermore, this chapter argues how Panikkar's cosmotheandric metaphysics is shaped by cross-cultural and inter-religious frameworks for understanding the nature of reality. Moreover it argues that his cosmotheandric metaphysics serves as a foil for articulating cosmotheandric theologies, while also giving expression to Panikkar's intuition into human religious experience.

DEFINING COSMOTHEANDRISM

Panikkar's idea of cosmotheandrism refers to a cluster of ideas. It refers to a tripartite structure of reality as patterned after the trinitarian doctrine of *perichoresis*, Hindu *advaita*, and Buddhist *pratityatsamudpada*, which are each encapsulated by his notions of advaitic trinitarianism and radical relativity, and posits that reality is irreducibly co-constituted by three dimensions of reality: World (matter), God (the divine), and Man (the human). These three dimensions of reality are relationally co-constitutive of the real. It states that each dimension of reality is real in and of itself, yet are not reducible to one another, while maintaining their inter-in-dependency upon one another to constitute reality as real. It is a metaphysical intuition into the nature of reality as well as a phenomenological intuition into the nature of human religious experience marked by a wholistic and integral experience of reality. It is governed by an insight into the trinitarian pattern or structure of reality—one that focuses on the harmony of inter-in-dependent yet non-reducible dimensions of reality. Furthermore, a cosmotheandric reality is advaitically mediated through the co-constitutive participation of three dimensions of reality in and with one another as the real without reducing reality to a singular dimension. Veli-Matti Kärkkäinen also states that for Panikkar, a cosmotheandric reality,

> [i]s multidimensional, [where] the various strands come together . . . [in a] technical sense in Panikkar's thought. . . . Panikkar himself defines [cosmotheandrism] in this way: "the cosmotheandric principle could be stated by saying that the divine, the human, and the earthly—however we may prefer them—are the three irreducible dimensions which constitute the real, i.e., any reality inasmuch as it is real." He can also state it in this way: "There is a kind of *perichoresis*, 'dwelling within one another,' of these three dimensions of reality, the divine, the human, and the cosmic—the I, the you and the it."[2]

Underlying Panikkar's cosmotheandric understanding of reality is not explicitly a reference to the triune God. Rather it refers to a trinitarian structure to reality. While the Christian *perichoresis* refers to the mutual subsisting of the triune persons in the Godhead, Panikkar's use of *perichoresis* does not refer to God, but applies the structural logic of *perichoresis* among the persons of the Godhead to his cosmotheandric understanding of reality. This means that reality is also not reducible to one dimension, and that each of the three dimensions of reality subsist in and with one another for reality to be real. A cosmotheandric reality follows the trinitarian logic of *perichoresis* as the mutual indwelling not only of the divine in itself, but also of the divine in relation to the cosmic and the human. Linked to his cosmotheandric vision of reality is the notion of advaitic trinitarianism—which paints a relational

The Cosmotheandric Intuition 11

understanding of reality that combines a non-dual experience of union with a trinitarian com-union and wholeness that allows reality to be experienced as a relational whole constituted in and through its diversity. At its heart Panikkar's understanding of an advaitic trinitarianism depicts reality, not just God, in ways to emphasize "the intrinsic relationality of reality as constituted by the relation."[3]

Panikkar's intuition into the relationally constitutive nature of reality is expressed in his cosmotheandric interpretation of the structure of reality. This "cosmotheandric intuition" is expressed in the Christian idea of *perichoresis*, Hindu *advaita*, and Buddhist *pratityatsamudpada*. Each of these ideas demonstrate the ideas of inter-independency, relationality, and holism. Panikkar's word for this is radical relativity. Panikkar's cosmotheandric metaphysics is guided by a trinitarian hermeneutic developed as a cosmotheandric intuition into the constitutive and intrinsically relational whole of reality. The cosmotheandric intuition serves in what could be understood of Panikkar as a cultural invariant common to world religions on the grounds of its triadic and holistic interpretations into the nature of reality.[4]

Jyri Komulainen argues that Panikkar's understanding of the trinitarian structure of reality is marked by harmony, relationality, and dynamism.[5] Komulainen argues that Panikkar's understanding of harmony allows him to move beyond monism and dualism and that his understanding of dynamism is characterized by an attunement to the rhythms of the cosmos and the dance of the trinity to create space for change and growth. However, Komulainen's understanding of Panikkar's emphasis on relationality is the most important here because it sheds light on the participation of human persons in and constituted by a cosmotheandric reality. This personal participation is intrinsically marked by the human person's relational co-constitution and participation in a cosmotheandric reality. It not only characterizes the human being as personal or relational, but also as constituted by relations with and in the other two dimensions of reality in non-reductive and harmonious communion.[6] Furthermore, Komulainen states that Panikkar's "relational ontology allows room for both unity in reality and differentiation"—central elements that tie into Panikkar's cosmotheandric metaphysics.[7]

Through Panikkar's cosmotheandric intuition into the nature of reality, the divine, human, and material world find their being in and through the experience of the law of their constitutive inter-relatedness—what Panikkar calls "ontonomy."[8] While we will examine Panikkar's notion of ontonomy more fully in the next chapter on Panikkar's relational ontology, what it implies is that there is a law of being and that law of being is expressed through Panikkar's intuition into the trinitarian or triadic structure to reality.

Ewert Cousins rightly characterizes Panikkar's trinitarian theology as advaitic trinitarianism implying the advaitic, or non-dual orientation to

12 *Chapter 1*

trinitarian theology.[9] Tied to this is also Panikkar's understanding of the Buddhist *pratityatsamudpada* as radical relativity. Panikkar's advaitic trinitarianism thus implies that reality is not only grounded in a trinitarian structure, but that it articulates a unitive and participatory holism. It is not merely that world, God, and humanity exist independently, but rather that their independence is *in*-dependence upon one another to be whole. Thus, the relational dependence of each dimension of reality upon one another constitutes their wholeness insofar as in their dependence upon one another they participate in one another.

This entails not only that for humans to be real they must be material and (at least have the potential to) be(-come) divine, but that for them to be whole they must participate in their practical embodiment as symbolically and ontonomously reflecting the divine in their actions. In turn, material matter not only constitutes human beings and is a material embodiment of the divine through Incarnation, but for the cosmos to be real it must constitute divine embodiment in and through human beings.[10] Likewise for the divine to be real it must not only constitute the human and material dimensions, but it must participate in the human and material dimensions freely as a divine immanence manifesting, or participating, in or of materiality and humanity. Panikkar's notion of ontonomy is grounded in his idea of radical relativity, stressing the inter-in-dependency of each dimension of a cosmotheandric reality. To unpack this trinitarian or triadic structure or pattern of a cosmotheandric reality, it is worthwhile to examine the notions of advaitic trinitarianism and radical relativity.

Advaitic Trinitarianism

Panikkar's intuition into the triadic structure of reality is grounded primarily in a re-interpretation of the Christian Trinity through the lens of advaita, that is, an advaitic trinitarianism. Advaitic trinitarianism signifies the harmony between a relationally co-constituted and co-constitutive reality marked by the absence of duality. In short, while advaita refers to the harmony and relational holism of reality without reducing reality to one substance or category of the real, Panikkar's trinitarianism refers to the relational diversity-in-unity of reality. Panikkar's advaitic trinitarianism points to the underlying harmony and holism not within God, but rather in what irreducibly constitutes reality as real—as material, human, and divine. Panikkar's advaitic trinitarianism shapes the possibility of a cosmotheandric reality in ways that applies both the Christian trinitarian idea of *perichoresis* and the Hindu notion of advaita to his cosmotheandric metaphysical interpretation of reality.

To understand Panikkar's advaitic trinitarianism one must understand his advaitic insight into the triadic structure of reality. Panikkar's conception

The Cosmotheandric Intuition   13

of advaita, unlike traditional Hindu *advaita*, is not merely non-dualistic, but emphasizes the not-two-ness of reality, thus emphasizing not only the absence of duality but the importance of harmony and the *relation* as constitutive of reality, and even of God.[11] Panikkar's advaitic trinitarianism interprets a cosmotheandric reality through this principle of non-duality primarily in the context of the relational, triadic structure of being and reality.[12] This ontological inter-connectedness of the triadic structure of reality as co-constitutive of one another implies what Panikkar calls "ontonomy," which refers to "the intrinsic inter-connectedness of the three dimensions of reality as integrally constituting what it means to be 'real.'"[13]

Panikkar's advaitic trinitarianism thus seeks not only to describe the real as cosmotheandric but also as a mediation between the one and the many, by which the trinity becomes a model for a non-dual oneness that "embraces the whole of reality" and completes it as the Source to which it all returns, is gathering into, and is generated out of.[14] Panikkar points to the harmonious relationship between creation to the Creator (as Source) wherein creation finds its completion as constitutively real through its relationship with the Creator. Panikkar's advaitic trinitarianism is not really about God but about the cosmotheandric structure of reality that transcends itself and yet remains immanent as it completes itself in the intrinsically co-constitutive ontonomy of the inter-in-dependent relations between the three dimensions of reality.[15]

Guiding Panikkar's understanding of a cosmotheandric reality, the advaitic insight into the experience of reality contributes to his phenomenological and trinitarian insight of *perichoresis* to explain the relational wholeness of reality as "the ceaseless and constitutive interpenetration of the three dimensions or three persons or three centers of reality . . . the 'three' of these metaphors refers to the fact that the three dimensions, the three persons, the three centers, etc. are all part of a heuristic device that refers to the whole."[16] Francis D'Sa articulates that the wholeness of reality points not merely to an experiential or phenomenological dimension of a cosmotheandric reality but also to the trinitarian structure of reality. Building from the advaitic insight into the not-two-ness of reality, Panikkar's advaitic trinitarianism points to the trinitarian structure of reality as constituted as a whole through the interpretive lens of *perichoresis*. D'Sa offers an insightful analysis worth examining:

> Reality refers to the inter-related whole, where every being is related to every being and so constitutes a continuum. Accordingly, where reality is concerned distinctions are in order but not separations. This attitude is born of a perichoretic vision. . . .
>
> The other point about *perichoresis* is that it is a holistic vision of Reality. It is in the context of *perichoresis* that we have to locate the symbolic character of the almost ubiquitous "three." Like the seven colors of the rainbow we speak

14   *Chapter 1*

of three persons, three dimensions, three centers of reality *because*, first of all, though *Reality is in fact a continuum*, the three persons, three dimensions, three centers, etc., *stand out* [as referring to the whole of reality]. . . .

The perichoretic insight ensures that the Trinity is not equated with tri-theism. Panikkar's cosmotheandric intuition is the contemporary, secular, expression of the Trinity. But the great difference is that whereas the original Christian Trinity referred to the divine (persons) alone, the cosmotheandric intuition embraces the whole of reality.[17]

This means that Panikkar's use of *perichoresis* is taken from the Christian doctrine of God and applied to his cosmotheandric intuition into the structure of reality. Whereas *perichoresis* is traditionally used to understand the divine dance among the triune persons of God, for Panikkar it refers to the inter-penetrative, co-constitutive dance of the dimensions of reality. Just as it is wrong to think of God as irreducible to one person in the Trinity, so also does Panikkar think that reality cannot be reducible to one dimension. Arguably, because Panikkar adopts the idea of *perichoresis* as key to his understanding of reality, it means that for something to be real, it is constituted in some way by the co-constitution of reality as divine, cosmic, and human without reducing reality to one mere dimension of reality alone. Rather reality is cosmotheandric—it is marked by a mutual indwelling of the divine in the cosmic and human, of the cosmos by human agents who participate in the divine and care for the cosmos, and of the human by material bodies that are relationally dependent upon the divine for their being.

The purpose of Panikkar's advaitic trinitarianism is not the search to know or experience God and the human dependence upon God in light of the Christian conception of the Triune God. Rather it offers a phenomenological insight into the nature of reality as cosmotheandric, as three irreducible dimensions of reality as ontologically (and mutually) constituting one another as real. Panikkar states that the cosmotheandric

vision tells us that reality is not formed from a single, indistinct block—whether it be divine, spiritual, or material—but neither is it formed from three blocks or a world on three levels—the world of the Gods (or of transcendence), the world of Men (or of consciousness), and the physical world (or that of matter), as though it were a building on three floors. Reality is made up of three dimensions in relation to one another—the trinitarian *perichoresis*—so that not only does one not exist without the other, but all three are inter-independently entwined. Either God or the World, or equally Man, if taken separately or in themselves, without relation to the other dimensions of reality, are simply abstractions of our mind.[18]

And yet, Panikkar also understands that this cosmotheandric reality is not merely constituted by three irreducible dimensions of reality but also by

The Cosmotheandric Intuition 15

what Christians have called the "trinitarian mystery." In Panikkar's terms, the trinitarian mystery is experienced not merely in the divine life, but also in the human and in the material. Gerard Hall states that,

> [i]n fact, he moves beyond the realms of both science and philosophy to speak of the Christian Trinity as the fundamental paradigm and ultimate mystery for understanding every ontological reality, whether divine or non-divine. In this view, creation and the material universe need to be understood with reference to some spiritual reality. Without an awareness of this transcendent dimension, he believes that we inevitably fall into the trap of "radical dualism" (the denial of unity) or "cosmological monism" (the denial of multiplicity).[19]

Here, in his advaitic insight into the experience of the not-two-ness of the relational whole of a cosmotheandric reality, Panikkar seeks to describe the perichoretic, trinitarian inter-penetration of the three dimensions of reality by pointing to the divine immanence and presence of God in and to humans and creation. Subsequently he is also pointing to the human and material participation in the divine as constitutively and relationally, but not as substantially, real. For Panikkar the constitutive relationality of reality includes not only the divine as subsisting *as relation* but also the relational subsisting between divine, human, and material through their co-constitutive participation in the whole.[20] Thus, for Panikkar all of reality is governed by a relational ontology, where not just the divine but each of the three dimensions of reality are, through their co-constitutiveness and inter-relationality, dependent upon one another as a relational whole *to be real*. In the turn to relational inter-in-dependency, or what Panikkar calls radical relativity, the analysis below will describe Panikkar's appropriation and development of the Buddhist idea of *pratityatsamudpada*.

Pratityatsamudpada and Radical Relativity

While Panikkar's intuition into the triadic myth is certainly influenced by his understandings of Trinity and advaita, another layer to Panikkar's cosmotheandric intuition is its appropriation of Buddhist *pratityatsamudpada* into his idea of radical relativity. Jyri Komulainen is clear that Panikkar's appropriation of the Buddhist *pratityatsamudpada* includes both the relativity of being captured in its emphasis on dependent co-origination, as well as the overcoming "the dilemmas of both determinism and indeterminism, and of oneness and pluralism."[21] But he argues that Panikkar's appropriation of Buddhist *pratityatsamudpada* goes beyond Buddhism insofar as it emphasizes the interwovenness of reality and the mutual interplay of a cosmotheandric reality. Panikkar's understanding of *pratityatsamudpada* does not so much emphasize the causal structure of reality, but rather its simultaneity and co-constitutiveness of reality as irreducible to one another—yet interrelated to and in one another at the same time.[22] This emphasis on inter-in-dependency is for Panikkar an understanding of the Buddhist *pratityatsamudpada* in terms of "radical relativity." In his commentary on Panikkar's radical relativity, Young-chan Ro states it is where:

> Each and every being is already pluralistically composed to become its own being. From the communal and collective point of view, pluralism is a way of recognizing that the nature of reality and being are mutually dependent on each other (*pratityatsamudpada*) . . . pluralism assumes the inter-dependence of all beings as both an external relationship with other beings and an intrinsic structure of every being. . . . Pluralism is an existential attitude of openness to others, to nature, [and to] heaven and earth . . . pluralism is a way of discerning the nature of reality and being. It is a way of finding wisdom to comprehend how to relate to each other without losing one's own being and identity.[23]

Panikkar's radical relativity articulates a pluralistic understanding of the inter-connectedness of all of reality. It is where all things are independent, inter-dependent, and relationally in dependence at the same time. They are wholly real in and of themselves insofar as their in-dependency is found through their inter-independency upon other co-constitutive relationalities. Panikkar states that "the inter-in-dependence of the three dimensions of reality is essential to the cosmotheandric experience."[24] Just as the Buddhist *pratityatsamudpada* articulates how reality is inter-dependently co-arising with all other aspects of reality, allowing causes and conditions to arise and constitute reality inter-dependently, Panikkar's radical relativity articulates the *relation* as that which constitutes reality as the constitutive thread that connects all things in reality to the rest of reality.

Thus far this chapter has described the cross-cultural interpretation of Christian, Hindu, and Buddhist ideas to help explain Panikkar's cosmotheandric intuition into the structure of reality. While a focus on the implicit relational ontology will be picked up again at the end of the next chapter, it is worthwhile to examine how Panikkar's cosmotheandric metaphysics can be articulated in particular theological expressions that are found among the human religious experience. The remainder of the chapter will focus on this and examine how Panikkar's cosmotheandric metaphysics can be understood as a cultural invariant that can be found in particular religious theological traditions, in particular the Christian theological tradition and Advaita Vedāntic traditions of Hinduism. These will be examined to understand how Panikkar's cosmotheandric metaphysics serves as a foil for a plurality of

The Cosmotheandric Intuition 17

cosmotheandric theologies that describe and illustrate aspects of the cosmotheandric experience.

COSMOTHEANDRIC METAPHYSICS

While the sections above have set the groundwork of Panikkar's cosmotheandric intuition into reality through an account of his advaitic trinitarianism and radical relativity, this section begins to develop Panikkar's cosmotheandric metaphysics, which gives account to the advaitic inter-in-dependency, or plurivocity, of his metaphysics and theology. The following argues that Panikkar's cosmotheandric intuition into reality is not only metaphysical, but also serves as a foil for particular theological expressions of religious incommensurability. To develop this, it is worth examining how Panikkar develops a plurivocal metaphysics that gives account to his inter-religious hermeneutics.

At its heart, Panikkar's plurivocal metaphysics is non-absolutist, allowing the possibility of religious truth in multiple religious traditions without positing either their reduction of one into another, nor the superiority of one over another. Beneath a plurivocal metaphysics is the Jain idea of *anekantavada*, the "many-sided-doctrine" of non-absolutism. Plurivocal metaphysics posits reading and understanding religious truths alongside one another without collapsing them into one another. It also entails reading and understanding religious truths in harmonious ways that are conducive to experiencing the beauty of the other's religious tradition and truth. It entails an openness to experiencing and understanding religious truth in multiple traditions without absolutizing one over or against another. Panikkar's cosmotheandric metaphysics of reality is a plurivocal metaphysics that posits a metaphysical mystery that transcends and remains immanent within particular cosmotheandric theologies. That is, Panikkar's plurivocal cosmotheandric metaphysics serves as a foil for understanding particular cosmotheandric theologies.

Panikkar's plurivocal metaphysics is described by the terms "incommensurability," "cultural invariants," and "homeomorphic equivalents" to describe how, across religious traditions and cultures, one may understand and grapple with religious difference without reducing it to the same. Panikkar's plurivocal metaphysics posits that: (a) homeomorphic equivalents refer to the similar forms and functions between particular religious contents, ideas, or structures in explaining reality—that is, a concept of the divine and how the human condition is resolved through an emphasis on salvation/liberation/flourishing; (b) cultural invariants refer to religious phenomena common across cultures that may be found concretely in and among many religious or cultural contexts—that is, cosmotheandrism, worship, meditation, and/or the belief in the sacred;

18 *Chapter 1*

and (c) incommensurability refers to the idea that religious ideas and beliefs are not reducible to one another, emphasizing that there are irreconcilable differences between religions that cannot be reconciled to one another—that is, that Abrahamic messianism cannot be reconciled to Hindu and Buddhist notions of rebirth or reincarnation.[25] These ideas help us to understand a plurivocal understanding of religious harmony that pays attention to difference-in-unity and unity-in-difference, not an univocal reduction of religions to the same conception of God, salvation, or the human condition or an equivocal differentiation between religious traditions that gives no account of common themes. Plurivocity posits the multiple points of interconnection and difference between religious traditions, theology, and culture without positing a monopoly on religious truth.

Following from this, the remainder of this chapter argues that Panikkar's cosmotheandric intuition into the mystery of reality is a cultural invariant common across human cultures, religions, and experiences that can be articulated theologically in different ways through its particular expressions in those cultures, religions, and experiences. If a cultural invariant is the articulation of a common cultural, religious, or here, metaphysical idea across human cultures, then a homeomorphic equivalent articulates how ideas in various traditions function similarly. A homeomorphic equivalent posits not a universal or univocal theology, but rather that in religious traditions we find particular ideas that function in similar ways across and within human religions. This means that, theologically speaking, the role of Allah, the Trinity, Brahman, nirvana and *shunyata*, the Dao, and Tian functionally do the same thing in particular traditions: they articulate the concept of the sacred. But the Trinity, etc., while they are homeomorphic equivalents, they are not cultural invariants: each concept of the sacred does not univocally map onto the concept of the sacred in or across other religious traditions. Rather, Panikkar's cosmotheandric metaphysics serves as a cultural invariant that allows us to understand the mystery found within the plurivocity of homeomorphic equivalents in cosmotheandric *theologies* that are expressed in incommensurable ways in particular religious traditions.

For Panikkar, the whole of reality—the cosmotheandric mystery—is displayed across particular religions as a cultural invariant that manifests as homeomorphic equivalents between religions. That is, for Panikkar, the cosmotheandric mystery is an intuition into not only the nature of reality, but is also manifested among and in particular religions and their theologies. Panikkar imagines the mystery of reality as manifested in the particular theologies while still transcending them. Likewise, Panikkar thinks that from the theologies we can posit the transcending mystery. But, according to Panikkar, while the pluralities of particular religious particulars may reveal the mystery, they are also transcended by the mystery because no religion has a monopoly on the expression of the cosmotheandric mystery.

Panikkar's cosmotheandric intuition into the nature of reality does not only try to explain the metaphysical structures of a triadic myth. It is also, arguably, a foil for understanding and articulating the particularities of cosmotheandric *theologies* found throughout and within particular religions because they tap into the triadic myth of a cosmotheandric reality. Panikkar's cosmotheandric intuition is a metaphysical *intuition* into the mystery of a cosmotheandric reality manifested in the particularity of a variety of cosmotheandric *theologies*. Thus, "theology" is not singular: there are a plurality of *theologies* constituted by various cosmotheandric interpretations across religious traditions that reveal the mystery of a triadic myth to the nature of reality.

The plurivocity of Panikkar's metaphysical intuition into the mystery of reality is not only manifested in its theological particulars. It is grounded in a trinitarian vision of reality (which transcends the Christian vision of Trinity): "Humanity has always been aware, with greater or lesser clarity, of a mystery that is higher, transcendent, or immanent in Man."[26] He goes further to state that

> the entire reality is trinitarian, and the three dimensions reciprocally co-penetrate one another. This *circumincessio* or *perichoresis* is so perfect that the three elements can be distinct but not separate. Sky, earth, and their "in-between"—or past, present, and future—might be cosmological formulations of it. *Sat*, *cit*, and *ananda*, the *trikaya*, the Christian Trinity, and so on, might be religious formulations of it. We are not claiming that all these conceptions are equal; we simply ascertain that these homeomorphic correspondences exist, without however going into any comparisons.[27]

What we see here is that Panikkar's metaphysical intuition allows the space for religious difference while also articulating its functional similarities. This plurivocal metaphysics of reality challenges the monism and dualism characteristic of many religious and philosophical traditions and argues for the harmony between the differences without reducing difference into sameness. So, what is the logic of Panikkar's metaphysics? To understand the logic from intuition to theology, it is worth noting how Panikkar, by studying multiple traditions, articulates a pluralistic mystery from the various homeomorphic equivalences among religious traditions that display the triadic insight into the structure of reality. It is to the study of two particular traditions, Hindu and Christian, that we now turn to articulate a concretization of Panikkar's plurivocal account of cosmotheandric theologies.

20   *Chapter 1*

HINDU AND CHRISTIAN
COSMOTHEANDRIC THEOLOGIES

Within Panikkar's thought there is a sense that if one were to speak of a cosmotheandric metaphysics of reality, then it serves to encompass the possibility and articulation of multiple theologies based on his cosmotheandric mystery. That is, Panikkar's cosmotheandric metaphysics serves as a foil for understanding and articulating World, God, and humanity within various religious traditions. From this, we can construct a variety of cosmotheandric theologies. This means that Panikkar's cosmotheandric *metaphysics* serves as a background for articulating various cosmotheandric *theologies*.

Panikkar's account of cosmotheandrism entails not merely the relational constitution of reality, that is, radical relativity, but that insofar as reality is constituted by material matter, being human, and divinity, humans are participating in a cosmotheandric reality. This implies two inter-related factors: embodiment and participation. The embodiment of divinity in a human and material reality can be seen through participation, manifestation, and/or Incarnation. Whereas religious traditions would articulate embodiment of divinity differently as homeomorphic equivalents (as Incarnation, *avatāra*, nirmanakaya, the world as manifestation of Brahman, etc.), what is striking of Panikkar's plurivocal understanding of cosmotheandrism is that it can be expressed not as an incommensurable whole, but rather as a metaphysical understanding of reality found in its religious manifestations as a cultural invariant. This implies not only that it intuitively grasps the inter-in-dependence and radical relativity of the three dimensions of reality, but also that each religion may or can express its own particular articulation of cosmotheandrism. This entails not only that a Hindu or Christian will articulate divine embodiment differently, but also how they describe God, creation, and humanity will differ while still supporting the triadic myth that constitutes a cosmotheandric reality as a cultural invariant.[28]

The extent or way in which humanity may be or become divine is determined particularly among world religions. Whether humans are intrinsically divine because we share the divine essence within us and one must realize and identify the union of *ātman* as Brahman or become divine through a process of *theosis* characterized by participation in liturgy, the experience of God, the cultivation of holiness, or rooted in the doctrines of justification, sanctification, and glorification, there remains an understanding of the essential or potential deification of humanity.[29] *Theosis* entails the potential deification of human beings through the trinitarian activity of God through the human participation in the spiritual sanctification of human beings by symbolically and practically conforming them into the image of the Son. This is achieved

The Cosmotheandric Intuition

through living a life of crucifixion and death to sin, and living to a new life of grace, forgiveness, and reconciliation in the Kingdom of God to fulfill and live according to the will of the Father in dependence upon the Spirit through faith in God through Christ. The extent to which creation displays the glory of God in the Christian context is in its being created *ex nihilo* as an other from God, yet suspended from and participating in God's own being as a created gift substantiated as other in love. This implies a Christian conception of cosmotheandric inter-in-dependence insofar as creation and humanity are given their worth as created beings other than God to freely receive God's redeeming love and be physically and mentally renewed proleptically by the Spirit in the eschaton with resurrected bodies. From the Christian context, divine embodiment condescends to material creation as a human person in Jesus of Nazareth as the Incarnation of the *Logos* as the Son of the Father via the work of the Holy Spirit conforming created existence to the *Logos* and the will of the Father. The eschatological end of a Christian cosmotheandrism ends in God deifying, glorifying, and redeeming creation by means of the particular historicity of Jesus Christ and the universal activity of the Spirit in drawing creation back into communion and shalom with God the Father.

By contrast, for an Advaita Vedāntic Hindu, not only would creation be the essential embodiment and veil of the divine, but as humans participate in reality as created out of or from the *lila* (play) of Brahman they find their liberation when they realize their oneness with creation and Brahman as an essential manifestation of or absorption into Brahman. But humans also participate in Brahman. In their participation in creation as the divine embodied in created form one may and can affirm the worth of creation, not in being other than Brahman, but in one's identification with and realization of essential oneness—as the same essence of Brahman participating and sharing essentially in the sacrality of creation and human life as an embodiment of the divine. The context of divine embodiment in the Hindu tradition thus implies that all of creation is an embodiment of the divine because it shares and participates in the essence of divinity and that it is redeemed insofar as one identifies their true self (*ātman*) with the underlying essence and ground of all Being (Brahman).

Above are two instances of cosmotheandric theologies within both Christianity and Hinduism. They are grounded in participatory ontologies which allude to what Panikkar calls homeomorphic equivalents: functional equivalents between religious traditions. Homeomorphic equivalents for Panikkar entail a resistance to both the homogenization of the other and the negation of difference because it places religious diversity within a plurivocal metaphysics that allows incommensurability. By demonstrating how cosmotheandrism functions as a cultural invariant through an analysis of Christian and Hindu homeomorphic equivalents, this chapter shows how a cosmotheandric metaphysics of reality can be theologically contextualized in particular religious traditions. What these cosmotheandric theologies imply of a cosmotheandric metaphysics is the possibility of a cosmotheandric experience developed below.

THE COSMOTHEANDRIC EXPERIENCE

For Panikkar, human religious experience is mediated through a cosmotheandric experience. Panikkar identifies reality as an inter-independent relational harmony and dynamism between Man (humanity), the World (matter), and the Sacred (God). Panikkar's cosmotheandrism emphasizes both a cosmic and mystical element in the human experience of the divine. The divine is present in all beings where everyone and everything is a *pars pro toto* reality that represents every dimension of the cosmotheandric reality because each part of reality is relationally and harmoniously reflected in the whole of reality. Humans experience a cosmotheandric reality as a non-dualistic religious experience, where they see within the experience of the divine not only the self in relation to the divine, but also both the self in relation to the world and in relation to other human beings. This non-dualistic religious experience is where humans are able to see their participation in both the cosmic and the divine throughout all aspects of their lives. Humans are not only human, but both the divine may dwell within them, and the material world constitutes the human being as a constitutive part of what it means to be human.

The cosmotheandric experience articulates that Man, God, and the World represent a whole, unified dimension of reality. When we reflect Reality as a whole, we encounter within ourselves a sense of oneness with reality. The non-duality of cosmotheandric reality is constantly lived and constantly experienced in ways that moves with the dynamism and rhythms of reality through a harmonious participation in and between all three dimensions of reality. Humans experience reality in an existential, material, and mystical way, in a non-dualistic way, where the differentiation and participation between God, human persons, and the material world are relationally constitutive to what it means to be *real*. This is an experience where every part of reality has as intrinsic irreducibility and uniqueness to itself while yet remaining relationally co-constituted by and co-constitutive of reality. It is an experience where what it means to be human cannot be conceived of as separated from God, the world, and other human persons—to experience being human means to experience the totality of reality as co-constitutively cosmotheandric and as intrinsically relational. It is to this question of a relational ontology that the next chapter will develop.

NOTES

1. Raimon Panikkar, *The Rhythm of Being: The Unbroken Trinity* (Maryknoll, NY: Orbis Books, 2010), 212–62.

2. Quoted in Veli-Matti Kärkkäinen, *Trinity and Religious Pluralism: The Doctrine of the Trinity in Christian Theology of Religions* (Burlington, VT: Ashgate, 2004), 119.

3. Andrew D. Thrasher, "A Glossary of Panikkarean Terms," in *Raimon Panikkar: A Companion to His Life and Thought*, eds., Peter Phan and Young-Chan Ro (Cambridge, UK: James Clarke and Co., 2018), 271–81, 271.

4. Panikkar, *The Rhythm of Being*, 224–32.

5. Jyri Komulainen, *An Emerging Cosmotheandric Religion? Raimon Panikkar's Pluralistic Theology of Religions* (Leiden and Boston: Brill, 2005), 183–88.

6. Komulainen, *An Emerging Cosmotheandric Religion?*, 184.

7. Komulainen, *An Emerging Cosmotheandric Religion?*, 187.

8. This notion of ontonomy has been developed by scholars through the lens of cosmotheandrism to articulate how reality is constituted by the inter-relatedness of the three dimensions of reality constituting their being as real through an act of *"perichoresis."* C.f. Fred Dallmayr, "Rethinking Secularism (with Raimon Panikkar)," *The Review of Politics* 61, no. 4 (1999): 715–35; Anselm Min, "Panikkar's Radical Trinitarianism: Reflections on Panikkar's Transformation of the Christian Trinity into Cosmotheandrism," *CIRPIT Review* 6 (2015): 75–100.

9. Ewert Cousins, "Panikkar's Advaitic Trinitarianism," in *The Intercultural Challenge of Raimon Panikkar*, ed. Joseph Prabhu (Maryknoll, NY: Orbis Books, 1996), 119–30.

10. Raimon Panikkar, *Hinduism: The Dharma of India*, ed. Milena Carrara Pavan, Vol. IV.2, XII vols., Opera Omnia (Maryknoll, NY: Orbis Books, 2017), 232–41.

11. C.f. Panikkar's understanding of substance as relation in: Panikkar, *The Rhythm of Being*, 218–19.

12. C.f. Panikkar, *The Rhythm of Being*, 61, 76–80, 85–86, 93–94, 99.

13. C.f. Dallmayr, "Rethinking Secularism," 726.

14. Panikkar, *The Rhythm of Being*, 226–27.

15. Panikkar, *The Rhythm of Being*, 277.

16. Francis X. D'Sa, "How Trinitarian Is Panikkar's Trinity," *CIRPIT Review* 3 (2012): 33–50, 41–42.

17. D'Sa, "How Trinitarian is Panikkar's Trinity," 42.

18. Raimon Panikkar, "Introduction," in *Trinitarian and Cosmotheandric Vision*, ed. Milena Carrara Pavan, Vol. VIII, XII vols., Opera Omnia (Maryknoll, NY: Orbis Books, 2019), xiii–xv, xiv.

19. Gerard Vincent Hall, "Raimon Panikkar's Hermeneutics of Religious Pluralism," Catholic University of America (Ann Arbor, MI: UMI Dissertation Services, 1994), 14.

20. The nuance in Panikkar's castigation of substance for and as relation is picked up most notably by Min: C.f. Anselm K. Min, "Panikkar's Radical Trinitarianism," 75–100; Anselm Min, "The Trinity and the Cosmotheandric Vision: Reflections on

Panikkar's Intercultural Theology," in *Raimon Panikkar: A Companion to His Life and Thought*, eds., Peter Phan and Young-Chan Ro (Maryknoll, NY: Orbis Books, 2018), 152–70.

21. Komulainen, *An Emerging Cosmotheandric Religion?*, 185.

22. Komulainen, *An Emerging Cosmotheandric Religion?*, 185.

23. Young-Chan Ro, "Relativism, Universalism, and Pluralism in an Age of Globalization," *CIRPIT Review* 3 (2012): 91–101, 100–101.

24. Panikkar, *The Rhythm of Being*, 277.

25. However, this is possible in fantastic literature: C.f. Andrew D. Thrasher, "Fantastic Inter-religious Resourcement in Robert Jordan and David Eddings," in *Theology, Fantasy, and the Imagination*, eds. Andrew D. Thrasher and Austin M. Freeman (Lanham, MD: Rowman & Littlefield, 2023), 133–53.

26. Panikkar, "Introduction," xiii.

27. Raimon Panikkar, "Man—A Trinitarian Mystery," in *Trinitarian and Cosmotheandric Vision*, ed. Milena Carrara Pavan, Vol. VIII, XII vols., Opera Omnia (Maryknoll, NY: Orbis Books, 2019), 93–118, 114.

28. C.f. Keith Ward, *Concepts of God: Images of the Divine in Five Religious Traditions* (Oxford: Oneworld, 1998); Keith Ward, *Religion and Human Nature* (Oxford: Clarendon Press, 1998); Keith Ward, *Religion and Creation* (Oxford: Clarendon Press, 1996).

29. C.f. Anantanand Rambachan, *The Advaita Worldview: God, World, and Humanity* (Albany, NY: State University of New York Press, 2006); Jared Ortiz, ed. *With all the Fullness of God: Deification in Christian Tradition* (Lanham, MD: Lexington Press, 2021).

Chapter 2

Panikkar's Relational Ontology
Being, Relation, and Ontonomy

While the previous chapter gave an account of Panikkar's cosmotheandric intuition, this chapter continues developments found there, but with particular attention to Panikkar's relational ontology in conjunction with Martin Heidegger, Jean-Luc Nancy, and Charles Taylor's understandings of fundamental, relational, and moral ontology. While the previous chapter focused on laying out definitions and ideas that shape Panikkar's cosmotheandric intuition, this chapter focuses on another side of Panikkar's cosmotheandric intuition—his relational ontology.

Panikkar's relational ontology posits that the nature of reality is relationally co-constituted as divine, human, and material. And yet it's co-constitution is irreducible to any one dimension of reality, whether that be the material world, humanity, or our conception of God or the sacred. If the relation cosmotheandrically constitutes reality, it does so by articulating the constitutive interconnectedness of: what it means to be human in light of the divine as a material being; of what it means to be material in communion with or as a human person graced by the supernatural; and of what it means to be divine, in some way related to the human and the material. But underlying a cosmotheandric reality is the relation that harmoniously connects all parts of reality to all other parts of reality without reducing reality to mere univocal identity or equivocal difference. In Panikkar's metaphysics, relationality or the relation replaces substance, creating new ways of thinking about the nature of reality.

And yet this chapter further develops Panikkar's relational ontology in two ways. First, it situates Panikkar's relational ontology into a discourse that builds upon the Heideggerian tradition of fundamental ontology and Charles Taylor's moral ontology. In doing so it grounds Panikkar's relational ontology in the question of the meaning of being—while expanding upon the meaning of being to include a cosmotheandric understanding of the human person.

26   *Chapter 2*

Second it analyzes Panikkar's relational ontology as grounded in an advaitic insight into the cosmotheandric structure of reality. After offering constructive building blocks of a relational ontology through the contributions of Martin Heidegger, Jean-Luc Nancy, and Charles Taylor, this chapter then develops more fully Panikkar's relational ontology through a thick description of what Fred Dallmayr has articulated as his cosmotheandric ontonomy.[1]

CONSTRUCTIVE ELEMENTS OF A RELATIONAL ONTOLOGY

A relational ontology requires understanding the constitutively relational nature of human identity as tied to the everyday search for meaning. This section articulates two elements of a relational ontology: Martin Heidegger's and Jean-Luc Nancy's fundamental ontology and Charles Taylor's moral ontology. Within both the Heideggerian fundamental ontology and Taylor's moral ontology are constitutive links between the meaning of being and a relational ontology. It argues that Heidegger lays out the importance of a fundamental ontology by positing the ontological question and that Nancy re-interprets the ontological question by emphasizing primordiality of the relation through his philosophical emphasis on being-with (*mitsein*). Heidegger's idea of a fundamental ontology is constitutive of a relational ontology that asks the meaning of being and finds a fuller expression via Nancy through his emphasis on being-with others. Furthermore, Taylor's moral ontology articulates the importance of constitutive goods and narrative identity as essential components of a relational ontology, because it offers a layer of moral discernment of what is considered as a good. Arguably, Heidegger, Nancy, and Taylor each offer constructive components that can shape a relational ontology, but what each lack, and what this chapter argues Panikkar offers, is the religious orientation of a relational ontology found in Panikkar's notion of cosmotheandric ontonomy.

Fundamental Ontology: From Heidegger to Nancy

Martin Heidegger develops the roots of a relational ontology in the fundamental ontology of his *Being and Time*. The early Heidegger deemed ontic existence as *existentiell*: an unquestioning of self-existence that fails to individuate from the crowd or to understand the depth of self-knowledge and authenticity needed for an ontological existentiality. The search for the authenticity of the self, for Heidegger, is engaged as an inquiry into self as one lives in everyday existence.[2] But it is within the ontic constitution of being-with (*mitsein*) others in the crowd, or the everyday, that we do not differentiate who we are from others. In contrast to this ontic everydayness where life is inauthentic, undifferentiated, and unindividuated, Heidegger argues that human existence can be ontologically meaningful, authentic, when we begin to differentiate and individuate ourselves from the everyday. This is done primarily through asking the ontological question—"what is the meaning of Being?"—and entails that meaningful existence comes through the *existential*, authentic possibility of *Dasein* as being-toward-death.[3] *Dasein* means to-be-here/there-in-the-world, inquiring into the meaning of one's own existence.[4]

A fundamental ontology is one that questions the meaning of being and attempts to live an authentic and meaningful everyday life. The everyday is the space where meaning is "appropriated from" in the constitution of authentic existence. Heidegger's use of *Dasein* represents the idea that it is always already thrown-into-the-world, where the everyday is the space where we can authentically differentiate ourselves from others and understand who we are as individuated beings. What Heidegger articulates is the necessity of inquiring into the meaning of being as a way of living authentically throughout everyday life: the search for meaning requires an inquiry into everydayness, differentiation from the crowd, and the authenticity of *Dasein* as oriented by its own-most horizon of meaning.

A fundamental ontology holds that the ontological question is grounded in everyday life insofar as the self is always already existing *in the world*. Our everyday existence can be seen as a place where we exist ontically without understanding the importance of the everydayness of our lives and relationships with others. To go beyond our ontic existence, we must inquire into the way and modes in which we act and live in our everyday life. Our everyday life becomes the place where our sense of self becomes authentic when we intentionally live toward an end in our everyday lives.

For Heidegger, to authentically exist means that we question the meaning of our being as *Dasein* when we become aware of our ownmost possibility as oriented toward our own death.[5] With death as the horizon of meaning, *Dasein* is able to authentically live-in-the-world because the anticipation of death as *Dasein's* ownmost end allows *Dasein* to authentically individuate and differentiate itself from others in everyday life. A life lived in anticipation of death allows one to meaningfully make sense of the world and exist in everyday life. This is because if the meaningfulness of existence comes through our orientation to death, and my death can only be my own death, *Dasein's* life can be authentically individuated and differentiated from others by anticipating and living life as if death is always already an inevitable possibility—but it is also one that can orient life as meaningful when we live always in anticipation of our own death.

28 *Chapter 2*

However, to understand the value of everyday existence, Jean-Luc Nancy offers a revisioning of Heidegger by reemphasizing the primordiality of being-with (*mitsein*) others in everyday life over *Dasein*'s individuation and differentiation from the everyday through its orientation to death.[6] For Nancy, everyday life may become authentic when being-with others displays the primordiality of the relation as the co-appearing and exposure of self-knowledge, self-identity, and authentic meaning.[7] The concept of being-with others implies the co-constitutiveness of a sense of self through relationship in which meaning and authenticity are exposed through relationship with others. That is, by being-with others, one can become authentically self-aware of who we are and what is meaningful to us.

If we want to know who we are by being-with others, there is an exposure to who we are in what Nancy calls "the between." The between for Nancy is the relational space between us where meaning originates and offers a sense of meaning and identity. The between exposes us to who we are as beings who are singularly plural. To be singularly plural means to be a singular being constituted by a plurality of relationships. It is by our relations with others that we ontologically exist as plurally constituted singularities.[8] It is by our being-with others as a singular existence within a plurality of unfolding relationships that we meaningfully exist.[9] The ontological paradox of being singularly plural is that when we exist as a singular plurality in relation with others, we exist as a plurally constituted singular being, originating meaningful existence with others who are also plurally constituted singular beings. It is within everyday relationships that meaning and authentic existence co-appear with others and are exposed to us through relationship with other singular plural beings.[10]

A relational ontology understands that how we live *toward* others is constituted by the knowledge *of* an other that informs us *of* ourselves and constitutes our lives as meaningful through the relationship *with* an other. The relational exposure to the meaning of being is apparent when we become aware that we are not all that is and that others are constitutive to our identities, just as a person may relationally constitute the meaning of being with, for, and of others. It implies that relationship with the other constitutes the other with meaning just as the other becomes constitutive to a person's own sense of meaning. Relationality implies a sense of meaning that allows us to relate with others in a way where every person has their own value; every person becomes invaluable and we can only find the sense of meaning by recognizing that the other also constitutes my own sense of self. It is through relationship that self and other become co-constitutive of each other; meaningful and authentic existence becomes constituted through relationship with others.

Ontologically, by being-with others we are exposed to who we are as a relating person and it is through relationships that we are able to live authentic and meaningful lives. Furthermore, our life-narratives define us and give meaningful orientation and direction to our lives. There is an orientation to life derived from the horizons of our life-narratives. The horizons of life-narratives and relationship-with-others in everyday life constitute central elements of a relational ontology. Moreover, narrative and relationship are constitutive of what we deem good. By building on Charles Taylor's moral ontology, the following section outlines the narrative and moral dimensions of a relational ontology. The following argues via Charles Taylor that self-identity and orientation to the good is derivative from life's moral sources found in narrative experiences.

Moral Ontology: Ontology and the Good Life

In Charles Taylor's understanding of a moral ontology, a narrative identity (in what Alasdair MacIntyre calls a narrative quest)[11] is that which moves us to action and serves as a constitutive good that identifies us as participating in the good life.[12] For Taylor, a moral ontology implies the notion that personal identity is tied to a conception of the good that reveals the implicit background frameworks not only of our self-identity but also of what orients us toward the good, whether that be in the affirmation of ordinary life, the betterment of human life or the environment, or in the experience of God as the *sunnum bonum*.[13] Furthermore, Taylor's idea of "making sense" states that the self is constituted by moral concerns for the good life that are grounded in moral sources found within narrative experiences that constitute a sense of meaningful identity. Ontologically, making sense indicates a meaning-making process, where personal identity is being made, as originating in and constituted by moral sources and concerns that move us. Thus, the question of making sense implies an ontologically constitutive process of meaning-making, self-referencing, and self-understanding.

Taylor states, "to be able to answer for oneself is to know where one stands, what one wants to answer. And that is why we naturally tend to talk of our fundamental orientation in terms of who we are. To lose this orientation, or not to have found it, is not to know who one is. And this orientation, once attained, defines where you answer from, hence your identity."[14] Taylor goes further to state that making sense "means articulating what makes these responses appropriate: identifying what makes something a fit object for them and correlatively formulating more fully the nature of the response as well as spelling out what all this presupposes about ourselves and our situation in the world."[15] Taylor identifies this process of making sense with what he calls webs of interlocution. A web of interlocution is where we are defined and constituted by our spheres of influence, our situations in life, and by our life experiences. All humans are found within, and are themselves, a web of

30 *Chapter 2*

interlocution. Leaning on Nancy, to be a web of interlocution is to be singularly plural. But Taylor's webs of interlocution also imply being constituted by our life-narratives and languages of self-understanding.[16] These languages of self-understanding imply certain frameworks in which we make sense of the world and articulate a web of relations through which our self-identity is constituted: and this is often done in social and communal relationships.

Charles Taylor offers the moral scope to a relational ontology in his articulation of the affirmation of ordinary life as the space where moral sources inform us of implicit meaning in our everyday life. The affirmation of moral sources in everyday life is not just an affirmation of the constitutive goodness or badness of everyday life, but rather it is the affirmation of the moral dimensions of a self as intrinsically having a sense of dignity. This sense of the dignity demands the respect that every "other" has an ontological sense of meaning and morality that a person respects as an invaluable part of life.[17] Taylor's moral ontology shows that everyday life offers a sense of meaning that is not just an ontic level of existence but has an ontological depth of *moral* meaning. The moral depth of the good implies that meaning-making must be made by every person insofar as they participate in the good life through the valuation of moral sources and the orientation to moral concerns. The process of meaning-making or making sense implies a moral depth to everyday life found within our conception of the good life, moral sources, and moral concerns. Moreover, the conception of the good life, moral sources, and moral concerns are dependent upon the communities we participate in, our conception of God, our life-narratives, and our everyday experience in and of the world.

Arto Laitinen argues that Taylor splits this moral depth into two levels: (1) the unexamined life, beliefs, or frameworks, (i.e., what I would characterize as Heidegger's ontic existence that has an existential depth if it is inquired into); and (2) an understanding and examination of both the sources of meaning and the frameworks that shape them, (i.e., what I would characterize as the ontological inquiry of Heidegger into the meaning of being).[18] Without moral evaluation by and through our conception of the good and its relation to our narrative identity and communal participation, everyday life remains alienated from authentic and meaningful existence. For Taylor the ontological is not a mere search for meaning; it is an affirmation of the meaningfulness of everyday life.[19] Our frameworks help constitute our lives as meaningful, but they must be examined. This examination includes the evaluation of moral sources and of the implicit moral concerns found within our ordinary lives. While there are three main moral sources by which we may order our lives (God, humanity, or nature), our moral concerns for the good life are contextualized by our life-narratives. He argues that the importance of belief or unbelief lies within the context of lived experience.[20]

Panikkar's Relational Ontology

In examining the good life, we must be aware of our world and deliberate between a plurality of goods, relationships, and concerns that implicitly articulate what is good for us, constitute our moral compass, and order our ordinary lives. For Taylor, a moral ontology is derivative of our background frameworks: our historical heritage, education, social relationships, and life-narratives. These frameworks constitute the meaning of being and orient us to a conception of a good life.[21] Taylor's ideas indicate that the good life is grounded in a plurality of moral concerns and conceptions of the good. This plurality de-centers our sense of self, meaning, and morality. If the West is defined by a plurality of possible options, moral frameworks, and authenticity, then these factors contribute to the created religious idiosyncrasies characteristic of what results from the cross-pressures of moral concerns in ordinary life.[22] That is, the contentions between our moral concerns and life-narratives determine what we imagine the good life to be, what moral sources work for us, and what moral sources become constitutive of our identity. We have a plurality of moral concerns, and meaning-making may be constituted by multiple moral sources, narrative identities, and communal belongings. These frameworks can be plurivocal, a melting pot of ideas or beliefs that may or may not realize or acknowledge incommensurable differences, or they can be holistic reflections of what it means to be human with others as a way of being in the world, showing us the truth of our moral frameworks for meaning-making via the examination, articulation, and exposition of the good life.

***

This section developed the constitutive everydayness of a relational ontology through analyses of Heidegger's, Nancy's, and Taylor's ideas of fundamental, relational, and moral ontologies. A relational ontology argues that in the affirmation of everyday life there is a necessary search for authenticity and the meaning of being where the self is morally constituted through narrative and relationship. Being-with others relationally becomes constitutive of who we are in "originary" ways. Relationships with others originate between myself and the other an authentic sense of meaning and identity. The good life, moral sources, and moral concerns found throughout our life-narratives refer a moral orientation of living wherein one's self-identity is constituted through moral deliberation and examination of ordinary life.

A relational ontology grounded in everyday life constitutes a moral sense of self in relation with others as an authentic experience of the good life. Heidegger shows us that we must question the meaning of being to authentically live. Nancy shows us that being-with others is relationally

32   *Chapter 2*

co-constitutive. Taylor shows us that the moral sources found among our life-narratives allow us to make-sense of meaning and offer us conceptions of the good life. From each of these there remains a *religious* silence however—one that Panikkar offers key ideas to flesh out through his religious innovations of sacred secularity and cosmotheandric ontonomy.

PANIKKAR'S RELIGIOUS INNOVATION

Panikkar's ideas of sacred secularity and cosmotheandrism emphasize a religious innovation to his relational ontology. His notion of sacred secularity entails the idea that humans remain existentially open to transcendence and that human, secular action may be transformed into religious action as an act of worship.[23] Sacred secularity entails that human action may be transformed into liturgical acts of worship in everyday life. Furthermore, Panikkar's sacred secularity fundamentally presupposes a cosmotheandric ontonomy which implies the integral relationship of the three dimensions of reality—world, God, and humanity—as ontologically and relationally constitutive of everyday human experience as a participatory religiosity of ordinary life. Developing Panikkar's idea of a cosmotheandric ontonomy, Fred Dallmayr states that it "stresses the integral connection between the divine, the human, and nature," and that "ontonomy construes . . . the tapping of the hidden potential" found in the realization of the law of our being as mirrors of the whole picture of reality.[24] Furthermore, "ontonomy refers to a perspective that shuns both internal and external constitutions and accentuates instead a web of ontological relationships."[25] Panikkar argues that human persons are a cosmotheandric symbol that manifests reality: humans are a symbolic reflection of a cosmotheandric reality, which affirms the reality of Being as represented in humans as a knot of cosmotheandric relationships that constitute their identity.[26]

Panikkar develops the *pars pro toto* as a means by which humanity symbolically reflects not merely a part of the whole but the in-finitude of infinite being by participating in reality as a microcosm of a cosmotheandric reality. Anthony Savari Raj states that "a symbol implies a function in the existential world," meaning that symbols create meaning to every person's existence and that "[a symbol] gradually reveals a whole world of relationships of which the knower is a part."[27] This means that insofar as humans participate in reality, they are not only a symbolic manifestation of God's purpose and meaning in everyday life, but also that through human action, everyday experience is sanctified. The symbolic meaning of sacred secularity indicates an entwinement of religious experience and ritual action with everydayness and ordinary life insofar as a human participates as a symbol of reality in the actions of their everyday life. What sacred secularity implies is a transformation of secular everydayness through human (liturgical) action in the world with others as a response to the divine insofar as each person is a manifestation of and constitutes relationally the whole of reality.

The symbolic nature of sacred secularity implies that as human beings participate in the whole of reality, they reflect a participatory and cosmotheandric sense of self-identity, meaning, and authenticity. Therefore, human identity is relationally constitutive of and constituted by participating in a cosmotheandric reality insofar as human action is transformed by its everyday participation and experience of an enchanted cosmos, by the presence of God, and through human action. Because a cosmotheandric reality is always already "en-spirited" and teleologically oriented toward its eschatological completion in the fullness of Christ through the human, liturgical participation in reality,[28] Panikkar's account of sacred secularity and cosmotheandric ontonomy connect a relational ontology to participatory experience which constitutes self-identity, authenticity, and meaning through its religious everydayness. Religious everydayness can be described as participating symbolically in a cosmotheandric reality through human liturgical action and secular experience as charged with religious significance and meaning.

For Panikkar lived experience is always a cosmotheandric experience where secular everydayness is transformed by humanity's liturgical action as participating in an experience of a cosmotheandric reality. Panikkar's conception of religious experience in everyday life is equally the transformation of secular experience through the liturgical action and participation in secular time. Lived experience and secular action as such, becomes sacramental and liturgical action insofar as human action and lived experience is symbolically transformed into a symbolic act of worship. Furthermore, secular experience is transformed insofar as it participates in divine Being through human liturgical action as an act of sacramental worship.

For Panikkar the Being of God is metaphysically found within the cosmotheandric, participatory nature of the tripartite experience of reality. Being is not limited to just what *my* being is, but it is also relative to all other beings. Being is participated in insofar as beings experience the threefold nature of reality. Our everyday existence is defined by the relational experience of our sense of self with and in a cosmotheandric reality where we understand ourselves as a being relationally identified with and in the continual relational unfolding of life and time. Our sense of self-identity requires an ontological experience of meaning that both transcends us and symbolically constitutes us as a ontonomic being through our liturgical participation in reality. Sacred secularity and cosmotheandric ontonomy ontologically indicate the symbolical participation of human action in the ontonomic rhythm of reality. Panikkar's sacred secularity opens the cosmos and human beings to the

34   *Chapter 2*

experience of God by stressing divine immanence to and in this world insofar as it transforms secular experience and religious identity. Likewise, Panikkar's cosmotheandric ontonomy implies an ontological inter-connectedness of all reality—and this will be developed below.

COSMOTHEANDRIC ONTONOMY

This chapter thus far has analyzed certain building blocks in a constructive account of a relational ontology. These have included Martin Heidegger and Jean-Luc Nancy's fundamental ontology and Charles Taylor's moral ontology—which are constitutive of a relational ontology. And yet, Panikkar's religious innovations emphasizes the ontonomic dimension to both his ideas of sacred secularity and cosmotheandrism. The remainder of this chapter will analyze in depth Panikkar's notion of a cosmotheandric ontonomy to flesh out more fully *Panikkar's* relational ontology.

Undergirding Panikkar's trinitarian intuition into the nature of a cosmotheandric reality are three theological themes found within Christianity, Hinduism, and Buddhism: *perichoresis*, *advaita*, and *pratityatsamudpada*. Beginning with *perichoresis*, Panikkar observed and articulated not only a trinitarian theology that perceives the three persons in the Trinity through the lens of *advaita* and *shunyata* from Indian traditions,[29] but through his understanding of the trinitarian theme of *perichoresis*, he argues not only for a tripartite structure to a cosmotheandric reality, but for a trinitarian intuition into the structure of reality as relationally co-constitutive. Panikkar argues that the trinitarian structure of reality is relationally co-constitutive of its reality: the relation is constitutively real and replaces substance for Panikkar.[30] The perichoretic principle of ontonomy for Panikkar is the relationally constitutive basis of not only what is real but of everything in reality as real.

The trinitarian overtones to this cosmotheandric reality are fundamentally oriented by an advaitic trinitarianism in which what is real becomes constituted as real when it relationally and intrinsically reflects, or is realized or actualized, in a cosmotheandric experience of reality. In essence, Panikkar's advaitic trinitarianism implies the relationally subsisting nature of reality as constitutively inter-relational in and of what it means to be human, material, or divine—as always constituted in and substantiated by the relation to each of the other two dimensions of the real. Anselm Min draws out the trinitarian implications of a cosmotheandric reality in that:

> The basic idea of the cosmotheandric Trinity is the intrinsic interconnectedness of the three realms, each regarded as irreducible to the other, the human, the cosmic, and the divine, or Earth, Heaven, and Man, which constitutes the

ontological solidarity of all beings. Man is not the world any more than Man or world is the divine. There is also differentiation and originality to each being, not only to each of the three realms, but each being is also intrinsically related to all others in the order of being as such or ontonomy. . . . The connection is neither monarchical nor logical nor causal, but ontological.[31]

A cosmotheandric conception of reality supported by an advaitic trinitarianism implies the importance of the relation and of every being as participating in and with one another, being constituted by relationships with other people, in and by the cosmic dimension of materiality and material existence, and by divine immanence, implying the manifestation of the divine's presence in and to the world within the very dimensions of materiality and a participatory anthropology. What a cosmotheandric reality maintains is not merely the irreducibility of each dimension into one another but rather the constitutive relationality of each to and with the other. This intrinsic inter-relatedness of reality allows differentiation and otherness in a way that safeguards each person and dimension of reality as its own in a greater network of *be-ing-in-relation.*

The culmination of the governing dimension of Panikkar's advaitic trinitarianism is in his cosmotheandric intuition. The term cosmotheandrism is etymologically rooted in understanding not only the material dimension of the cosmos, the human species, and the sacred, divine, God, and/or transcendence, but their radical interconnectedness in constituting what is *real.* For Panikkar to be truly real means to be constituted in and through the inter-relatedness of the three irreducible-yet-interpenetrating dimensions of reality.[32] Moreover for Panikkar, each dimension of reality is constitutive of the other two, just as each dimension is not irreducible to the other two. The particular dimensions of a cosmotheandric reality, whether materiality, humanity, or the divine are constitutive parts of a whole cosmotheandric reality. For Panikkar every person cosmotheandrically participates with and in reality, in an advaitic experience where we consciously experience this reality. Panikkar's cosmotheandric experience implies that our existence is understood as a microcosm of reality; but we are also a being that reflects symbolically the whole of reality.

Cosmotheandrically, we are intrinsically constituted as a microcosm reflecting the inter-in-independent relationality between matter, humanity, and God. Each dimension of reality reflects a distinct dynamic within which we participate with and partake in reality as a microcosmic cosmotheandric person experiencing and symbolically reflecting and manifesting the macrocosm of a cosmotheandric reality. Panikkar articulates that every human person exists ontonomically, reflecting the cosmotheandric reality as a whole. Reality is not only reflected in us as human persons intrinsically representing

Chapter 2

a microcosm of reality but that reality itself is macrocosmically interrelated within us as we display the ontonomic inter-independency of the intrinsic cosmotheandric relationship that constitutes reality itself. Subsequently, this means that to be truly human also means both to be material and divine. For matter to be real requires its human mediation to, and participation in, the divine immanence permeating throughout physical reality. Finally, and most controversially, for the divine to be real requires some form of inter-in-dependence, presence, and/or incarnation or mediation of the divine to humanity in the material world. The true cosmotheandric being, person, or reality manifests itself through participation and/or Incarnation.

Panikkar's conception of a cosmotheandric reality implies a certain scope in which everything that *is* is seen holistically as a whole in which every part and dimension of the whole participates ontonomically. Panikkar's conception of participation is grounded in his idea of a cosmotheandric ontonomy wherein not only is humanity constituted by matter (world) and God, but finds their completion in this wholistic experience of participation in the material and divine dimension. The importance for Panikkar is the experience of wholeness in a fragmented modern world, where he sees cosmotheandrism as offering a stabilizing and redeeming vision to a damaged and fragmented reality.[33] Panikkar's cosmotheandric ontonomy thus values wholeness, relationality, identity, and otherness experienced in a tripartite understanding of reality that mutually informs and constitutes what it means *to be real*. Here the cosmotheandric reality finds its best expression in that what is real is constitutively composed of world, God, and humanity in a way that allows each to express itself holistically and ontonomically, each in its own way as itself participating within a reality that finds itself in the relationships that constitute it. For Panikkar reality is constituted cosmotheandrically. Panikkar states that:

> The [ontonomic] intuition [of a cosmotheandric reality] does not claim that these three dimensions are three modes of a monolithic, undifferentiated reality, nor does it say that they are three elements in a pluralistic system. Rather [they are] one, though intrinsically threefold, [a] relationship [that] expresses the ultimate constitution of reality. Everything that exists, any real human being, presents this triune structure expressed in three dimensions. I am not only stating that everything is directly or indirectly related to everything else—as in the radical relativity or *pratityatsamudpada* of the Buddhist tradition. [But] I am also stressing that this relationship is not only constitutive of the whole but that it shines through, ever new and vital, in every spark of the real. The cosmotheandric intuition is not a tripartite division of beings but an insight into the threefold core of all that is insofar as it is.[34]

Each dimension of reality reflects a distinct dynamic within which we participate with and partake in a cosmotheandric reality as a microcosm symbolically experiencing the macrocosm of a tripartite, inter-related, and co-constitutive reality. Panikkar argues that reality is not only reflected in us as a human person intrinsically representing a microcosm of reality but that reality itself is macrocosmically interrelated within us as we display the ontonomic inter-independency of the intrinsic cosmotheandric relationship that constitutes reality itself. Joseph Prabhu offers an understanding of cosmotheandric reality by stating that:

> [The main thesis of Panikkar] is the triadic structure of reality comprising the divine, the human, and the cosmic in [a] thoroughgoing relationality. In saying that, "God, Man, and World are three artificially substantivized forms of adjectives which describe Reality," Panikkar is pointing to his own version of the Buddhist *pratityatsamudpada*, the espousal of what he calls "radical relativity." There are no such things or beings as God or Man or World considered as completely independent entities. Not only are they dependent on each other, but this dependence is not just external but rather internal, i.e., constitutive of their being. Panikkar coined the term "inter-in-dependence" to express this relationship. . . . The mutual dependence of the divine, Human, and the cosmic are co-constitutive of their very "being."[35]

However, for Panikkar, not only is reality irreducible to merely the human, divine, *or* material dimension, but rather that each is in some way constitutive of each other dimension and constituted by the other dimensions. The human dimension is not only irreducible to the exclusion of the material or divine dimensions, but it is also inseparable from the material and divine dimensions. Likewise, the material dimension does not exclude the divine or human dimensions but in some way is constituted by the divine and constitutive of the human dimension, just as the divine dimension does not exclude the human or material. Rather the divine dimension constitutes both the material and human dimensions as derivative from it.

The human person is constituted not only by material embodiment, but also in some way as divine or dependent upon the divine. To be truly human means to be not merely alive, rational, relational, etc., but also to be material and in some sense divine. Panikkar states that, "a person . . . is a center of relationships based on the qualitative distinction of uniqueness. A person is unique and incomparable, and so in some way a mystery, for uniqueness is the phenomenological expression of any ontological mystery; it cannot be compared, there is no point of reference, it remains a mystery . . . [the person] is all but [a unique] bundle of relations."[36] The constitution of a cosmotheandric person is the fact that we exist *pars pro toto* within reality as an experiencing person that derives his or her sense of self as participating in a cosmotheandric reality: a human being is a cosmotheandric person that reflects microcosmically the macrocosm of a cosmotheandric reality in ways that reflects an ontonomic order of inter-in-dependency that generates ever new laws of being both between a cosmotheandric reality and within a cosmotheandric reality.[37]

Panikkar's idea of the ontonomy implies that the cosmotheandric experience of reality is participatory. Cosmotheandric ontonomy refers to an understanding of how reality is inter-in-dependent, constituted by the tripartite dimensions of reality while intrinsically constitutive of each dimension of reality. Panikkar's understanding of reality as cosmotheandric implies that reality is ontonomically constituted as an intrinsic threefold unity of an inter-in-dependent reality that is experienced through the perichoretic inter-penetration and radical relativity between cosmotheandric dimensions. Ontonomy expresses that each dimension of reality lies within every dimension as a *pars pro toto*, fundamentally representing the whole of reality in each dimension as a part of reality that is intrinsically and inter-independently presented as a cosmotheandric reality. Panikkar states that reality is:

> Ontonomically intended to express the recognition of the inner regularities of each field of activity or sphere of being in light of the whole. The whole is, in fact, neither different nor merely identical with any one field or sphere. Ontonomy rests on the assumption that the universe is a whole, that there is an internal and constitutive relationship between all and every part of reality, that nothing is disconnected and that the development and progress of one being is not to be at the expense of another.[38]

Panikkar's understanding of reality as ontonomic highlights that "according to [the ontonomic] vision we *are* inasmuch as we participate in the whole and allow the whole to participate, i.e., to express itself in us. I am, inasmuch as the others are in me, inasmuch as I am involved and committed to the whole of reality, inasmuch as I take part, i.e., I participate in the entire process of the universe."[39] Within this participatory framework of an ontonomic vision, Jacob Parappally argues that ontonomy for Panikkar is linked to his notion of radical relativity:

> Ontonomy recognizes the radical relativity [the inter-in-dependency] of all beings, sees reality as non-dualistic polarities, and opens the way for the integration of every being into [a] harmonious whole. . . . It is this ontonomic intuition that reveals the radical relativity of everything. The symbol of this ontonomy which reveals the radical relativity is [the] person. [The] person is neither singular or plural. *A person is a conjunction* . . . Panikkar affirms that a person is a bundle of relationships and a knot in the network of relationships.[40]

Within this framework, advaitic trinitarianism, radical relativity, cosmotheandric reality, and ontonomy stress Panikkar's vision of reality as inherently co-constitutive, relational, and participatory. His emphasis on the relationally constitutive harmony of reality is one marked by a participatory ontology in which each dimension of reality participates in some sense with and/or in another dimension, mutually constituting reality as cosmotheandric. Relationally, each part of the tripartite dimension of a cosmotheandric reality constitutes in some way the other two dimensions, implying not only the mutual interpenetration between the three dimensions of reality but their participation in one another as a constitutive, relational harmony. Panikkar defines this cosmotheandric harmony as an experience of reality when he states that:

> The experience of harmony is a primordial experience that cannot be reduced to unity and multiplicity. In order to perceive harmony, pure unity is not needed and mere diversity is not enough. . . . [The experience of harmony] requires the experience of rhythm, which is neither the repetition of an identical movement nor its negation. Our atrophied artistic culture makes it harder for us to realize that neither rhythm nor harmony can be reduced to something external; neither can [it] be perceived without our participation, without us "becoming part" of them and without our complete identifying with them. The second "movement" of rhythm repeats the first but is not identical to it, coming in second place as it does. We are a part; we "participate," but we are not the whole.[41]

Within this context, the relational harmony implies the co-constitutive ontonomous participation of reality with and in each of the tripartite dimensions of reality in ways that allows both their differentiation and otherness from one another, as well as their co-constitutive participatory unity.

TOWARD AN ADVAITIC RELATIONAL ONTOLOGY

While Heidegger, Nancy, and Taylor each offer important insights in the development of a relational ontology, this chapter has argued how Panikkar offers a religious interpretation of a relational ontology through analyses of his cosmotheandric ontonomy and sacred secularity. While Heidegger remains fundamental for asking the question of the meaning of Being, both Nancy and Taylor offer important insights into both the relational co-constitution of beings as well as the moral commitments of making sense of meaning throughout our life-narratives. Building on these, if Panikkar's relational ontology articulates the *relation* as the constitutive link that connects all of reality, then we find in Panikkar's relational ontology an interpretation

40 *Chapter 2*

of being that sees reality as cosmotheandrically interconnected and inter-in-dependent. For the remainder of this chapter the emphasis however will be on an underdeveloped theme—the advaitic emphasis of Panikkar's relational ontology.

Fred Dallmayr's understanding of Panikkar's relational ontology is one that articulates the ontological constitution between a web of relationships which constitute what it means to be human. While the meaning of being has been a central question throughout this chapter in the development of a relational ontology, Panikkar's unique contribution to this discourse is the human person's ontonomic experience of a cosmotheandric reality. This ontonomic experience implies a co-constitutive non-dualistic relationship between infinite and finite existence. It implies an ontonomy in which we exist as a being governed by the non-dualistic relationality, harmony, and dynamism of cosmotheandric reality—but not as an experience of a divided autonomous self that is separated from others, God, and the world. Non-dualistic experience is one that is concerned with relations, and more specifically of the human relation to an ultimate reality or the mystery of being. Panikkar states that "inter-relatedness is what I call the ontonomic relatedness of a universal inter-independence, which is another way of explaining the advaitic insight."[42] Panikkar's understanding of a relational ontology as the advaitic insight points to the essence of the relation that unites the experience between humanity, the world, and the divine in a way that authentically portrays the ontonomic experience of a cosmotheandric reality as constitutive of what it means to be human.

Furthermore, what Panikkar's ontonomic relatedness of reality indicates is that we are in fact a part of reality that relationally participates and reflects the whole of reality because we exist in and as (a cosmotheandric) reality. A non-dual experience is an experience in which human persons are able to realize the *pars pro toto* of reality; that the part speaks to and re-presents the whole to itself in a way that identifies itself with, in, and as the relational and unitive factor that demonstrates the relationality of a cosmotheandric reality that informs human persons of their relationally ontological constitution as material, human, and divine. This *pars pro toto* of reality is one that reflects the co-constitution between the sacred and the human in a relationally wholistic and harmonious way.

The *pars pro toto* of reality in an advaitic relational ontology provides a sense that we are able to become a whole, unified reality through finitude's participation in infinitude. Non-dualistic experience articulates an inter-relational interaction between reality, where the Sacred, the human, and the material relate to one another in ways that participate in one another. What this implies is how finite beings can be relationally constituted by and participate in infinitude. It is to the question of the relationship between finitude

Panikkar's Relational Ontology   41

and infinitude that we will examine next through a comparative analysis of the metaphysical implications of Raimon Panikkar and Martin Heidegger's understandings of being and time.

NOTES

1. Fred Dallmayr, "Rethinking Secularism (with Raimon Panikkar)," *The Review of Politics* 61, no. 4 (1999): 715–35.

2. Martin Heidegger, *Being and Time*, trans. John MacQuarrie and Edward Robinson (New York: Harper Collins Publishers, 2008), 1–35.

3. Heidegger, *Being and Time*, 33, 149–68.

4. Heidegger, *Being and Time*, 32, 78–90.

5. Heidegger, *Being and Time*, 279–311.

6. Heidegger, *Being and Time*, 161; opt. cit. Jean-Luc Nancy, *Being Singular Plural*, trans. Robert D. Richardson and Anne E. O'Bryne (Stanford, CA: Stanford University Press, 2000), 26–27; Ian James, *The Fragmentary Demand: An Introduction to the Philosophy of Jean-Luc Nancy* (Stanford, CA: Stanford University Press, 2006), 104.

7. For a fuller account of Nancy's ontological position c.f. Nancy, *Being Singular Plural*, 28–41; and Jean-Luc Nancy, *The Sense of the World*, trans. Jeffrey S. Librett (Minneapolis: University of Minnesota Press, 1997), 4–9, 27–29.

8. Jean-Luc Nancy, *The Inoperative Community*, trans. Peter Connor, Theory and History of Literature 76 (Minneapolis, MN: University of Minnesota Press, 1991), 27–28.

9. Nancy, *Being Singular Plural*, 94.

10. C.f. Nancy, *Being Singular Plural*, 1–41.

11. Alasdair MacIntyre, *After Virtue: A Study of Moral Theory*, Second Edition (Notre-Dame, IN: University of Notre-Dame Press, 1984), 215–21.

12. Charles Taylor, *Sources of the Self: The Making of the Modern Identity* (Cambridge, MA: the Belknap Press of Harvard University Press, 1989), 3–104.

13. These four "goods" partition four background frameworks and their moral concerns. The four background frameworks describe four ways of being modern and their moral concerns: the theist, the exclusive humanist, the Romantic-idealist-expressivist, and the neo-Nietzschean anti-humanist. While the theist posits God as a moral source, the exclusive humanist and neo-Nietzschean anti-humanist posit an anthropological moral source (self for neo-Nietzschean and others for exclusive humanist), and the Romantic-idealist-expressivist posits self and nature as a moral source. Thus, there are four possible moral sources in three categories: God is a moral source in the theistic category, nature is a moral source in the ecological category, and self and others are moral sources in the anthropological category. C.f. David McPherson, "Re-Enchanting the World: An Examination of Ethics, Religion, and Their Relationship in the Work of Charles Taylor" (Milwaukee, WI: Marquette University, 2013), 61–64.

14. Taylor, *Sources of the Self*, 29.

15. Taylor, *Sources of the Self*, 8–9.

42 *Chapter 2*

16. Colin Jager, "This Detail, This History: Charles Taylor's Romanticism," in *Varieties of Secularism in a Secular Age*, eds., Michael Warner, Jonathan VanAntwerpen, and Craig Calhoun (Cambridge, MA: Harvard University Press, 2010), 166–92, 185–86; Taylor, *Sources of the Self*, 36.

17. For Taylor's understanding of "dignity": c.f. Taylor, *Sources of the Self*, 15–16.

18. For a more in depth understanding of Taylor's tiers of moral value c.f. Arto Laitinen, "A Critique of Charles Taylor's Notions of Moral Sources and Constitutive Goods," *Acta Philosophica Fennica* 76 (2004): 73–104.

19. Taylor, *Sources of the Self*, 3–8.

20. Charles Taylor, *A Secular Age* (Cambridge, MA: The Belknap Press of Harvard University Press, 2007), 13.

21. C.f. Taylor, *Sources of the Self*, 8–9.

22. Taylor, *Sources of the Self*, 17.

23. C.f. Raimon Panikkar, *Worship and Secular Man* (Maryknoll, NY: Orbis Books, 1973).

24. Dallmayr, "Rethinking Secularism (with Raimon Panikkar)," 726.

25. Dallmayr, "Rethinking Secularism (with Raimon Panikkar)," 725.

26. Panikkar, *Worship and Secular Man*, 20–21.

27. Anthony Savari Raj, *A New Hermeneutic of Reality: Raimon Panikkar's Cosmotheandric Vision* (New York: Peter Lang, 1998), 58–59.

28. C.f. Gerard Vincent Hall, "Raimon Panikkar's Hermeneutics of Religious Pluralism," Catholic University of America (Ann Arbor, MI: UMI Dissertation Services, 1994), 66.

29. C.f. Raimon Panikkar, *Trinity and the Religious Experience of Man* (Maryknoll, NY: Orbis Books, 1973), 41–69.

30. Raimon Panikkar, *The Rhythm of Being: The Unbroken Trinity* (Maryknoll, NY: Orbis Books, 2010), 218–19.

31. Anselm Min, "Panikkar's Radical Trinitarianism: Reflections on Panikkar's Transformation of the Christian Trinity into Cosmotheandrism," *CIRPIT Review* 6 (2015): 75–100, 76–77.

32. Joseph Prabhu, "Panikkar's Trinitarianism and His Critique of (Mono) Theism," *CIRPIT Review* 5 (2014): 79–87, 81, 84–85.

33. Raimon Panikkar, *The Cosmotheandric Experience: Emerging Religious Consciousness*, ed. Scott Eastham (Maryknoll, NY: Orbis Books, 1993), 32–53.

34. Raimon Panikkar, *Mysticism and Spirituality: Mysticism, The Fullness of Life*, ed. Milena Carrara Pavan, Vol. I.1, XII vols., Opera Omnia (Maryknoll, NY: Orbis Books, 2014), 28; C.f. Panikkar, *The Cosmotheandric Experience*, 60.

35. Prabhu, "Panikkar's Trinitarianism and His Critique of (Mono) Theism," 81, 84–85.

36. Raimon Panikkar, *Myth, Faith, and Hermeneutics: Cross Cultural Studies* (New York: Paulist Press, 1979), 377.

37. Panikkar, *The Rhythm of Being*, 53.

38. Panikkar, *Worship and Secular Man*, 41–42.

39. Panikkar, *Worship and Secular Man*, 47.

40. Jacob Parappally, "Panikkar's Vision of Reality and Contextual Theology," *CIRPIT Review* 4 (2013): 217–26, 224.

41. Panikkar, *Mysticism and Spirituality*, 143.

42. Panikkar, *The Rhythm of Being*, 220.

Chapter 3

Heidegger's Ontology, Panikkar's Advaita

Ontology, Metaphysics, and Tempiternity

While the previous chapter analyzed Panikkar's relational ontology, and started with Heidegger's fundamental ontology, this chapter will continue the dialogue between these two thinkers. Without a doubt, the crux of Heidegger's philosophy is the questioning of being in time—what Heidegger calls fundamental ontology and its onto-theological critique of metaphysics. But how Heidegger asks the question of being in time offers important foundations for Panikkar's reformulations of Heidegger around the question of the ontological distinction between God and created beings, as well as the ontological difference between Being and beings.

While Heidegger argued that these ontological questions pose a univocal problem, this chapter argues that Panikkar's advaitic metaphysics and tempiternal reconciliations solve this problem because Panikkar does not adhere to the ontological distinction between God and (created) Beings. Whereas Heidegger adopts a univocal onto-theology that separates metaphysics from theology, Panikkar offers an advaitic metaphysics that non-dualistically reads Being, God, and Reality as co-constitutive of one another. Furthermore, Panikkar's tempiternal understanding of reality, where eternity and time are co-temporaneous and participate in one another, resolves Heidegger's univocal problem centered around the impossibility of speaking of God as Being because it creates an ontological problem when we speak of God as conditioned by temporality.

This chapter argues that Panikkar is deeply indebted to the thought of Martin Heidegger and describes both Panikkar's advaitic reformulations of Heidegger's onto-theology as well as Panikkar's tempiternal solution

46   *Chapter 3*

to Heidegger's problem of being in time. The problem of being in time is situated in how finitude participates in infinitude (Panikkar) or how finitude transcends its finitude through the temporal existing of being-in-time (Heidegger). At the heart of this chapter is an advaitic meditation on metaphysics and Panikkar's tempiternal reconciliation of being and time. It argues that Panikkar's advaitic reformulations of Heidegger open up the limits of thinking about Being, God, and Reality in ways that do not necessitate the ontological distinction between God and creation—and indeed overcomes the problems Heidegger poses about the temporality of God and Being.

THE PROBLEM AND THE SOLUTION

Both Panikkar and Heidegger were concerned with the relationship between Being and time. How Being exists in time is a central question for both. For Heidegger, Being is understood as *Dasein*, the being-here/there of a being in time. But *Dasein* is also embedded and embodied in-the-world in ways that Heidegger posits both its finitude and its temporality. But for Heidegger the positioning of *Dasein* in time is something that can only be bound to finite existence. To be bound to time is to be bound to finitude, which is marked by the totalization and individuation of *Dasein* in its orientation to its death. *Dasein* for Heidegger is ontological, aware of itself as authentically distinct from the crowd of entities not aware of their own meaning of Being. If *Dasein* questions the meaning of Being, entities do not. Entities merely live in the world of the crowd and are unable to stand above it, authentically know who they are apart from it, or authentically live in the world as individuated beings.

If, for Heidegger, Being is understood temporally and as finite, then for Panikkar, Being is understood *in*-finitude and includes the eternal presence of divine immanence in temporal life. Panikkar's "tempiternity" is a term used to articulate how Being exists in time marked by the presence of eternity. Panikkar does not accept the univocity of Being that Heidegger does, stemming from the tradition of Duns Scotus.[1] Rather Panikkar reverses the Christian trajectory toward divine transcendence in modernity with an awareness and articulation of divine immanence in and with beings in time. The eternal presence of divine immanence to, in, and with time allows beings the ability to live tempiternally. Indeed, Panikkar's theological understanding of Being, God, and Reality is something that exists in-finitude. Infinitude enters into finitude for Panikkar, allowing beings to be found in their finitude in the presence of God's infinitude. Tempiternity is Panikkar's word for theologically explaining the problem of Being in time by allowing beings to be found in their finitude through their participation in the presence of divine infinitude.

HEIDEGGER'S FUNDAMENTAL ONTOLOGY

Heidegger coined the term *"Dasein"* to refer to the ontological nature of a being who is here/there in the world. For Heidegger, the essence or whatness of existence is found in its "that-ness" or the mode of a being's being-in-the-world.[2] Heidegger states that the "'essence' of *Dasein* lies in its existence."[3] For Heidegger we are already thrown into the world: the world is something *in* which we (already) live. This means our world is not something we construct, but rather is something we already exist within: a world is always already presupposed by the very conditions of situated existence in which we live. Heidegger further makes ontological distinctions between Being (Sein) and beings/entities (Seiendes), and existential (authentic) and existentiell (inauthentic) existence to refer to his distinction between ontological (Sein and existential) and ontic (Seiendes and existentiell) existing.[4]

These ontological distinctions are constitutive of what Heidegger called the ontological difference: the questioning of the difference between Being (itself) and beings. Heidegger's notions of "Being" and "existential" are linked and imply the ontological question of "what does it mean to be," or rather, "what is the meaning of being?" These questions imply an inquiry into why "I am here" (*Dasein*) and what gives *Dasein* meaning, identity, and purpose.[5] By contrast, Heidegger's notions of "existentiell" and "beings/entities" are linked and imply the lack of the ontological questioning of the meaning of being. By not asking after the meaning of being, Heidegger understands beings/entities as lacking differentiation from others in the crowd of being (*Das Man*). Heidegger's argues that when beings ask the *ontological question* by contrast they are marked by the individuation and totalization of *Dasein*.[6] We become individuals when we differentiate ourselves from the crowd. And we do this by asking the ontological question, giving us a unique identity that is oriented toward an end that is uniquely "my own." This "ownmost end" is for Heidegger death: by embracing the possibility and anticipation of our own death as something that individuates every person as "my own" is how we authentically live according to Heidegger.[7]

Heidegger's fundamental ontology depicts a reality of everyday life as always already presupposing a world of meaning we make sense of and in through the lived experience of temporality. To be, for Heidegger, means to be here/there already in the world—a world in which we are always already temporally enpresenting/enpresented. For Heidegger, we are not just enpresented in a world that already is, but so also are we enpresented through *Dasein*'s ecstatic experience of time in ways that transcends *Dasein*. The temporal structures of *Dasein*'s experience for Heidegger entails the temporal experience of past, present, and future in ways that not only characterize

Dasein's experience in the world, but in and through the spatial application of *Dasein*-in-the-world, the temporalization of *Dasein* implies its transcendence from itself as it experiences the world. The temporalization of *Dasein* is ecstatic insofar as *Dasein* experiences time in ways that take *Dasein* beyond itself—in relation to others, the world, as well as its own subjective experience of time. In these senses, *Dasein* transcendends itself through its experience of the world, others, and of itself in and through time. Heidegger argues that the enpresencing of *Dasein* is temporal: *Dasein* is enpresented in time in ways that ecstatically transcends itself. It is in the temporal structures of everyday life that Heidegger fundamentally demonstrates the structures of Being in time.[8]

Dorothea Frede argues that in Heidegger's omission of Division III of *Being and Time*, he failed to provide the reversal of Being and Time as Time and Being. She argues that the first two Divisions of Heidegger's *Being and Time* describe a static ontology of what it means to exist in time.[9] By contrast, she suggests that if there were the reversal to Time and Being in the unfinished parts of *Being and Time*, a dynamic ontology would open how humans find themselves produced or arising within the temporality of the world. Frede states that "the 'meaning of being' as it is constituted by our understanding is thus grounded in the temporal structure that underlies our understanding."[10] Frede argues that:

> By temporality (Heidegger) does not mean that we are, as are all other things, confined to time, nor that we have a sense of time, but rather that we exist as three temporal dimensions at once: it is being ahead of ourselves in the future, drawing on our past, while being concerned with the present that constitutes our being. The way we project ourselves into the future (ahead of ourselves) while taking with us our past (being already in) in our immersion into the present (being at home with) is what Heidegger designates as the "*ekstasis*" of temporality.[11]

In further commentary on Heidegger's notions of the temporality of Being, Robert Dostal identifies the temporal structures of *Dasein* as "1) ahead of itself (understanding), 2) already in (disposition), and 3) alongside. Heidegger often refers to these three structures as existentiality, facticity, and fallenness." Dostal links "this three-dimensionality of lived experience of time" in Heidegger "as the 'ecstatic' unity of time."[12] Furthermore, how *Dasein* lives itself out in time may be authentic or inauthentic, where what separates them is that the authentic anticipates its future from its past in the present, whereas the inauthentic cuts itself off from its future and its past.[13]

And yet, Heidegger does in part offer the reversal of Being and time, even if he does not complete it.[14] Heidegger argues in *The Basic Problems of Phenomenology* how *Dasein* exists in time in ways that the finitude of its being is transcended through a turn to its temporal experience of existence. The temporal structure of the existence of *Dasein* is fundamentally characterized as an ecstatic appearing, or a presencing that appears in time in ways that distends and transcends the finitude of *Dasein*. To ecstatically appear or presence itself, *Dasein* is conditioned by temporality insofar as it exists in time in ways that experiences the temporal duration of time. Furthermore, in this duration of time, *Dasein* temporally transcends the experience of past, present, and future in ways that the presence of *Dasein* temporally appears in and through time. Here we see that *Dasein* is able to transcend the temporal structures of finitude insofar that its appearance in time allows *Dasein* to be *in time*. *Dasein* is marked by temporality and immanence and rejects a transcendent God as constitutive of *Dasein*'s being. Because of this, *Dasein*'s finitude is temporally structured and constituted.

It is in the temporal structures of everyday life and experience that Heidegger's ontology manifests important intersections with the thought of Raimon Panikkar. For the purposes of this chapter, the problem with Heidegger's fundamental ontology is not so much whether finitude can be transcended. Heidegger has already made a case as to how the temporality of *Dasein* ecstatically appears and enpresents in time in ways that transcend an immanent experience of time through the finite experience of time.[15] Rather the problem is how infinitude and finitude can co-exist in time. Panikkar offers solutions to Heidegger's fundamental ontology by promoting the lived experience of faith as a tempiternal experience where God condescends to exist alongside temporality through the eternal enpresenting of divine immanence in-finitude. Before turning to this tempiternal reconciliation of Being in time, the following section analyzes the problem of the ontological distinction through analyses of Heidegger's onto-theology and Panikkar's advaitic metaphysics to articulate Panikkar's advaitic reformulations of Being, God, and Reality.

ONTO-THEOLOGY AND ADVAITIC METAPHYSICS

While the previous section offered an account of Heidegger's fundamental ontology, this section offers a comparative account of Heidegger's onto-theology and Panikkar's advaitic metaphysics to examine the relationship between God and Being for Heidegger and how Being, God, and Reality are intimately co-constitutive for Panikkar. Underlying Heidegger's onto-theology is a univocal problem between God and Being, while underlying Panikkar's advaitic metaphysics is a plurivocity that works with both

50 *Chapter 3*

Western and Asian metaphysics to understand the relationship between Being, God, and Reality. A central metaphysical problem for Heidegger is that God cannot be in time. This stems from the ontological distinction between God and creation, which for Heidegger is linked to the ontological difference between Being and beings. This section argues that Heidegger's problem of God's infinitude and eternity, as incompatible with the temporality and finitude of beings, can be overcome through Panikkar's rejection of the ontological distinction between God and creation, thus offering pathways in which to rethink the relationship between eternity and temporality and infinitude and finitude in Panikkar's advaitic metaphysics.

Heidegger's Onto-Theological Problem

Heidegger situates his fundamental ontology within a univocal tradition of metaphysics that he calls "onto-theology" which posits the difference between metaphysics and ontology, and theology and philosophy. When Heidegger talks of Being and beings, of ontology and onticity, Heidegger makes a distinction between questioning what it means to be (ontology) and the mere existing of beings (onticity).[16] This is done to explain what it means to be and what it means to articulate how we exist in the world and in time. Heidegger argues that onto-theologically this creates a problem when we talk of God as Being in the same way, especially if God is eternal and not bound to time. To speak of God and Being univocally does not make sense when it comes to the temporal structures of Being in time. For Heidegger, univocity poses a theological problem for Being that is only exposed in the aftermath of Martin Heidegger: how can God be Being if Being is temporal?

David Burrell surveys the univocity of onto-theology, drawing out its theological tensions with analogical conceptions of the creator/creation distinction.[17] Theologically, Catherine Pickstock argues that Duns Scotus opens the door for the problem of onto-theology because: (1) "'being' can now be regarded as transcendentally prior and 'common to' both God and creatures"; and (2) he "prefigures the possibility of being without God, and as more fundamental than the alternative of finite vs. infinite or temporal vs. eternal."[18] But Michael Wiitala argues that to conflate the univocal difference of Being with beings fails to give adequate weight to Heidegger's ontological difference and Duns Scotus's univocal semantics.[19] The problem the ontological distinction between God and creation poses for Heidegger is that one cannot speak of the univocal difference between the Being of God and the Being of beings when we take into account both the temporal structures of the latter and the theological problem posed by the former if God temporally exists. What Heidegger builds on from Duns Scotus' univocal semantics is a univocal ontology that questions the consistency between speaking of the temporality of beings' Being in time and the possibility of God's Being in time. The problem this univocal difference poses is central to Heidegger's onto-theological critique of metaphysics.

By situating onto-theology in the epochal heritage of a metaphysics of the ontological question, Heidegger's onto-theology historicizes metaphysics as the history of how ontology and theology contextualize beings or entities asking the meaning of their existence and their historical way of being in the world.[20] Moreover, Ian Thomson shows how Heidegger's metaphysics implies an onto-theological historicization where being is thought as "the same" throughout the history of metaphysics. The "same" is the univocal thinking of Being in the sense of both being thought and/or to be thought, implying that Being is the fundamental question of Western metaphysics. Thomson traces the onto- and theo-logical dimensions of Western metaphysics throughout a series of dual terms as the grounding by which the presencing of presence elusively un-conceals the truth of Being being thought. In doing so, the truth of theology is manifested in the Being of beings—and the questioning of the mode of being factically reveals or un-conceals how Being is thought univocally throughout the history of Western metaphysics.[21] Building on his analyses of Heidegger's onto-theology, Thomson argues that Heidegger's onto-theology constitutes a turn in metaphysics to ontological pluralism. This ontological pluralism, or rather, a plural realism, is traced throughout epochs of history to un-conceal the elusive nature of Being within variations of thinking the same onto-theologically.[22] This means that the metaphysical grounding of their being implies a plurivocal onto-theology in which time, finitude, and temporality is understood in ways that point to the overcoming of the univocal problem of how we can conceive and think the difference between God and Being.[23]

It is at this point that Panikkar's advaitic metaphysics can take the argument further and more fully flesh out a reconciliation between the problem of God and Being. This is because, while Heidegger sees the problem between the two over the ontological relationship between eternity and temporality, infinitude and finitude, that is, of the ontological distinction between God and created beings, Panikkar, by contrast, does not hold to the ontological distinction between God and created beings, and sees Being, God, and Reality as co-constitutive of both infinitude and finitude, of both eternity and temporality. It is this "tempiternal reconciliation" between Being and time that Panikkar's advaitic metaphysics offers important insights into the relationship between finitude and infinitude.

52 *Chapter 3*

Panikkar's Advaitic Metaphysics

If Heidegger sets the stage for Panikkar's advaitic metaphysics, it does so by positing several tensions inherent to the ontological distinction that Panikkar resolves: the tensions between time and eternity, between being and becoming, and between presence and absence. Panikkar's advaitic metaphysics resolves these tensions through his advaitic spin, which posits a two-tiered metaphysics that allows the space for ontological presence of Being and eternity in the ontic experience of becoming in time. Furthermore, this section nuances Panikkar's advaitic metaphysics as advocating for plurivocal understandings of Being, God, and Reality exhibited through a metaphysics of religious experience. By a close reading of Panikkar's metaphysics of religious experience primarily from Panikkar's magnum opus, *The Rhythm of Being*, this section shows how his cosmotheandric vision links to his ontology, metaphysics, and theology.

Panikkar argues in *The Rhythm of Being* for the inter-dependency between three metaphysical and theological themes: Being, God, and Reality. The advaitic interpretation of these themes highlights the inadequacy of Western metaphysical concepts of univocity, analogy, and equivocity. Panikkar's advaitic spin on metaphysics demonstrates the how these three Western metaphysical theories in varying ways can describe the nature of Being, God, and Reality. But it is important to note, that for Panikkar, Being, God, and Reality at times, and in various ways and contexts, *ought* to be understood univocally, analogically, *and* equivocally. But underlying these Western metaphysical approaches is more fundamentally a plurivocal approach found in Panikkar's advaitic metaphysics as an attempt to describe the co-constitutiveness of Being, God, and Reality. For Panikkar, Being is constitutive of both God and Reality, while God constitutes a dimension to Reality as Being itself. Likewise, Reality is not only experienced, but is both constituted by Being and encompassed by God. For Panikkar, God is Being itself which constitutes his cosmotheandric reality as one of the three central dimensions of Reality itself. Being, God, and Reality are horizons of the Real in such a way that they are intrinsically constitutive of what *is*. This section thus unpacks Panikkar's nuanced advaitic spin on Being, God, and Reality.

Panikkar's cosmotheandric insight into the nature of reality implies that Reality itself includes an understanding of Being and God. What Panikkar identifies as Reality is a plurivocal synthesis of Indian, Western, and Christian positions that represent a phenomenological understanding of the very experience of reality. What Panikkar linguistically demonstrates through analyses of the Greek *physis*, Latin *rerum natura*, and Sanskrit *idam sarvam* and *tattva-satya*, is an understanding that Reality itself indicates an external and constitutive nature of what we are and that in which we are, which indicates an ontological identity with and in the reality of the world as all this that is.[24]

Panikkar argues that Reality, in the sense that it is the space where we live, is the material space of our everyday world, that is primordially here, there, and all around us. Like Heidegger, Gadamer, and Merleau-Ponty we are thrown into a world, or rather we find ourselves always already here/there, embodied,[25] and spatially finding ourselves diachronically across the horizons of particular places and times.[26] Reality for Panikkar is phenomenologically experienced as an embodied experience of the three dimensions of reality within a horizon of becoming-in-the-world that remains open to transcendence in such a way that divine immanence constitutes and enpresents existence in time.[27]

Panikkar's cosmotheandric reality implies a sense of divine transcendence as mediated through divine immanence. Reality is both present to us, immanent to and in us as constitutive of our reality. Reality also transcends its immanence as something always wholly ungraspable.[28] We may grasp ontically at the experience of reality, but when we do, it still eludes us ontologically because its transcendence is beyond our (in-)finite experience of the Real. For Panikkar, Reality is both finite and in-finite, transcendent and immanent, real and elusive to us because it is all around us, constituting us, and is yet beyond us. Panikkar states that, "our contact with reality cannot be mediated by anything other than reality itself. The insight into reality can be only an immediate experience."[29] In its immediacy of experience, it remains ineffable. Reality itself is experienced as an immediate transcendence and experiential immanence that positions us with and in the frameworks of a cosmotheandric reality. Panikkar states that humans are conscious of living as embodied creatures who live out a *mythos* that helps us make sense of reality—indeed this *mythos* is lived and is the reality that we live.[30] Even as we exist with and in reality, constituted by reality, Reality implies a sense of Being, a presence of God, to us and around us. It transcends us, while yet giving us a sense of our own reality, making present to us our reality. Our being then is lived and experienced as being-in-reality—as both ontically immanent and ontologically transcendent to us. For Panikkar, the ontic nature of reality—the pre-reflective experience—is more primordial than the ontological—the reflective situated experience of being-in-reality.

Unlike the early Heidegger's emphasis on the ontological, and in agreement with the later Heidegger's insight and recovery of the primordial ontic experience of being in time, Panikkar emphasizes the ontic experience of being-in-reality over ontologically understanding what it means to be in reality. If the ontic experience of being-in-reality entails the presencing of the real, then the ontological experience of what it means to be in reality

54   *Chapter 3*

entails the presence of being real. It is with this sense of being-in-reality that we exist in this world experiencing this world, experiencing reality, and experiencing the Being-of-reality. Reality is not merely ontic but also ontological. Panikkar's notion of the ontic and ontological dimensions of reality is determined by his advaitic spin of both classical Indian metaphysics and Heideggerian onto-theology.

Drawing on his Indian and Heideggerian influences, Panikkar makes central to his metaphysics the ontological question. He highlights the centrality of the ontological question as a common human phenomenon across the world and history. For Panikkar, the reality of being is understood precisely through the human questioning its existence. Panikkar states that Western tradition articulates Man as a questioning being and that Asian traditions approach the human condition as an ontological sharing in the real that resists the questioning of human Being because it leads to alienation.[31] As such, Panikkar opts for the onticity of Asian traditions as more primordial than the ontological concerns of Western tradition.

Like Heidegger, Panikkar's link between the ontic and ontological lies within the question of the meaning of being, or rather, whether we both question who we are *as* we experience reality or whether we question and reflect on our experience *of* reality. But while Heidegger tends to castigate the ontic in his early works by emphasizing the ontological questioning of the meaning of being as key to existential authenticity, Panikkar agrees more with the later Heidegger, who emphasizes the ontological depth of ontic existence in such a way that warrants the ontic as more fundamentally real.[32] In the transition from the early to the later Heidegger, the shift to onticity in Heidegger's understanding of everydayness is one that describes ontic experience as the authentic presencing that allows the ontological authentication of one's Being through language and art.[33] The inquiry into Being for Heidegger is one that finds its source in the ontic facticity of existence while simultaneously individuating from the crowd and consequentially authenticating the meaning of being through the questioning of *Dasein*'s own-most being-toward-death.[34]

Being per se, as *Dasein*, is understood in the early Heidegger as derivative from the ontic existence of being-with (*mitsein*) while remaining ontologically distinct from being-with the crowd because one's authenticity is found in the questioning of, and individuating search for, the meaning of being by one's relationship towards the possibility of being. For Heidegger, meaning is derivative from the inquiry into the possibility of being, and to live authentically is to know as my own the possibility of my own death as the horizon of meaning—and orienting the meaning of my existence as toward-death implies that *Dasein* differentiates itself from the thrownness of the everyday world through its orientation toward its own-most end.

Heidegger's ontological distinction between the onticity of existentiell life and the ontological, existential questioning of *Dasein*'s own-being high-lights the reality that for the early Heidegger, onticity is merely the surface of existence and life and that ontology implies the authentic depth, facticity, and intentional determination of one's own existence, being, and life toward death. For Heidegger in *Being and Time*, the ontic is castigated as inauthentic, unquestioning its own being, merely floating with the crowd of undifferenti-ated beings/entities. By contrast, the existential questioning of *Dasein*'s own being signifies an ontological depth to its own-most being that reveals the meaning of its existence as not merely ontic, but ontological. Not merely is *Dasein* thrown into the world, but *Dasein* is authentically and ontologically self-determined through its questioning of the meaning of its own-most being in its orientation toward its own death as the constant horizon of authentic self-determination.[35]

But when we turn to India, classical Indian two-tiered metaphysics sup-ports Panikkar's advaitic spin upon onticity and ontology. For Nagarjuna, Reality has two tiers, conventional reality, *saṃvṛti-satya*, and ultimate reality, *paramārtha-satya*.[36] Within Nagarjuna's logic, not only is conven-tional reality governed by the law of *pratityatsamudpada*, or dependent co-origination, but it logically implies that nothing in reality has independent own-being or existence (*svabhāva*). Richard Jones argues that in Nagarjuna's polemic against Abhidharma philosophy, his logic involves the emptiness of *svabhāva*.[37] That is, the self, time, being, and reality are empty of any *svabhāva*, implying that the ultimate nature of reality is empty of indepen-dent existence. The ontic nature of *saṃvṛti-satya* would reveal the emptiness of ultimate reality—meaning the ultimate nature of reality, or its ontological depth, is in fact revealed through the logic of its onticity as the emptiness and inter-dependence of existence.

Applying this to Panikkar's advaitic spin on ontology and onticity, reality is not only ontic in the conventional sense, but rather reveals its ontological reality and depth through the very phenomena of its ontic conventional-ity. Like classical Indian metaphysics of a two-tiered reality, Panikkar sees onticity as conventional, and yet this onticity reveals Reality's ultimacy and ontological depth. Nagarjuna's concept of *saṃvṛti-satya* reveals the reality that dependent co-origination is not merely conventional, constitutive, and descriptive of reality, but also ultimate because it reveals the emptiness of *svabhāva* as the deeper understanding of reality as ultimately empty of any self-existence: everything is dependent on and constitutive of its depen-dency for it to be, implying its emptiness and the inter-in-dependence of its own-being.[38]

But the ontological depth of ontic reality for Panikkar not only *reveals* its ultimate ontological Reality, but its ontological Reality is found precisely within its onticity. The primordial experience of conventional, ontic reality for Panikkar re-veils the ontological appearance of the real. Where Panikkar and the later Heidegger agree is in the idea that onticity reveals its ontological Reality precisely through the ungraspable, illusory, eluding, and ineffable nature of language.[39] There is something we can grasp of Reality, and while it remains immanent to our experience, it also transcends our experience, eluding us completely, while we yet may grasp it in part in the silence of the experience of reality through our bodies, minds, and wills.[40] Just because Reality is elusive does not mean it is unreal. Rather as we experience Reality, we realize our experience of reality is not the whole of reality, while yet a part of reality is experienced by us in our experience of the openness to/of the transcending absence. The onticity of Reality's presence in and to our experience of Reality is both eluding and ungraspable—it is experienced as an absencing. But it also displays an ontological depth to the Real as something hidden yet manifested in the experience of the Real's presencing of absence. Reality's ontological nature always exists both as immediately present to us in our ontic experience of it and as ineffably beyond us as we experience its Reality.

Fundamental to Panikkar's notion of experience are the transcendental and immanent characteristics of Reality that point us to Being. Being for Panikkar is understood twofold. First it is understood as being-ness which is constitutively experienced in an identifiable way as we participate within reality. The second is Being as such, which is the Being of Reality as both transcendent and immanent to us. It is transcendent because it is an experience that is beyond us, while yet it remains immanently present to us through our ontic experience of Reality itself. Being is something we understand ourselves as experiencing, and Being is something we experience within reality as the constant unfolding of the Real. Panikkar argues that Being is the source of all beings and being-ness and is constitutive of all reality because it is a symbol for God.

It is also worth introducing how Panikkar's plurivocal interpretation of Being invokes the medieval notion of quiddity, Daoist metaphysics of creation from *wu* (nothingness), and the Heideggerian notion of "enpresenting" tied to the Deleuzean notion of becoming. Underlying Panikkar's notion of Being is not the functional understanding, characteristic of modernity, of something's purpose. Modern notions of being or essence are often grounded in foundational epistemological frameworks and are functionally conflated with the instrumental means of production or technological ends. Instead, Panikkar's notion of being-ness emphasizes the what-ness or quiddity of something's being: what makes the thing essentially real. Rather than collapsing being into its function, Panikkar seemingly stresses that there is a real form to created being that is essentially constituted by the reality of God. But Panikkar challenges both the classical Christian notion of the ontological distinction between God and creation, *and* the modern trend of making God functionally irrelevant or separated from immanence.

Rather, Panikkar sees the quiddity of humanity and nature in terms of ultimacy in their inter-in-dependence and participatory relationship to God. If a secular notion of cosmotheandrism separates God by the line of transcendence that separates the divine from humans and nature, Panikkar's cosmotheandrism denies a line of transcendence, allowing both the immanence below the line its own transcendence to/in God and the transcendence above the line its own immanence to/in creation. Within this framework, not only does Being itself have being-ness, a quiddity incarnating as a being or entity, but also beings or entities participate constitutively and inter-in-dependently in the divinity of Being itself as beings themselves experiencing divinity.

Likewise, Panikkar offers an advaitic spin upon creation, incorporating into his understanding of the absence of duality both the Buddhist notion of *shunyata* and the Daoist notion of creation from nothingness (*wu*) as a theological position that mediates the Christian *creatio ex nihilo* with the Hindu *creatio a deo*.[41] Accepting the Buddhist emptiness of being as an *affirmation* of its dependent co-origination and the Daoist notion of the Dao as nothingness (*wu*) from which all creation is created, Panikkar sees Being as originating out of nothing, and this nothingness is in fact an origination coming out of God.[42] Underlying the law of conventional and phenomenal reality for Panikkar are the laws of Karma and dependent co-origination as governing this world.[43] Panikkar's notion of Being implies that the manifestation of divine immanence comes when the reality of Being empties itself of divine transcendence into creation, just as the Father empties the fullness of Himself into the Son.[44] This in turn negates the separation between Creator and created, and sees both as constitutively real precisely through the immanence of the divine to and in creation.

Moreover, Panikkar's notion of Being utilizes Heidegger's notion of enpresenting and Gilles Deleuze's notion of the dynamism of becoming. In a Panikkarean spin on Heidegger, the notion of the enpresenting of being implies not only presence but participation in absence. This participation in absence implies an experience of the elusivity and becoming of what *is* as it presences Reality. The reality of absence implies that being is present precisely in the ontic experience of its becoming real. Likewise, for Panikkar, "being is becoming,"[45] in such a way that reflects the Deleuzean notion of life as an immanent experience of the ever-new dynamism of the creative becoming of who we are without representational reference to transcendence or God.[46] Contra Deleuze, however, for Panikkar, immanence does not exist apart from transcendence. Rather for Panikkar, divine transcendence and immanence are both mutually constitutive to the unfolding of Being as we experience the dynamism of life as we participate in what we are becoming.

Panikkar's notion of Being is linked to God, but in such a way that radically challenges with an advaitic spin both classical Christian thought *and* twentieth century philosophy. However, his advaitic understanding of Being points to a theological understanding of God that is grounded fundamentally in medieval theology while also offering his own spin upon classical notions of being. Panikkar understands that to talk of the Being of God we must start with our experience of beings—which includes the "things" we perceive (*entia*), the formal concept of the *ens commune*, and the most real sense of all being (*ens realissimum*) found uniquely in transcendence—which becomes the symbol of Being as we experience the onticity of being-ness in and through immanence.[47]

The symbol of Being(-ness) then gives an understanding of both who we are as beings or entities, an ontic idea of existing as beings per se, as experiencing the Being of God in and through immanence, *and* the presence of Being within the nature of our experience. Panikkar argues that God is the immanent and transcendent quality to the real that we experience in the experience of life. God becomes the source of all experiences and the source of Reality as it is Real. Being as it is understood as God "is the root, the dwelling place, and the foundation of everything."[48] Panikkar's conception of Being indicates that God is both with and in Reality—and constitutes Reality. But God is also symbolically beyond Reality and Being while representing them. Panikkar states that, "it is we human beings who speak—or hear—of divine transcendence and by this very fact already transgress such transcendence and incorporate it into the immanence of our being."[49] The experience of God is an ineffable immediacy of immanence to life that yet transcends us.

Panikkar argues that "Being indwells, enlivens and supports everything that is. It has a core, as it were, which is the being-ness or truth of everything."[50] Panikkar continues to say that: "Being, in short, is that symbol that embraces the whole of reality in all the possible aspects we are able to detect," and we are co-participants and co-agents in that reality.[51] Being, as God, necessarily implies a relationship with and in reality, and as we exist with and in Reality we are with and in a relationship with God. Reality becomes the space where God works, and humanity and the cosmos become the embodied presences that experience and manifest God because God is present within Reality. The phenomenal world we live in ontically implies God because the phenomenal world ontologically reveals the Real. It is within our experience of the Real that we experience God as a presence with and in the world and to us. When we search for Being it is already present to us as Being-with, to, and in us.

For Panikkar, it is in the experience of being-with and in the Real, with Being, and thus *with* God, that Life becomes the space where the experience of Being, God, and Reality is known as the source and symbol of the Real. Our experience, defined by the constitutive, participatory, and relational inter-in-dependency of a cosmotheandric reality thus is an experience of the becoming of the Real, of Being, and of God. Panikkar argues that the becoming of being "is the coming to be of the being that is precisely becoming."[52] Thus the nature of reality is in its becoming; what we identify as Being, as God, and as Reality is in its becoming as we live in the experience of the Real. Our life is understood as life precisely because we are becoming with, in, and through life. Without the experiential becoming of be-*ing*-with Being, God, and Reality we would not exist. Our existence as such is marked by the experience of the presence and the unfolding of the Real through the horizons of Being, God, and Reality in a way that describes the ontological and metaphysics reality of the experience of Life.

A TEMPITERNAL RECONCILIATION?

In Heidegger's ontology lies a problem that Panikkar overcomes: whether God can be understood as Being in time. Panikkar's advaitic metaphysics does not only overcome the Heideggerian problem of ontological difference between the univocity of Being and beings with Panikkar's advaitic spin on Being, God, *and* Reality. It also overcomes a univocal metaphysics of Being and God in ways that point to an advaitic experience of Reality, where God is experienced as Being present in and to time in the creature's experience of reality. The enpresencing of eternity to and in beings in time is Panikkar's notion of tempiternity. At its heart, Panikkar's metaphysics of experience offers a reconciliation between God and Being in time through the tempiternal experience of Reality, where time and eternity meet in the temporal structures of lived experience.

Panikkar's coining of the term "tempiternity" is based on an understanding of the contingency between the divine and creation. Tempiternity indicates that God exists alongside his creation as a continuous presence that is actively seeking and creating Man and matter. It is not that God created and stepped to the side, but rather that the living God of creation is eternal just as much as it participates with and in temporality. Panikkar even goes so far as to affirm that the divine is nothingness defined as a symbol characterized by the Hindu *ākāśa* (space) or Buddhist *shunyata* (emptiness) in which the advaitic (non-dualistic) experience of the divine allows anthropocosmic reality to exist in the space of the divine's own existence.[53] Panikkar understands that all of reality is present to the presence of God because divine immanence's presence with and in creation in time also implies creation's presence with and in God as an eternal co-presence. He states that for creatures, "creation is con-temporal and co-extensive with the creator because time and space are created in the very act of creation" but paradoxically that "creatures . . . are temporal and spatial [while] from the side of God, so to speak, creation is coeternal, continuous with and contiguous to God."[54] Tempiternity implies that the divine is intrinsically related to creation and the creature as it co-exists eternally alongside temporal reality. The dynamics of the divine mystery, as Panikkar calls the *theos*, indicates that the divine is always present with and in creation; just as we participate with and in reality, the divine is there participating with and in us as we are intrinsically constituted as real. Panikkar uses "tempiternity" to,

> refer to the mediation of the eternal in the temporal, transforming the temporal with eternal significance in and through the presence of the divine to temporal existence. Thus, divine presence transforms temporal existence in the participation of divine immanence and transcendence in time. Tempiternity implies that the sacred transforms the temporal, mediates the eternal to time, and indicates the presence of the eternal in time.[55]

For Panikkar, the experience of eternity is found within the very structures of temporality. That is, to experience the Reality of God's Being, all one must do is recognize the divine immanence within the very temporal structures of reality. Temporality is where time and eternity meet for Panikkar. Temporality is the space in which we meet, find, and experience God. Temporality is where the meaning of being is known precisely in our relationship with the divine in the very structures of the tempiternal experience of reality.

The Heideggerian question of being as such, is not only a question of the temporality of lived experience as constitutive of a being's Being. For Heidegger the Being of beings is found in the temporality of a being's experience of Being in the situated experience of everyday life. The ontic experience of Being for the later Heidegger is primordial. But as the later Heidegger realized the primordiality of ontic experience over ontologically articulating what it means to be, Panikkar realized that the ontic experience of reality is where Being of God is experienced. The primordial experience of Being, God, and Reality for Panikkar is experienced in the temporal structures of daily life as it participates perichoretically in eternity's transformation of temporality. Francis D'Sa argues that for Panikkar, "tempiternity is the full moment in which the past is operative and the future magnetic, and the present perceives with the help of the two eyes its trans-temporal depth-dimension. Living in such an ontologically dense moment is to live tempiternally."[56]

Heidegger's Ontology, Panikkar's Advaita   61

For Panikkar, the tempiternal experience encompasses eternity in tension with the temporal structures of time. That is, to experience God is to experience God within the experience and reality of time. As Frede points out, if Heidegger offered a reversal of the Time of Being in Division III of *Being and Time*, one would see how Being is produced and arises *in* time.[57] This is precisely what Panikkar does with his concept of tempiternity. Not only does Being arise in the becoming of time, but it also arises *in* time. But for Panikkar, the experience of Being in time is also theological. The experience of God and the mediation of the Being of God in time allows us to become *with* God *in* time. The tempiternal experience offers a mediation of the eternity of God—the Being of God—within the contours of the lived experience of Reality. Panikkar's tempiternal metaphysics reconciles Being and God in time through his advaitic metaphysics in ways that allow us to experience the dynamics of Being, God, and Reality through the very becoming of lived experience in the temporal structures at the intersection of time and eternity.

CONCLUSION

This chapter demonstrated: (1) Panikkar's indebtedness to and solutions to Heidegger's problem of being in time found in his fundamental ontology and onto-theological critique of metaphysics; (2) how Panikkar's advaitic metaphysics offers plurivocal reformulations of Being, God, and Reality through his advaitic spin; and (3) how Panikkar's tempiternal metaphysics reformulates the possibility of experiencing the co-eternity of creatures with the Being and Reality of God through the temporal structures of lived experience through the conscious experience of divine immanence. Panikkar's tempiternal experience and advaitic metaphysics resolve the ontological problem Heidegger's univocal differentiation between Being and beings and their experience of temporality produced through the onto-theological separation of temporality between Being and God.

Panikkar's advaitic metaphysics reformulates Heidegger's onto-theology by demonstrating how we can experience God within the temporal structures of everyday experience, precisely on the basis of divine immanence, where the eternal Being of God exists alongside, with, and in the temporal structures of created experience. Panikkar's understanding of the tempiternal experience and his advaitic metaphysics of religious experience where Reality, Being, and God meet demonstrates his indebtedness to, and transformation of, Heidegger's fundamental ontology and onto-theological critique of metaphysics. His advaitic spin on metaphysics orients us to how we can experience God in the temporal structures of Reality and lived experience. What this points to is the question of how we make sense of transcendence from the experience of immanence, to which we turn in the next chapter through an analysis of how Panikkar and William Desmond offer analogous accounts of this experience through their ideas of *metaxu* and *advaita*.

NOTES

1. C.f. Philip Tonner, "The Univocity of Being: With Special Reference to the Doctrines of John Duns Scotus and Martin Heidegger" (Glasglow: The University of Glasglow, 2006).

2. C.f. Taylor Carman, "The Principle of Phenomenology," in *The Cambridge Companion to Heidegger*, ed. Charles Guignon, Second Edition (Cambridge, UK: Cambridge University Press, 2006), 97–119.

3. Martin Heidegger, *Being and Time*, trans. John MacQuarrie and Edward Robinson (New York: Harper Collins Publishers, 2008), 67.

4. Heidegger, *Being and Time*, 33.

5. Martin Heidegger, *Being and Time*, 32; C.f. Michael Gelven's commentary on Heidegger's *Being and Time*: Michael Gelven, *A Commentary of Heidegger's Being and Time: A Section by Section Interpretation* (New York: Harper and Row, 1970), 23: "the meaning of existence [for Heidegger] can be significant only to the one who asks about his own existence. For this reason, the question of being itself is possible only because *Dasein* can reflect upon its existence."

6. Piotr Hoffman, "Death, Time, History: Division II of *Being and Time*," in *The Cambridge Companion to Heidegger*, ed. Charles Guignon, Second Edition (Cambridge, UK: Cambridge University Press, 2006), 222–40, 226.

7. Heidegger, *Being and Time*, 283–84.

8. For this paragraph: C.f. Martin Heidegger, *The Basic Problems of Phenomenology*, trans. Albert Hofstadter, Revised Edition (Bloomington: Indiana University Press, 1982), 168, 228, 261, 263–68.

9. Dorothea Frede, "The Question of Being: Heidegger's Project," in *The Cambridge Companion to Heidegger*, ed. Charles Guignon, Second Edition (Cambridge, UK: Cambridge University Press, 2006), 42–69, 62–63.

10. Frede, "The Question of being: Heidegger's Project," 64–65.

11. Frede, "The Question of being: Heidegger's Project," 64.

12. Robert J. Dostal, "Time and Phenomenology in Husserl and Heidegger," in *The Cambridge Companion to Heidegger*, ed. Charles Guignon, Second Edition (Cambridge, UK: Cambridge University Press, 2006), 120–48, 135.

13. Dostal, "Time and Phenomenology in Husserl and Heidegger," 135–36.

14. C.f. Heidegger, *The Basic Problems of Phenomenology*.

15. C.f. Heidegger, *The Basic Problems of Phenomenology*, 168, 228, 261, 263–68.

16. Heidegger, *Being and Time*, 32–34.

17. David B. Burrell, "Creator/Creatures Relation: 'The Distinction' vs. 'Onto-Theology,'" *Faith and Philosophy* 25, no. 2 (2008): 177–89.

18. Catherine Pickstock, "Postmodern Scholasticism: Critique of Postmodern Univocity," *Telos* 33, no. 4 (2003): 3–24, 7.

19. Michael Wiitala, "The Metaphysics of Duns Scotus and Onto-Theology," *Philosophy Today* 53 (2009): 158–63, 158. Wiitala seeks to open up a pathway for the exoneration of Duns Scotus from being onto-theological through an analysis of Heidegger's onto-theology to show how Duns Scotus' metaphysics, as the act and will to love God, defies a Heideggerian onto-theological categorization that conflates God's Being with human Being in time.

20. Ian D. Thomson, *Heidegger on Ontotheology: Technology and the Politics of Education* (Cambridge, UK: Cambridge University Press, 2005), 7–43.

21. Ian D. Thomson, "Ontotheology? Understanding Heidegger's Destruktion of Metaphysics," *International Journal of Philosophical Studies* 8, no. 3 (2000): 297–327.

22. Ian D. Thomson, "Ontotheology," in *Interpreting Heidegger: Critical Essays*, ed. Daniel Dahlstrom (Cambridge, UK: Cambridge University Press, 2011), 106–31.

23. Martin Heidegger, *Identity and Difference*, trans. Joan Stambough (Chicago, IL: The University of Chicago Press, 2002), 70–71.

24. Raimon Panikkar, *The Rhythm of Being: The Unbroken Trinity* (Maryknoll, NY: Orbis Books, 2010), 76–78.

25. Maurice Merleau-Ponty, *Phenomenology of Perception* (New York: Routledge, 2013).

26. Hans-Georg Gadamer, *Truth and Method*, trans. Joel Weinsheimer and Donald Marshall, Second Revised Edition (New York: Continuum, 1999), 173–379.

27. Contra Husserl, Panikkar does not think we can bracket out religious belief or experience. Rather, religious experience and belief becomes central to the phenomenological experience of the divine. C.f. Raimon Panikkar, *The Intra-Religious Dialogue* (New York and Ramsey, NJ: Paulist Press, 1999), 73–84.

28. One can posit that Panikkar's eschatological vision remains silent because of the mystery of being at the limits of the experience of the survival of being. C.f. Peter Phan, "Raimon Panikkar's 'Eschatology': The Unpublished Chapter," in *Raimon Panikkar: A Companion to His Life and Thought*, eds., Peter Phan and Young-Chan Ro (Cambridge, UK: James Clarke and Co., 2018), 242–57; Panikkar, *The Rhythm of Being*, 404.

29. Panikkar, *The Rhythm of Being*, 79.

30. Panikkar, *The Rhythm of Being*, 79–80.

31. Raimon Panikkar, *Myth, Faith, and Hermeneutics: Cross Cultural Studies* (New York: Paulist Press, 1979), 273.

32. C.f. Heidegger, *Being and Time*; Martin Heidegger, *Introduction to Metaphysics*, trans. Gregory Fried and Richard Polt (New Haven, CT: Yale University Press, 2014), 34; Heidegger, *Identity and Difference*; Martin Heidegger, *Poetry, Language, and Thought* (New York: Harper Perennial Modern Classics, 2013).

33. Martin Heidegger, "The Origin of the Work of Art," in *Basic Writings*, trans. David Farrell Krell (New York: Harper Collins, 2008), 139–212; Martin Heidegger, *On the Way to Language* (New York: HarperOne, 1982).

34. Howard N. Tuttle, *The Crowd Is Untruth: The Existential Critique of Mass Society in the Thought of Kierkegaard, Nietzsche, Heidegger, and Ortega y Gasset* (New York: Peter Lang, 1996), 53–82.

64 *Chapter 3*

35. C.f. Heidegger, *Being and Time*, 279–311; Piotr Hoffman, "Death, Time, History: Division II of *Being and Time*," 222–40.

36. C.f. Nagarjuna, *The Fundamental Wisdom of the Middle Way: Nagarjuna's Mulamadhyamikakarika*, trans. Jay Garfield (New York: Oxford University Press, 1995); Douglas Berger, "Acquiring Emptiness: Interpreting Nagarjuna's MMK 24:18," *Philosophy East and West* 60, no. 1 (2010): 40–64; Jay Garfield, "Dependent Arising and the Emptiness of Emptiness: Why Did Nagarjuna Start with Causation?," *Philosophy East and West* 44, no. 2 (1994): 219–50; Jay Garfield and Graham Priest, "Nagarjuna and the Limits of Thought," *Philosophy East and West* 53, no. 1 (2003): 1–21.

37. Paul Williams, "On the Abhidharma Ontology," *Journal of Indian Philosophy* 9, no. 3 (1981): 227–57; Richard Jones, *Nagarjuna: Buddhism's Most Important Philosopher*, Revised and Expanded Edition (New York: Jackson Square Books, 2018), 171–77.

38. Garfield, "Dependent Arising and the Emptiness of Emptiness."

39. Heidegger, *On the Way to Language*; Panikkar, *The Rhythm of Being*, 323–37. I have presented on this at the Eastern Regional meeting of the American Philosophical Association in Montreal, Canada in January 2023, and intend to flesh this out in another book on Panikkar and Continental Philosophy.

40. Panikkar, *The Rhythm of Being*, 323–37.

41. Raimon Panikkar, *Hinduism: The Dharma of India*, ed. Milena Carrara Pavan, Vol. IV.2, XII vols., Opera Omnia (Maryknoll, NY: Orbis Books, 2017), 239–41.

42. Panikkar, *The Rhythm of Being*, 312–15.

43. Raimon Panikkar, "The Law of Karman and the Historical Dimension of Man," *Philosophy East and West* 22, no. 1 (1972): 25–43; c.f. Raimon Panikkar, *Myth, Faith, and Hermeneutics*, 375–76, 375.

44. Raimon Panikkar, *Trinity and the Religious Experience of Man* (Maryknoll, NY: Orbis Books, 1973), 44–51; Panikkar, *Hinduism: The Dharma of India*, 237–38.

45. Panikkar, *The Rhythm of Being*, 90–93.

46. C.f. Gilles Deleuze, *Difference and Repetition*, trans. Paul Patton (New York: Columbia University Press, 1994); Gilles Deleuze and Felix Guattari, *What Is Philosophy?*, trans. Hugh Tomlinson and Graham Burchell (New York: Columbia University Press, 1994).

47. Panikkar, *The Rhythm of Being*, 85–86.

48. Panikkar, *The Rhythm of Being*, 93.

49. Panikkar, *The Rhythm of Being*, 61.

50. Panikkar, *The Rhythm of Being*, 94.

51. Panikkar, *The Rhythm of Being*, 94.

52. Panikkar, *The Rhythm of Being*, 99.

53. Panikkar, *The Rhythm of Being*, 313–14.

54. Panikkar, *The Rhythm of Being*, 286.

55. Andrew D. Thrasher, "A Glossary of Panikkarean Terms," in *Raimon Panikkar: A Companion to His Life and Thought*, eds., Peter Phan and Young-Chan Ro (Cambridge, UK: James Clarke and Co., 2018), 271–81, 281.

56. Francis X. D'Sa, "Time, History, and Christophany," in *Raimon Panikkar: A Companion to His Life and Thought*, eds., Peter Phan and Young-Chan Ro (Cambridge, UK: James Clarke & Co., 2018), 171–93, 184.

57. Frede, "The Question of being: Heidegger's Project," 62–63.

Chapter 4

Desmond's Metaxu, Panikkar's Advaita

Opening to Transcendence

Raimon Panikkar's advocation for a cosmotheandric vision of reality challenges modern Western metaphysical and theological visions of reality. He argues that Western thought reduces reality to either monism or dualism, collapsing difference into identity, negating difference, or absolutizing the difference between divine transcendence and this-worldly immanence. In an attempt to mediate between identity and difference, transcendence and immanence—without negating otherness and difference for monism—Panikkar argues for an advaitic mediation of reality. *Advaita* produces the mediation between dualism and monism—it produces the space for harmony between identity and difference, between sameness and otherness. Panikkar's advaita promises the space of communion with the other based on not only tolerance of difference, but also, through exposure and experiencing the other as myself, we are able to see ourselves as an other to not only ourselves, but also to an other as another other. The promise of Panikkar's advaitic metaphysical vision is that it foresees a vision of reality where not only difference and identity are harmoniously in relation to and with one another, but also to transcendence and the immanent experience of it.

But while Panikkar's metaphysical vision articulates an advaitic metaphysics of reality that mediates difference and identity without reducing it to univocal sameness and violence against the other, we also find something analogous to Panikkar in the metaxological metaphysics of William Desmond. Desmond's metaxological metaphysics is at once dialectical, dialogical, and agapeic. Desmond's idea of *metaxu* refers to the "between" which holds the space for agapeic love and an openness to transcendence. *Metaxu* is dialectical and dialogical because it moves from the concern for identification with the same, a concern for the other's difference, a concern for self-reference in relation to difference, and culminates in the between (*metaxu*) that is open to the other's transcendence of me in ways that the transcendence of the other exceeds my finitude and existence. This metaxological space is marked for Desmond by agapeic love where the self-referencing self is sacrificed for the sake and goodness of the other's excess beyond me. But this excess of the self toward the other for Desmond is not only oriented toward another human being—it is also pulled toward the otherness of transcendence as an over-determinate excess that transcends the self and calls us to an agapeic responsibility to love God and neighbor.

What bridges Desmond and Panikkar are not only their metaphysics that mediate difference in their attempts at articulating the harmony and rhythm of being and reality (Panikkar) and the over-determinacy of the immanent between through the fourfold (Desmond), but more importantly their reformulations of modern philosophy and theology as *open to transcendence from immanence*. If Panikkar remains open to the experience of God as a divine immanence that always transcends us, then Desmond argues likewise that within immanence, there is an over-determinate excess that posits and points us beyond ourselves toward our transcendence. Hence, this chapter is a comparative examination of William Desmond and Raimon Panikkar's metaphysics of reality to argue how they argue, within their own fields, against the problems of modern thought and for the openness of transcendence from immanence.

PANIKKAR'S CHALLENGE TO MODERN THOUGHT

Raimon Panikkar's advaitic metaphysics of reality articulates a challenge to modernity. If modernity is marked by the competing tensions of overcoming difference and otherness and reducing it to a univocal sameness, or even of overcoming homogeneity for difference and otherness, then Panikkar's advaitic vision of reality—grounded in his cosmotheandric cosmovision of reality as a relationally tripartite and constituted by God, materiality, and humanity—sees modernity as a failure insofar as it fails to allow space for the harmonious interplay of difference without reducing it to homogeneity. Panikkar argues that his "cosmovision" of reality challenges both monism (prone to reducing reality through reason to oneness) and dualism (which separates reality into the natural and supernatural and is marked by temporality and becoming). Panikkar argues that "if monism grants preeminence to the static, the immutable and the absolute, then dualism tends towards the dynamic, to change and to temporariness. In both cases it is a flight from irrationality."[1] By contrast, his advaitic vision marries knowledge with love as a cross-cultural mutation in today's culture that produces harmony.[2] In the cross-cultural marriage of knowledge and love, Panikkar argues that reality not only allows the space for otherness, but in understanding and loving the other, we can come to appreciate the incommensurabilities of difference in a globalizing world.

But if Panikkar's advaitic cosmovision of reality allows and cultivates the harmony between difference and sameness, otherness and identity, it also demonstrates through cross-cultural fertilization and inter-penetration the possibilities of understanding transcendence. In Panikkar's cross-cultural examination of "deity," he argues that it can be explained through three meta-horizons—cosmological, anthropological, and ontological—which correspond to three underlying characteristics of "Deity": infinity, freedom, and transcendence and immanence.[3] Panikkar's cross-cultural analyses of the meta-cosmological horizon initiates the possibility of infinity. The cosmos projects in its finitude an infinite excess that is yet beyond the finite stretches of our visions of the cosmos, while also meeting us in-finitude. Likewise, the meta-anthropological horizon projects the transcending excess of freedom. Unlimited human freedom leads to ethical violence toward others, God, self, and creation. And yet, divine freedom allows the possibility of expressing itself in the givenness and gift of creation. Finally, the meta-ontological horizon posits not the separation of divine transcendence and this-worldly immanence, but their intersection through divine immanence. Here we find in Panikkar the possibility of a divine immanence within the world and humanity that transcends itself and points beyond itself to divine transcendence at the limits of finitude.

If modernity challenges the immanence of God, and indeed articulates the irrelevance and impossibility of divine transcendence through developments since the Enlightenment and before, Panikkar challenges modern philosophy's eclipse of God's transcendence by articulating divine immanence to and in creation, mediating the divine in and through the tension between God's presence and absence. If God's presence is immanent within creation, it implies that creation is imbued with divine glory. Moreover, if God's absence is immanent to creation, it implies the hiddenness of God within creation in ways that can only be articulated through an apophatic theology of absence—through a theology of absence, we can affirm the silence of God and experience God in that silence. For Panikkar, silence speaks through the presence of its absence. At the excess of divine silence, circling around it, are the expressions that vibrate through created life, the manifestations of divine presence in the midst of divine hiddenness. Within this we can begin to articulate how Panikkar's metaphysics remains open to transcendence. To do so, this chapter examines Panikkar's theologizing on faith and transcendence, and then,

70   *Chapter 4*

before turning to Desmond, articulates Panikkar's pluralistic metatheological advocation for a primordial human experience that opens to transcendence.

Theologizing on Faith and Transcendence

In his analysis of faith as searching for understanding, Panikkar states that it is a "striving, searching, and even praying to understand, not to prove or justify, but just to implore intelligibility. This belief in God is a gift, a grace, and can eventually turn out to be an experience . . . [of] an awareness that is neither inhuman nor irrational; it is possible to understand that faith does not demean our faculties but enhances them."[4] Panikkar continues: "faith itself is looking for understanding both its own nature and of what faith believes" (*RB*, 131). But faith is also something that displays the limits and frailty of human reason in our search to find solutions. At the limits of human reason is faith as a prayer and hope to continue trusting in God throughout our lives in ways that we are aware that we cannot understand. Faith becomes an openness toward the infinite (*RB*, 131).

Panikkar goes further to state that in light of our existential openness, faith is an openness to mystery (*RB*, 131). This mystery erupts into our lives as something that has been preparing our lives for the reception of the mystery of God (*RB*, 154). While the philosopher's search is for the intelligibility of God as totality and truth, according to Panikkar, apophatic theology only lets us affirm God's nothingness: "we are looking for the Infinite, even when we come to the discovery that there is no such Entity, that heaven is empty, and the Void is its name. If in our search for Being we find an Entity, even the highest one, we shall not be satisfied" (*RB*, 155). But Panikkar is not reducing Being to nothingness or *shunyata* or the void of beings. Rather he is arguing that the divine transcends all that we could grasp and understand of it. The divine is always beyond what we can imagine it to be in ways that point to the limits of human understanding and the reality that human desire always transcends the limits of our desire. Whether we search for a ground or source of being, what we find is the search "for a Presence that presents itself to us and is not our projection" (*RB*, 155).

Panikkar rhetorically argues that at the limits of existence lies not only the essence of divine Being and Infinitude, but an essential Be-*ing* that cannot be explained by existence. Supreme, divine essence transcends existence in ways that it remains ungraspable and unknowable precisely because it does not exist (*ek-sist*) substantially like creatures exist substantially through their *be-ing*. The Being of God is an essence without substantial ek-sistence outside of its being (*RB*, 155). Ultimately for Panikkar, God remains ungraspable, and ultimately beyond our understanding. This is why Panikkar posits the emptiness of God: it essentially transcends all that we can grasp of it. God

Desmond's Metaxu, Panikkar's Advaita 71

remains unknowable in essence because God does not exist as we do as other than and from God. To "ek-sist" is to substantially be outside of oneself by extending who we are temporally in life and through time. But to essentially Be means to be substantially "sistent" in and of itself. Its essence is not existing, but rather "sisting" beyond us and our grasp and understanding of it.

And yet, Panikkar argues that this distance between transcendence and immanence, between essence and existence, is a problem that can only be overcome through adualistic space. Panikkar argues by contrast for the ungraspable Infinitude of the Transcendent Being of God in that it is found both outside us and within us as an immanent presence that "discloses an ever more mysterious absence." For Panikkar, transcendence cannot be thought without immanence, and yet when we distinguish God from ourselves, we begin to "recognize a certain transcendence in its immanence" (*RB*, 178–79). By recognizing the transcendence immanent within and without us, we begin to experience how transcendence becomes infinitude while yet not encompassed by finitude.

For Panikkar the nature of the divine is not some otherworldly transcendence that cannot be grasped, nor should it be confused or reduced to something merely immanent to us, as us, or our experience of the world. Panikkar argues that the problem of our world is the prevalent hiddenness of God and the absence of consciously experiencing Him (*RB*, 312). The overemphasis on divine transcendence to the exclusion of divine immanence leads to a nihilism that fails to see and appreciate the hiddenness of God in the visible, where "the roots are always invisible and the awareness of the invisible already fills the invisible with some meaning" (*RB*, 312). In the experience of divine absence, this is not a nihilistic experience of negation. Rather, Panikkar describes the divine absence as the Spanish *nada*, which implies not the negation of being, "but the awareness of the emptiness surrounding Being, as it were, the awareness of an Absence that only makes sense together with the Presence of whose absence we are aware" (*RB*, 314). It is in this advaitic space that the harmony of divine Presence and Absence evokes the freedom of Being (*RB*, 315). Panikkar states that the freedom to be "is the expression of the identity of a being with itself" in the authentic spontaneous flow of being in time (*RB*, 316). And this authentic flow of time is one that it experiences infinitude through the very life of the interconnectedness of human experiencing the rhythms of material and spiritual dimensions of a cosmotheandric reality.

Metatheology and Religious Experience

If Panikkar's theologizing of transcendence and faith situates Be-ing in time, this implies that Panikkar starts from immanence to God-talk. But in

72   *Chapter 4*

Panikkar's critique of a fundamental theology, he argues that it "claims to disclose the very basis of understanding theological self-understanding."[5] This requires both an assumption that we can know what theology discloses and the assumption that it's knowability is outside of itself. The dualistic ways of thinking—separating "God and the World, uncreated and created, Being and beings, the ground and the structure built upon it . . . [describes a] two story construction of nature and supernature, grace built on nature, faith on reason, theology on philosophy"—presupposes that the first in each category is presupposed in fundamental theology.[6] The problem with dualistic thinking is not only its aim to universalization, but constructs in its dualistic vision the subordination and violence of the many under the one.

By contrast, Panikkar's cross-cultural hermeneutics critiques this position of fundamental theology as a Western construct because it universalizes a singular definition of faith and theologizing about God. By contrast, Panikkar develops a metatheological position that does not take God for granted nor does it deify reason.[7] Rather in a pluralistic, metatheological, or advaitic perspective, we search "to understand that primordial human relatedness we perceive in dealing with ultimate problems from the fruit of a pluri-theological investigation."[8] This pluri-theological investigation neither asserts absolutes or monism over others, nor merely differentiates the many from an equivocal perspective. The advaitic metatheology Panikkar proposes addresses how religious traditions are harmonized—it is where difference is not reduced to univocal sameness, nor where identity voids difference. Rather it is where difference allows the space of tension with identification, and when identity allows the space for difference without doing violence to either. It provokes an advaitic, trinitarian intuition into the harmony between similarity and difference in ways that opens us to transcendence in the midst of immanence. For Panikkar this openness to transcendence in the midst of immanence is the search for supreme experience.

For Panikkar, the supreme experience must be understood, and be conscious of, through an advaitic, trinitarian vision of the harmony of reality, where one recognizes the link between myth and experience, the subject and the object, the knowable and the known. Panikkar argues that the supreme experience is authentically validated by the concrete experience itself: to experience the ultimate is something primordial to human faith—we are conscious of the experience of life and being in time. For Panikkar, experience is primordial to what it means to be human.[9] But when we seek to articulate a metatheology of supreme experience, what we find in Panikkar is a categorization of religious and secular traditions according to a fourfold of transcendence and immanence.[10]

Panikkar articulates this fourfold as: (1) transcendent transcendence (characterizing Abrahamic faiths); (2) immanent transcendence (characterizing

Hindu traditions); (3) transcendent immanence (characterizing Buddhist traditions); and (4) immanent immanence (characterizing Chinese and secular traditions). If transcendent transcendence emphasizes the distinction between a personal God and his creation, immanent transcendence emphasizes the absorption of immanence into and as transcendence (*ātman* as Brahman). Moreover, if transcendent immanence emphasizes realizing the transcendence of immanence through the very experience of transcendence *in* immanence (nirvana), then immanent immanence emphasizes the acceptance of what it means to be immanent with the orientation toward its flourishing.

Between each of these fourfold orientations is an underlying questioning of the separation between transcendence and immanence. Panikkar discerns that, through the study of a plurality of theological and religious traditions that to speak of a metatheology, one must recognize the difference between religious conceptions of transcendence and immanence, their various combinations, and how they all speak to the divine mystery as manifestations of the divine Spirit tempiternally present to human experience. Human experience of the divine through their immanent experience of the transcending nature of transcendence is a concrete manifestation of where the divine is known and transcended. That is, transcendence reveals itself to human experience through its immanent presence to and in our immanent experience of God in the world. To harmonize transcendence and immanence is to experience how immanence opens itself to, and opens unto, its transcendence within immanence.

***

If Panikkar's cosmotheandric metaphysics and advaitic cosmovision of reality critiques modernity's reduction of reality to this-worldly immanence and its eclipse and abandonment of divine transcendence, then his theologizing of divine immanence articulates not only the presence and hiddenness of God in immanence, but also the excess of divine immanence and the transcending of singular beings, religious conceptions of God, and their experience of God in reality. Panikkar's advaitic metaphysics and critique of modernity opens the door for the possibility of participating in, and the rearticulation of, the divine in a world that fights to reconcile difference and otherness with sameness and identity.

Furthermore, Panikkar's metatheology of human experience points us to the complex and plurivocal interplay of how religious and secular traditions imagine transcendence and immanence, their harmony, and their openness to otherness without reducing it to a singular monistic conception of reality. Advaita speaks of harmony between identity and difference, and its

74   *Chapter 4*

metatheology speaks of a plurivocal vision of reality where the experience of the divine not only transcends human religious experience as mystery, but presents itself to human experience as the manifestation of divine immanence. Arguably, William Desmond's metaxological metaphysics offers another metaphysical spin, this time from within Western thought, that seeks to overcome the overcoming of metaphysics. And in the rearticulations of a viable metaphysics, William Desmond articulates the possibility and openness of transcendence from within the excesses of immanence. It is to Desmond that we now turn.

WILLIAM DESMOND'S METAXOLOGICAL METAPHYSICS

Brenden Thomas Sammon and Christopher Ben Simpson argue that William Desmond's metaxological philosophy of the between offers a modern recovery of metaphysics that opens to theology. Furthermore, they argue that theological inquiry can benefit from Desmond's metaxological metaphysics in ways that open the doors of theology to the recovery of metaphysics. They situate Desmond's metaphysics within and alongside, or between, the Romantic idealism of Hegel, the phenomenology of Being as lived experience in Heidegger and Jean-Paul Sartre, and the postmodern concerns for difference and otherness.[11] Moreover, James L. Marsh argues that Desmond's metaxological metaphysics first overcomes the Heideggerian trend of overcoming metaphysics and second, challenges postmodern deconstructionists and their deconstruction of difference in its collapse into univocity.

By doing the first, Marsh argues that Desmond offers a fundamental philosophical possibility for thinking God without reducing God to valueless being. Rather Desmond argues for the value and possibility of God as not reduced to function or univocity. Instead, Marsh argues that Desmond's *metaxu* overcomes the negation of metaphysics precisely in the openness of metaphysics to the hyperbolic excess of being, not as reducible to univocity because of the postmodern deconstruction of otherness and difference, but rather as oriented to the possibility of Being in its open finitude, astonishment, and perplexity of being—the value of being.[12] Corey Tutewiler argues that Desmond expresses wonder at being something rather than nothing. He points out that the potential openness to wondering at being something has theological implications toward something more, implying not the uncertainty of being but rather its over-certainty—that being a Being produces an excess that overflows its becoming into a potential for more, like the possibility of God.[13] Tutewiler argues that this wondering at being something rather than nothing challenges the modern narrative of pessimistically resigning to being something rather than nothing. He argues that Desmond's openness to the excess of being offers a gift of being from God that does non necessitate God's creative act of creation, and yet because God did create, this act is a free gift to creation of its own being without compulsion or expectation of creation to respond to that gift.[14] In a sense, metaxological metaphysics opens up for creation to freely receive the gift of being and to freely respond to the gift of being as an act of love. This is true wonderment.

The excess of being found in Desmond's metaxological metaphysics is something D. C. Schindler points out as something already given in the midst of existence and as an intimate/hyperbolic excess of the overdetermined nature of being that remains central to being.[15] Schindler states that for Desmond, "the intimacy of being, its immanence in the self or its familiarity, nevertheless always remains what Desmond calls an 'intimate strangeness,' for *what* is intimate to me is precisely what I will never get to the end of, never have finished with."[16] Linking Desmond's emphasis on community to Emmanuel Levinas implies that for Desmond, "an ethical responsibility to and for the other," is not alienating, but inviting.[17]

What Desmond's philosophy opens us to is the intrinsic openness of his metaxological metaphysics "to theology, without any pre-emptive setting of the conditions of possibility."[18] D. C. Schindler argues that Desmond's metaphysics metaxologically mediates the seeming irreducibility and incompatibility between philosophy and theology precisely because he articulates a *metaphysics* of being where reason is positively present in the intimacy of Being's being. By articulating how we wonder at being and how we reason positively *by* being, Schindler argues that Desmond mediates between philosophy and theology through a metaphysics of wonder that is fundamentally ontological and open to being's excess and the making sense of it. To explicate Desmond's metaxological metaphysics, the following sections address his notions of the between, the fourfold, and the turn to transcendence.

The Between

William Desmond states in *Being and the Between*, that "there is a thinking about the beyond in the between itself. What gives the between surpasses the between, though we face towards it, in and through the between."[19] Patrick X. Gardner states that "metaxological metaphysics is, in this sense, hyperbolic: it is the realization that the between itself constitutes a kind of sacrament of what lies beyond it. Thinking metaxologically involves, in other words, attention to the forces in the between that are not of the between."[20] Desmond states that the between implies a primordial openness of being, one that is always already porously open to the experience of being in the between.[21]

76   *Chapter 4*

Desmond argues in *Ethics and the Between* that the between is marked by an over-determinacy that takes "form in a plurivocal interplay between otherness and sameness, openness and definition, and yet excessive to final fixation."[22] He argues for a "sense of the 'between' in which we always are: not so much at the limit of origin or verging on the 'beyond' of given immanence, but constitutively in that given immanence, relative to our daily being just so in the midst of things."[23] While the Between yields "an interconnected web of thoughts, or happenings, each related to the others" it also questions the sphere of immanence as mere immanence.[24] Rather Desmond questions whether immanence "gives witness to another sense of between that is at the boundary of immanence, or itself between immanence and transcendence."[25] These "hyperboles of being" are "happenings in immanent finitude that yet cannot be determined completely on the terms of immanent finitude. They point beyond . . . in terms of the excesses given to showing in the immanent between itself. The immanent between is porous to something other to it."[26] That is, in the excesses of immanent finitude, there lies in the between its transcendent excess. To understand Desmond's move from Being, to ethics, and to God and the between, it would help to articulate his understanding of the fourfold, a central theme to his metaxological metaphysics.

The Fourfold

For Desmond, "the metaxological is the truth of the univocal, equivocal, the dialectical" in ways that each dialectically carries over into the following progression, building on what comes before, opening Being to being in the between (*BB*, xii). Desmond suggests "that as dialectic tries to redeem the promise of univocity beyond equivocity, so the metaxological tries to redeem the promise of equivocity beyond univocity and dialectic. It keeps the space of the between open to mediations from the other irreducible to any mediation from the self . . . the mediation from the other converges on the middle out of its own excess of being and integrity for itself" (*BB*, 178). Brenden Thomas Sammon argues that "the richness and the ambiguity that cannot be accounted for by the univocal, equivocal, and dialectical ways of being and mind precisely is the excess of being, the plenitude of determinate content that constitutes the givenness of being itself."[27] In another more substantial space at the beginning of his trilogy on the between, Desmond states that while "the univocal sense of being stresses the notion of sameness, or unity," the equivocal allows difference to thrive. Furthermore, he states that "the dialectical sense emphasizes the mediation of the different, the reintegration of the diverse," while the *metaxu* mediates difference and sameness, not in terms of self-mediation, but rather in terms of an openness of self to a pluralized intermediation to others and God (*BB*, xii).

The fourfold as such describes univocity as the diminution of difference, the equivocal as its reaffirmation (but to its endless differing and differentiation to otherness without mediation), and of the dialectical as its open mediation to include identity and difference.[28] The metaxological in turn "stands in openness to over-determinacy, even as it recurs to the interplay of sameness and difference. It re-engages with the pluralism of inter-mediations, finding the 'inter' itself to be irreducible. The participants in the inter-mediations are themselves not reducible to one all-inclusive self-mediation. There is no whole of wholes that includes [the] everyday in the majestic solitude of the immanent one" (*GB*, 10). This immanent one is not the mere passing of wholes in their similitude and differences and self-mediations from immanence to immanence. Rather the passing of immanence transcends itself, opening itself porously to transcendence, community, and being. Immanence points beyond itself "to ultimate transcendence as other to the immanent between" (*GB*, 10). In the openness of being to the experience of the whole, Desmond argues that the between is fundamentally open to the interplay between wholes that transcend themselves toward others without subsuming the other (*BB*, 163).

To explain the fourfold, Desmond describes certain adjectival descriptions that prescribe tendencies that metaxologically find their fulfillment in the midst of the between. While the fourfold implies four metaphysical sensibilities of the between, attached to each are (not in pejorative senses) the descriptions of idiocy, aesthetics, erotics, and agapeic conditions of selving in light of the fourfold. If idiocy is linked to univocal sameness, it invokes a sense by which we assert our own identity as a singular and in rebellion against otherness (*BB*, 379–84). Thus, the idiotic self is concerned for itself and creates an ethical concern for its own being. If aesthetics is linked to equivocal difference, it articulates an authentic selving in light of the other (*BB*, 384–88), opening the self to the happening of its excess completed through the dialectical erotics of self-mediation where we love ourselves in light of difference (*BB*, 385–406). Overcoming the erotic selving of dialectical happening, we turn to the agapeic selving focused in its excess in community and love for others (*BB*, 406–15). But agapeic selving does not only complete the fourfold. It also realizes the aspirations of each of the other selvings and opens us to God. If the agapeic self realizes the singularity of univocal being and the incarnation of equivocal selving of itself in light of the other, it also realizes the dialectical self's promise of transcending self-possession for the other.

In the over-determinacy of Desmond's *metaxu*, he also develops in *Ethics of the Between* the fourfold's orientation to the Good. Through analyses of the univocal, he draws out the positive surplus of the ethical out of the same (*EB*, 51–77). Equivocally, he argues for the negative indeterminacy of the good in the nihilistic confusion of coming to nothing (*EB*, 79–115). Dialectically,

78   Chapter 4

he argues that the ethical indeterminacy produces the determinations of the antinomy of autonomy (*EB*, 117–62). Metaxologically, the good culminates in the over-determinacy of the indeterminate determination of transcendence, where the good reconciles univocal positive surplus with equivocal coming to nothing and dialectical autonomy and self-mediation. He does so through the otherness and ethical responsibility of the between with its Platonic grounding of goodness in the origin of Being as transcendence (*EB*, 163–220).

In more positive light, later in *Ethics and the Between*, he argues for a fourfold model of community of his ethical selvings (*EB*, 221–384). He moves from the familial intimacy of the idiotic (*EB*, 385–414), and the instrumental network of aesthetics (*EB*, 415–42), to the erotic sovereignty of striving after excellence (*EB*, 443–82) and the agapeic community oriented to service of the transcendent Good (*EB*, 483–514). Arguing for the Platonic Good over against the Enlightenment contrast between transcendence and immanence, between heteronomy and autonomy, Desmond articulates that the problem of modernity is neither (*EB*, 17–47).[29] Rather it's problem is the relation between "the good and the valueless whole" (*EB*, 158). By contrast, Desmond argues that there is a reversal in the potencies of the fourfold where the ethical dynamics of the idiotic, aesthetic, dianoetic, transcendental, and eudaimonistic are transcended when transcendence "possibilizes all transcending" as not only good but the good. This good communicates itself in the space between "that sustains the community of finite being" and all of their self-becoming difference is determined as each strives toward the good. This good is determinative of each finite being's good, while also promising all finite beings' good through their agapeic community with other beings (*EB*, 219).

Furthermore, Desmond links these attributes of the *metaxu* to demonstrate how their excess points them to God. If the idiotic self opens us to Being's transcendence and the aesthetic, and the equivocal self opens us to the possibility of experiencing the happening of God in excess of difference, then the erotics of self opens us to transcending the possibility of evil and the contingency of life within immanence. That is, the idiocy of being articulates the sheer givenness of being, while the aesthetics of happening incarnates the astonishment and appreciation that the finite exceeds itself (*GB*, 11–12).

Moreover, the erotics of selving surpasses itself in its finitude while the agapeics of community point us to the gift—of receiving and giving of our being to others (*GB*, 12). That is, the agapeic selving in light of otherness opens us to the excess of not just ethical concern for community, but also to the excess produced out of the between of its limits that transcend it, opening us to the possibility of God. Building on the singularity of human freedom in light of the idiocy of singularity, Desmond argues that through a community of equivocal desire and an erotic community of sovereignty, the metaxological community opens us not just to the other and the good, but also to God (*GB*, 168–69). The ethics of an agapeic community of service for the other's good is Desmond's climax of metaxological metaphysics, ethics, and theology of the between. He argues that it promises freedom as the highest, incarnate form of the good in creation, transforming otherness into an infinite good, drawing together in intimacy the diversity of each singularity through which "the infinite valuing of self also becomes an infinite valuing of the other as other" (*GB*, 169). This comes through the agapeic service of a human community into a mystical communion of a coming to be into the unknown through the exceeding excess of love between human persons (*GB*, 169).

Desmond's fourfold consists of a metaphysics that moves from univocity and equivocity, their dialectic self-mediation into the between of *metaxu*. *Metaxu* is an idea that mediates between univocity, equivocity, and dialectics—drawing out the best of each in a metaxological space of the between. *Metaxu* culminates through the fourfold in the between of how to live for others, for oneself, for God, and for creation. The metaphysical movement reasons through *metaxu* in concrete situations of lived experience in the tension between unity, difference, self-mediation, and inter-relationality. Its openness of being is both determinate and indeterminate: it is over-determinate.

The openness of being is determinate because it is concretized within lived experience of the tensions of the between which produce the contingency of its existence. But it is also indeterminate and over-determinate because the openness of being transcends its conditions—it is always more, or rather, there is always a more to being. It is marked by the wonder or astonishment of be-ing something rather than nothing, or rather of becoming something more through life. The experience of being in the between for Desmond is a position of fundamental openness to Being, the Good, and God and becoming through life in the metaxological conditions and space *for* Being, *for* the Good, and *for* God. It is not just the astonishment of Being something rather than nothing but also as being *for* something in concrete experiences of everyday life.

The Turn to Transcendence

Desmond argues that the logic of *metaxu* is to articulate what it means to be at all. But more specifically in his theological work, *God and the Between*, he argues for the over-determinacy of the between where the fourfold has a given community of being where we are unsure of its beginning and already participate in it—which communicates the openness to the possibility of transcendence (*GB*, 9). His articulation of transcendence is threefold. His T[1] refers to the exteriority of creation and the world as other, while his T[2] refers

80   *Chapter 4*

to the interiority of self-transcendence and his T^3 refers to the superiority of the otherness of transcendence itself (*GB*, 22–23).

But between these transcendences are not only their metaxological excesses pointing beyond their transcendences consecutively from exteriority to interiority to superiority, but also to the sheer givenness of being as *passio essendi* (the patience of Being) over against the *conatus essendi* (the endeavor to be). Desmond highlights that *in* the sheer givenness of being, *there* is its transcendence in our experience of the between. In our astonishment at experiencing being, we need not endeavor to be: it is already here/there, present to our experience, opening us to the experience of transcendence in the immanent between.

But the threat of autonomy for Desmond is linked to the endeavor to be in ways that challenges what it means to be in the between. Desmond rhetorically argues that the danger is to idolize ourselves and create the world in our own image. He argues that the danger in the will to power is an ontological necessity that presumes the valuelessness of being and that we must make it worthy of ourselves, and this results in nihilism if all we are trying to do is make being worthy in our image because it is for ourselves and not the other: the self becomes the center of reality, reducing all of reality's worthiness to the determinations of the self (*GB*, 22).

By contrast, Desmond argues that nihilism is not the point of Being in the between. Being in the between, in its transcendencing from exteriority to interiority and superiority, is grounded in a fourfold understanding of its givenness of being created. First, creation is given as an other, not as for us, but has value and being in and of itself. Second, in the excess of creation's being for itself, we are released from "the abyss hidden in self-being" (*GB*, 43). Third, we are released "towards the community of creation and self-being" culminating a rapport between beings in the between, of self, creation, and other in ways that delivers us to wonder about the possibility of a superior, transcending other found in God (*GB*, 43–44).

The transcending of being in the between is found in Desmond's articulations of the communicativeness of being. Not only is being communicated through world as something here determinate by a primordial determinacy that exceeds its coming to be by pointing to its origins, but it is also communicated through human coming to be in the world where the world is presupposed as we come to be in the world. This determining is not self-determining, but a givenness of being that we involve ourselves with throughout our lives. Finally, the transcending of being in the between points beyond relatedness to world and humans in the excess that points to the possibility of God.

For Desmond, the ambiguity of the asymmetrical relation between God and world plays with the possibility of God being for us and for himself, of relating to us as we relate to him in the excess of life's ambiguity that shades the possibility of his concern for us (*GB*, 107). Metaxological metaphysics points us not only to God over and above, but also in the midst of us. In doing so it communicates "something double: from the 'midst' of immanent being a passage (*poros*) is opened, and we may become porous to something communicated of what is 'beyond' or 'above.' The 'above' is not 'beyond' as a dualistic opposite or a void inaccessible transcendence, and its signs of fullness serve to enable some metaphorical prefiguration of what transcendence as other might be" (*GB*, 123).

Continuing an analysis of Desmond's theology as against the dualism between transcendence and immanence, he argues rather that God determines the world in an asymmetrical relation, like himself, to be good. If God were absolutely other than the world, then this would dedivinize the world: "nothing in the world is God; without God the world is nothing, and has nothing to do with God" (*GB*, 252). He articulates three consequences of the utter separation between world and God. First, the "earthly traces of the divine are extirpated." Second, the "earth appears as the godless place of our mastery." Third, "the godless earth earns less respect." And fourth, "creation is made [for] our means, mere matter for exploitation: in itself nothing good, we impose our value on it. We are God's gift to the world, the world worthless until we give ourselves" (*GB*, 252).

But Desmond argues that though the world is other than God, it is good as other when God stands back after creation to deem it "Good." In God's affirmation of creation as Good, we do not find him congratulating himself on creating something good. We see God beholding the goodness of creation as something worthy and "esteemed . . . by the creator" (*GB*, 252). Desmond links the asymmetrical relation of God's hyper transcendence above and beyond, and in the midst of the world, as something that suggests not that God is dependent on the world, nor merely that the world is dependent upon God. Rather it highlights divine freedom to create and gift creation its own freedom through the "free release [of his] free giving" (*GB*, 253). Desmond argues that the metaxological asymmetry of relations between God and creation is something of a doubling and interplay between two spheres of an inclusive whole. He states God and the world are marked by an asymmetrical relation, an agapeic community between God and world that gives to the creature their being in ways not to dominate the creature but for God to freely and agapeically give beyond himself and his own community the freedom of creatures their finite otherness (*GB*, 255).

So, what does Desmond offer us? Theologically, John Betz makes a distinction between Heidegger's ontological distinction and Aquinas's creaturely distinction: "the real, ontic distinction between essence and existence is not immanently self-contained but (to adopt Desmond's idiom) porous, being

82   *Chapter 4*

intersected by a still profounder, ontological difference between the creature, whose being [is] inherently in becoming (*in fieri*), and God, who simply IS (*Ipsum Esse*)."[30] Betz argues that the tradition of overcoming metaphysics forgets the theological frameworks of the relationship between essence and existence. Betz distinctly develops a Christian metaphysical critique of Heidegger's onto-theology, drawing out alongside Desmond how Being and beings and the ontological distinction is not just a question between and about the what and that of Being (which conceals Being/essence in existence/beings). Rather the ontological distinction must also remember the creaturely distinction between the Being of God and the becoming of creatures as a rebuttal for forgetting the creational theology and what it ontologically implies of God and creature.

***

In *God and the Between*, William Desmond builds on his work in *Being and the Between* and *Ethics and the Between*, drawing his metaxological metaphysics of Being and Ethics into Theology. Like his developments there, he develops and links the notions of idiocy to univocity, aesthetics to equivocity, erotics to dialectics, and of agape to *metaxu*. In part one of *God and the Between*, Desmond argues that godlessness and nihilism are theological questionings and by-products of developments in modern theology and philosophy, implying how exterior transcendence, interior transcendence, and superior transcendence are frameworks for rethinking God and the between. He highlights how the modern philosophical emphasis on autonomy is antimonious to self-transcendence's focus on interiority and produces nihilism and godlessness. Like *Being and the Between* and *Ethics and the Between*, Desmond develops his fourfold, problematizing and building from univocity, equivocity, and dialectics to their metaphysical consummation in the *metaxu*.

His metaxological metaphysics produces through the fourfold four ways to God and highlights the inadequacy of univocity (through analyses of its history in philosophy as producing problematically the by-product of irreconcilable difference), equivocity (because it produces the fragmentation of being, ethics, and God), and dialectics (because it fails to intermediate sameness and difference for the other). In further analyses, he argues how dialectics fails to adequately address the determinacy and indeterminacy of God—culminating in his metaxological reformulations of over-determinacy of God as the hyperbolic excess as both above and beyond, and in the midst of, finitude. It is in this hyperbolic excess that God is over-determined and superior to, while immanent in, finitude. While part three of *God and the Between* addresses different theisms and their articulations and inadequacies in light of theological over-determinacy, part four develops a theology of over-determinacy. This theology of over-determinacy articulates theologically the more and superiority of God in asymmetrical relation to creation as the Being prior and superior to nothingness. Furthermore, creation is gifted existence apart from, yet dependent on, God's over-determinacy.

ADVAITA AND METAXU

Between Panikkar and Desmond, we find two metaphysical systems and orientations that posit the openness to transcendence from immanence. Both Panikkar and Desmond articulate the centrality of infinity, freedom, and transcendence and immanence as core elements of philosophizing about God. While Panikkar develops his philosophical theology from a cross-cultural perspective, Desmond develops his metaxological metaphysics from within Western philosophy. Not only does this demonstrate Western philosophy's critique from within and a cross-cultural critique from both without and within, but it demonstrates how Panikkar and Desmond philosophically imagine the possibility of divine immanence as a critique of modern philosophy and theology's overemphasis on divine transcendence.

But if Desmond articulates a metaxological critique of modernity from within Western philosophical tradition, then Panikkar offers an advaitic critique of modernity that situates divine immanence as tempiternally present in human experience. That is, divine immanence for Panikkar enpresents divine transcendence because it's infinitude is *in*-finitude, divine freedom is hidden within immanence, and its transcendence has condescended into, and participates in, time and human experience. Because transcendence is tempiternally experienced in time, divine transcendence's tempiternity and immanence opens itself primordially to human experience and to the co-temporaneity between transcendence and immanence of the cosmotheandric mystery of reality.

Likewise, Desmond's fourfold and the between articulates that from the hyperbolic excesses of being we have an opening from immanence to transcendence. Desmond's ontological, ethical, and theological concerns and reflections offer insights into the nature of reality that opens us to the possibility of God from the very conditions of immanence and the between. The between is the intermediate over-determinate space of immanence that exceeds itself and opens us to the possibility of living for God, Others, and the Good throughout an immanent experience of creation that exceeds itself in a turn to transcendence. It combines what it means to be, to be good, and to be open to God from within immanence in light of what its excess exposes with what it means to wonder at being, what it means to live for, and how

84 *Chapter 4*

the between opens us already to the excessive over-determinacy of immanent experience to wonder at transcendence.

Reading Desmond and Panikkar together generates two instances of how Desmond's *metaxu* and Panikkar's advaita hold open the space for divine transcendence within immanence and for the gift of and participation in divine transcendence for and from immanence. While Panikkar's emphasis on divine immanence sees divine transcendence as co-temporal and co-participatory in created immanence, Desmond's emphasis on the excesses of transcendence found within the immanence experience of metaxological space—the between—is where immanence is able to transcend itself in the porosity of being's excessive participation in the agapeic gift of its being for others, the good, and God. Desmond's understanding of transcendence is both horizontal and vertical—it's transcending excess is found in agapeic community with both other (created/immanent/finite) beings as well as with God as a transcendent other who gifts each created being with their being as an act of agapeic love that does not demand compulsory love. Rather the gift of being is a free gift that is not only to be received but lived in astonishment and response to the excesses of God's over-determinate love. This over-determinate excess of agapeic love from God not only gifts created beings their being, but also creates a space between transcendence and immanence where immanent, finite beings are called out of themselves to freely receive and gift themselves in agapeic community for others.

Panikkar's advaitic contributions by contrast see the divine as co-temporaneous within immanence in ways that draw human beings to recognize their co-participation in a cosmotheandric reality. But Panikkar's advaitic critique of modernity also wrestles with the problem of identity and difference in ways that focus on the harmonious interplay between identity and difference. His understanding of divine immanence entails both a sense of difference between created and divine immanence, as well as the identity of created immanence as participating in divine immanence. This participation opens the space for both sameness and difference and generates an understanding that created immanence may share in and act in harmony with divine immanence. Panikkar's critique of modernity is centered around the advaitic overcoming of monism and dualism in ways that generate a participatory ontology that holds open the space for created immanence to cosmotheandrically experience reality tempiternally through immanence's participation in transcendence.

The difference, however, between Panikkar and Desmond's understanding of the relationship between transcendence and immanence is not only in Panikkar's rejection of the ontological distinction between God and creation through his understanding of the immanence as tempiternally co-participating in transcendence. It also lies in Desmond's understanding of immanence's transcending excesses that poses inter-mediate excesses beyond immanence to the other, whether that is human or divine. The other both transcends the immanence of finite beings and exceeds finite beings in ways that open up the space between transcendence and immanence in the transcending excesses and over-determinations of being. While both Desmond and Panikkar understand being as porous in the senses that they (a) exceed their finitude through transcending excesses of their immanence (Desmond), and (b) harmoniously participates in a reality that tempiternally sees transcendence *in*-finitude— that is, that immanence participates in and is imbued with divine transcendence (Panikkar), their understandings of the porosity of being do differ in significant ways.

While Desmond understands the porosity of being to exceed and transcend itself, Panikkar understands the porosity of being insofar as beings participate in a cosmotheandric understanding of reality where divine transcendence permeates immanence in ways that immanence is imbued with the sacred. Desmond's metaxological metaphysics creates a space where immanence exceeds itself in the over-determinacy of (its) transcendence. Panikkar's advaitic critique of modernity sees immanence as imbued with and participating in the mystery of transcendence. Desmond accepts the ontological distinction between God and creation, and yet articulates a space where they may meet in the *metaxu*. Panikkar rejects the ontological distinction between God and creation, and articulates how divine immanence permeates all of reality where its presence is hidden in creation, opening up immanence to transcendence because of immanence's participation in transcendence.

However, whether we accept the ontological distinction between transcendence and immanence or not, both Desmond and Panikkar articulate two ways of thinking theologically and metaphysically about immanence's openness to transcendence. The transcending excesses of immanence in Desmond create a metaxological space, a between, where immanence remains open to transcendence. Panikkar's advaitic critique of modernity articulates how creation and immanence are always already open to its harmonious participating in transcendence. Both Desmond and Panikkar struggle with modernity's problem of identity and difference through their understandings of transcendence. Desmond sees transcendence as over-determinate and this creates an excess governed by the reception of the gift of Being as a gift from God to be agapeically astonished and live for the good of the Other. Panikkar sees divine transcendence in-finitude in ways that generate an alternate solution to monistic emphases on sameness and dualistic emphases on difference. It is here that Panikkar's critique of modernity generates ontological problems and promises in what is developed below through the idea of a postmodern ontology.

86 Chapter 4

***

Between the last two chapters, Panikkar's advaitic metaphysical vision has been developed in dialogue with Martin Heidegger and William Desmond. Core to Panikkar's metaphysics is the tempiternal presence of divine immanence to human religious experience, which points beyond itself in faith as excess to the hiddenness of divine transcendence in immanence. Divine transcendence in turn is marked by infinitude and freedom to become with and alongside creation, creating an advaitic, trinitarian harmony between the material world, God, and humanity. In Panikkar's advaitic spin on metaphysics we not only see the possibilities of understanding a metatheology of divine mystery, but also of particular theologies as particular manifestations of the divine mystery. In Panikkar's refrain from absolutizing and universalizing religious Truth, what we find in human religious experience is an advaitic, trinitarian, cosmotheandric metaphysical vision of reality defined by rhythm and harmony among and between religious incommensurabilities, open to the possibility of transcendence precisely because of its immanence and its excess that points beyond itself to the mystery of the divine.

In contrast to these chapters on Panikkar's metaphysics in dialogue with Heidegger and Desmond, the following chapters mark a turn to understanding further developments of Panikkar's in dialogue with "postmodern ontology" which are especially refracted through accounts and critiques of modernity. The turn from metaphysics to postmodern ontology and sacred secularity situates a turn in this book that situates the focus in subsequent chapters to Panikkar's ontological confluences with Charles Taylor, Heideggerian tradition, and the Radical Orthodoxy Movement alongside the contributions of Panikkar's critique of modernity. The turn to these dialogue partners will begin to reveal how Panikkar represents an advaitic postmodern turn that is both theological and philosophical—and one that reveals his implicit critique of modernity's closure and eclipse of divine transcendence through his agonistic affinities with Charles Taylor, Martin Heidegger, and the Radical Orthodoxy Movement.

NOTES

1. Raimon Panikkar, "Introduction," in *Trinitarian and Cosmotheandric Vision*, ed. Milena Carrara Pavan, Vol. VIII, XII vols., Opera Omnia (Maryknoll, NY: Orbis Books, 2019), xiii–xv, xiv.

2. Panikkar, "Introduction," xiv.

3. Raimon Panikkar, "Deity," in *Trinitarian and Cosmotheandric Vision*, ed. Milena Carrara Pavan, Vol. VIII, XII vols., Opera Omnia (Maryknoll, NY: Orbis Books, 2019), 5–27.

4. Raimon Panikkar, *The Rhythm of Being: The Unbroken Trinity* (Maryknoll, NY: Orbis Books, 2010), 130. Henceforth in text as *RB*.

5. Raimon Panikkar, *Myth, Faith, and Hermeneutics: Cross Cultural Studies* (New York: Paulist Press, 1979), 323.

6. Panikkar, *Myth, Faith, and Hermeneutics*, 323.

7. Panikkar, *Myth, Faith, and Hermeneutics*, 331.

8. Panikkar, *Myth, Faith, and Hermeneutics*, 331.

9. On Panikkar's phenomenology of Experience see his mathematical equation of "E=(e.l.m.i.r.a)": C.f. Raimon Panikkar, *Mysticism and Spirituality: Mysticism, The Fullness of Life*, ed. Milena Carrara Pavan, Vol. I.1, XII vols., Opera Omnia (Maryknoll, NY: Orbis Books, 2014), 167–86.

10. Panikkar, *Myth, Faith, and Hermeneutics*, 311–15.

11. Brenden Thomas Sammon and Christopher Ben Simpson, "Introduction," in *William Desmond and Contemporary Theology*, eds., Christopher Ben Simpson and Brenden Thomas Sammon (Notre-Dame, IN: University of Notre-Dame Press, 2017), 1–13.

12. James L. Marsh, "William Desmond's Overcoming of the Overcoming of Metaphysics," in *Between System and Poetics: William Desmond and Philosophy after Dialectic*, ed. Thomas A. F. Kelly (London and New York: Routledge, 2007), 95–105.

13. Corey Benjamin Tutewiler, "On the Cause of Metaphysical Indeterminacy and the Origin of Being," in *William Desmond and Contemporary Theology*, eds., Christopher Ben Simpson and Brenden Thomas Sammon (Notre-Dame, IN: University of Notre-Dame Press, 2017), 93–116.

14. Corey Benjamin Tutewiler, "On the Cause of Metaphysical Indeterminacy and the Origin of Being," 109.

15. D.C. Schindler, "The Positivity of Philosophy: William Desmond's Contribution to Theology," in *William Desmond and Contemporary Theology*, eds., Christopher Ben Simpson and Brenden Thomas Sammon (Notre-Dame, IN: University of Notre-Dame Press, 2017), 117–37, 121–23.

16. Schindler, "The Positivity of Philosophy," 123.

17. Schindler, "The Positivity of Philosophy," 123.

18. Schindler, "The Positivity of Philosophy," 132.

19. William Desmond, *Being and the Between* (Albany, NY: State University of New York Press, 1995), 44. Henceforth in text as *BB*.

20. Patrick X. Gardner, "God Beyond and Between: Desmond, Przywara, and Catholic Metaphysics," in *William Desmond and Contemporary Theology*, eds., Christopher Ben Simpson and Brenden Thomas Sammon (Notre-Dame, IN: University of Notre-Dame Press, 2017), 165–90, 173.

21. William Desmond, "Wording the Between," in *The William Desmond Reader*, ed. Christopher Ben Simpson (Albany, NY: State University of New York Press, 2012), 195–227, 196.

22. William Desmond, *Ethics and the Between* (Albany, NY: State University of New York Press, 2001), 1. Henceforth in text as *EB*.

23. William Desmond, "Between System and Poetics: On the Practices of Philosophy," in *Between System and Poetics: William Desmond and Philosophy after Dialectic*, ed. Thomas A. F. Kelly (London and New York: Routledge, 2007), 13–36, 15–16.

24. Desmond, "Between System and Poetics," 27.

25. Desmond, "Between System and Poetics," 27.

26. Desmond, "Between System and Poetics," 27.

27. Brenden Thomas Sammon, "The Reawakening of the Between: William Desmond and Reason's Intimacy with Beauty," in *William Desmond and Contemporary Theology*, eds., Christopher Ben Simpson and Brenden Thomas Sammon (Notre-Dame, IN: University of Notre-Dame Press, 2017), 15–56, 47.

28. William Desmond, *God and the Between* (Malden, MA: Blackwell, 2008), 9–10. Henceforth in text as *GB*.

29. Desmond critiques through the fourfold the modern Enlightenment and its trends as against metaxological metaphysics and as for nihilism.

30. John R. Betz, "Overcoming the Forgetfulness of Metaphysics: The More Original Philosophy of William Desmond," in *William Desmond and Contemporary Theology*, eds., Christopher Ben Simpson and Brenden Thomas Sammon (Notre-Dame, IN: University of Notre-Dame Press, 2017), 57–91, 80.

Chapter 5

The Problems and Promises of a Postmodern Ontology

Theological Critiques of Modernity

While the previous two chapters addressed Panikkar's advaitic metaphysics in engagement with Martin Heidegger and William Desmond, this chapter and the next focus on the question of a postmodern ontology. Whereas this chapter addresses the problems and promises of a postmodern ontology, the next chapter will address a postmodern ontology at the limits of modernity. In particular, this chapter offers several critiques of modernity centered around the ontological question and its problems of autonomy, individualism, and violence, all the while problematizing theological and ontological resolutions found in David Bentley Hart, Emmanuel Levinas, and Raimon Panikkar around the role of analogy, otherness, participation, and faith. Hence, this chapter offers an analysis of the critique of modernity this book is centrally addressing. As we have seen throughout this book, this chapter also takes a dialogical approach to its analysis of the critique of modernity and engages Panikkar with several key interlocutors around the problems and promises of a postmodern ontology.

THE PROBLEM OF A POSTMODERN ONTOLOGY

Notions of the ontological question of the meaning of being often fail to connect it to faith. We are at a stage in history where what it means to know, exist, and be, is questioned, relativized, and disorientated from accounts of human nature and dignity. Certain theologians characterize the "postmodern self" as characterized by the fragility and fragmentation of a sense of self after the eclipse of the *imago dei* and the collapse of the modern centered self into the poly- and de-centered self of postmodernity.[1] Furthermore, the nihilism and lack of orienting purposes in human life opens the question of the meaning of being to an ever increasing abyss sought to be filled by the various idiosyncratic constructions of meaning and religious belief.[2] This results in the pluralization of religious belief (Charles Taylor's Nova Effect) where religious expression is emancipated and explodes from the bounds of traditional religion for more individual, expressive, and authentic expressions of religious identity and practice.[3]

Christian theologians argue that postmodernity is marked by generations that are burdened by the inability to reason, the loss of innocence, and the ontic affirmation of feeling.[4] Contemporary society struggles with meaning, indeed even paradoxically in the affirmation of ordinary life. Ordinary life is seen as empty of depth, living off of the surface of ontic experience as that which matters most to us, when in reality it has no lasting meaning beyond the comforts of the possibilism of experience. We affirm something in the embrace of experience of that which is ultimately lacking and empty of any ultimate meaning.[5] Within the postmodern mind there is a threat of understanding the meaning of being as inherently valueless and meaningless, leading to despair and the radical affirmation or denial of life in the face of absurdity when we expect meaning in a meaningless world.[6]

Thus the postmodern self not only suffers from a de-centered and poly-centered self,[7] but is fundamentally characterized by a certain lack, emptiness, ennui, and nothingness that may be filled through the pursuit of depth in the ontic experience of what Jean Baudrillard and Graham Ward call the "virtual reality": a simulation of the real that blurs the lines between the actual, the virtual, and the imagined.[8] Tied to the ontic search for meaning is the fear of death, which can be defined as the horizon of an eternal nothingness, as the negation of existence that is always waiting.[9] The threat of our mortality is not something that merely authenticates our existence by living toward death, but it is something courageously defied in the "courage to be" and the drive to experience all this world has to offer.[10] By living in a meaningless world, one may courageously affirm that the nihilism of life and meaning can be something, even when its possibilities defy the logic that it is still nothing.[11]

This "nihilism of meaning" is tied to the modern developments of autonomy, exclusive humanism, and the focus on human flourishing to the exclusion of religious frameworks for meaning. Furthermore, the nihilism of meaning is expressed when the postmodern self devalues the possibility of a transcendent and governing God as irrelevant and even offensive while modern conceptions of autonomy eliminate the possibility of participating in God because God is seen as against human flourishing.[12] Modern, exclusive humanists reject the theists' emphasis on humanity's createdness,

The Problems and Promises of a Postmodern Ontology   91

dependence, and contingency upon God for meaning and worth through their turn to this-worldly flourishing and postmodern negations of absolute truth.[13]

This nihilism is situated in common sensibilities of postmodern relativism. Postmodern relativism implies that there is no standard by which we can adjudicate truth, the good, or the right, because in advocating for particular local truths and rejecting metanarratives of universal truth,[14] we lose the ability to judge something to be good, true, or right. This is because by denying absolute truth we deny any standard by which to judge truth beyond our own personal desires or particular, contextual horizons by which we create and understand our values and what we find meaningful. Because of this, postmodern nihilism entails that there is no longer any universal value because everything is unhooked from any foundation upon which a standard can judge something to be true, right, or good. This invokes the emptiness of any depth to what we deem right, good, and true. It implies becoming slaves to desires and rejecting any authority by which judgement could be passed. In this context, everyday life may see the destruction of any sense of inherent or given meaning; it is when our desire to determine ourselves over against religious, social, familial, biological, and cultural constructs becomes the norm.

If we accept relativism, this does not mean that we cannot do good. Rather it means that there is no *absolute* standard by which the good could be judged good. This results in nihilism precisely because we would no longer have an absolute standard by which we could determine something as good or evil, violent or peaceful. This postmodern ontology does not only declare that we can believe what we want because nothing can determine for us and tell us what to do. It also entails that meaning and value can be devalued, because there is no standard by which they could be determined as having any substantial value. Value and meaning can be destroyed by our passions at the expense of truth. We are open to whatever we want, desire and feeling rule us, and anything going against what we want is castigated and seen as intolerant to our individualistic and authentic self-expression. Western history shows that the autonomous self not only divides and individuates the self from the others, but in essence it negates the other in favor of/for the self. This results in an ontological violence towards the other and a gradual devaluation of human dignity and one's ability to attribute ontological value to the human person.[15]

Part of this problem stems from the process of secularization that, according to the Radical Orthodoxy Movement, found a crucial turn in univocity where creation was unhooked from its participation in its creator and was granted its created autonomy. This later resulted in the shift from a created *physis* to an ordered nature subject to human technocratic and instrumental reason as the universally applicable and providential purpose of humans to master their world when the relevance of God is eclipsed, displaced, and

92 *Chapter 5*

replaced in modern society.[16] Conor Cunningham states that a world given its autonomous existence apart from God:

> becomes the purely ontic realm. Existence is separated from constitutive purpose, becoming divorced from any notion of a non-arbitrary *telos*. In consequence existence becomes "doubled," and can now be said to exist purely on its own. . . . Even finite existence exists without any lack or deficiency in being, because to exist is no longer inextricably linked with a teleological structure which would admit degrees in being. As a result, one can essentialize existence. Of course, the world was still created by God but what "to be created" meant has changed. It was now taken to mean determined in its nature by absolute power, not as exhibiting the absolute truth by virtue of its very existence. Thus, while creation had been rendered abjectly subject, the heart of the mystery, its being, is now allowed unproblematically to be its own possession. Hence in its increasingly autonomous existence it is also deprived of ontological worth.[17]

Univocity entails a nihilism of meaning where the separation between God and created existence doubles God and created existence in which the latter becomes not merely ontologically autonomous, but through this there came ontic repercussions. In becoming autonomous, the immanence of creation became its own being separated from transcendence—creation lost its depth and quiddity of being—and God became equivocally differentiated from creation to the point that God became subjectively irrelevant and ontologically inaccessible. Creation now struggles to affirm its onticity as truly real and ontological in the aftermath of an equivocal separation between God and creation because in being unhooked from the transcendence of God it has lost the ground on which the depth and meaning of its existence can be ontologically based.

The process of secularization moves from creation's participation in the Being of God to its created autonomy, and finally not only to the autonomous divide between human beings as masters of nature through the use of instrumental reason, but even to human violence toward the other and the anthropocentric vision of reality that negates God. Before modernity, the human person was seen as ontologically embedded and participating in a social, moral, and cosmic order characterized by the spiritual, which temporally ordered all aspects of human life according to its participation in eternity through the human engagement in religious practices and an embodied, liturgical faith.[18] If secularization is understood as the disembedding of humanity's social, moral, and cosmic embedding within an ordered cosmos, then its replacement by a modern moral order characterized by the public sphere, the citizen state, and the market economy entails a new experience of the flattening of vertical relations into the horizontal field of a direct access society.[19]

The Problems and Promises of a Postmodern Ontology   93

Thus, the secularization of belief theoretically denies the belief in God as a sovereign ruler over human history. It denies not merely God as a creator who providentially orders creation toward its eschatological end, but also denies God as having any bearing or authority over human existence. This does not deny religious experience, but rather denies the relevancy of God to, and rejects God's authority over, human life. The human relationship with God went through a continual intellectual disillusionment wherein God was gradually deemed unknowable via human reason and the meaning of being was no longer grounded upon a notion of faith. Belief in God was rejected because God was no longer seen as relatable and relevant to and with humanity and creation.[20] During the modern era of human history, the divine's basis for being the source of the meaning of being began to crumble while divine transcendence was infinitized and eclipsed: the process of the secularization of belief implied the gradual disillusionment and critique of the ontological affirmation of divine presence.

But this is not condoning a "return" to religion. We cannot go back to the medieval Christendom after modern discoveries and movements in naturalism, science, and atheism. Secularism, science, atheism, naturalism, and materialism have declared the irrelevancy of God to a postmodern ontology and have devalued the dignity of Man as created in the image of God.[21] We have devalued the relevancy of God as a possible horizon of meaning from which we can understand what it means to flourish and answer the question, "why we are here?" With the death of God, we have negated the actualization of ontological/created invaluability as created in the image of God and replaced it with an open abyss to the possibility of meaninglessness. But we can recover pre-modern theological trends that could reconstruct and renew a postmodern ontology: an existential openness and porosity toward the possibility, experience, and reality of God in ordinary life and experience. And this existential openness and porosity to faith may be recovered through an imagined openness to the everyday re-enchantment of ordinary life and experience.

Where do we ontologically ground the meaning of being when meaning and existence have been devalued? How can we renew a sense of ontological worth when the given nature of humanity, world, and God have been devalued by the hubris of reason? This renewal may happen when we search for and re-evaluate the meaning of being through the way we perceive and imagine our world, ourselves, and God. If we remain open to the possibility, recognition, and affirmation of the experience of God in the everydayness of ordinary life, this implicitly transforms how we imagine our world and God in ways that re-enchant our social, cultural, and religious imaginary. We can reconstruct meaning when we reexamine the possibility for God, by recognizing and affirming the gift and inherent value of our everyday lives as creatures created in the image of God and by participating in the life of God and his purposes for this-worldly human fullness and flourishing. Charles Taylor states that "we want our lives to have meaning, or weight, or substance, or to grow towards some fullness . . . [b]ut this means our whole lives. If necessary, we want the future to 'redeem' the past, to make it part of a life story which has sense of purpose, to take it up in a meaningful unity."[22]

SELF-KNOWLEDGE, PARTICIPATION, AND OTHERNESS

Central aspects of what it means to be human are the ontological concerns for identity, relating, and knowing. The ancient Greeks were constantly concerned with the metaphysical question of "being" through the search for a common substance by which the unity and diversity of reality could be explained.[23] The Delphic oracle called the Greeks to self-knowledge: "Know Thyself!" The Greek dictum of knowing thyself has pervaded the entire history of the West by inspiring a search for the reason for our existence.[24] Charles Taylor's and Michael Hanby's historical accounts of self-knowledge demonstrate the movement through stages from Augustine's self-reflexivity to Descartes's *cogito sum* and to Locke's punctual self when the human becomes a thinking thing with the ability to doubt itself and is able to determine its world through the use of instrumental, autonomous reason.[25] If the turn to modern autonomy in Descartes is tied to his questioning of his own existence and affirming it by the cogito, in the affirmation of a thinking existence we have a turn to representational epistemology which shifts the "knowledge *of* the self" (marked by self-reflexivity) into a "knowledge *about* the self" (marked by the objective self) insofar as it represents the reality of the self as an object to be objectified as something knowable and constructed.[26]

Making a distinction between knowledge "of" the self and knowledge "about" the self means that there is something participatory in being "of" something and something representational in being "about" something. The knowledge "of" self implies that the self participates in something. This links knowledge of self to participating in being known as other with a sense of shared "embeddedness" as the self participates within the real. Knowledge of the self "participates" in a sense of "participating-with" the community, culture, and society in ways where the self "shares" its existence with the other, the more-than, and the world in which it lives. Knowledge "of" self implies a participatory ontology with that which the self is embedded in.

By contrast, knowledge "about" self implies the epistemological representation and objectification of the self. What we know about reality or the self is objectified and constructed as real or as self, insofar as it can be something

The Problems and Promises of a Postmodern Ontology   95

known through its free autonomy and construction of what "I" am and desire to be or become. This results in a constructed identity that is autonomously centered in the rational capacity of the self in ordering itself as it determines and re-presents the self to be in the world as an autonomous individual in control of its own destiny or morality. The danger that modern representational "knowledge about the self" implies is the turn toward a neutral, aloof, and objectified reality of an autonomous self-identity disconnected from self, other, and God, and disconnected from the world in its mastery over and above the world.[27]

In the shifts from the pre-modern to modern and then to the postmodern, representational knowledge "about" has become dominant over the participatory knowledge "of," while postmodern ontology emphasizes the loss of a centered self. But insofar as Heidegger opens the hermeneutical horizon that doubts representational knowledge and seeks to articulate existence as always already existing in the world, the Heideggerian question of the meaning of being locates self-knowledge of its existential being-in-the-world. This self-knowledge embedded and informed by how we are already always in the world re-orients the postmodern self not only as re-oriented existentially toward an end. Moreover, by orienting the self toward its end, it makes a human agent participate intentionally in the world into which it is "thrown." The postmodern self not only recovers the participatory shared embeddedness of self-in-the-world which is eclipsed by modern representational knowledge about the self, but also recovers the ontological facticity of experience and human agency as constitutive of the meaning of being.

In the turn to otherness, another problem arises from the modern autonomous way of understanding the self. The modern autonomous self rejects the other both by (1) setting themselves above the other as a centered, buffered, and rationalized self and (2) by dominating or subverting the other through objectification and rationalization of the other as someone fundamentally inferior. Insofar as the modern autonomous self sees itself as being the centerpiece of reality in which "I" am all that matters, we necessarily leave out the possibility of existence in relation to other persons who are themselves a center. The problem with autonomy is that it lacks the ability to have a meaningful relationship with other autonomies because my individuation separates me from the other and implies that "I" am the only thing that matters and that "I" become "invulnerable" to the other. Autonomy can teach us social atomism, which entails that the individual is seen as above community and denies the inherent worth of participating with others, belonging to others, or caring for others.

Modernity lost the essential link between being and identity, the link between the way we exist and what makes us a human agent. A human agent is endowed with a self-reflexive identity that intentionally participates in community with others. Self-identity is derivative from how we exist in the world, which in turn tells us about ourselves and who we are. It implies a constitutive link between how we exist and how we understand ourselves. Self-identity implies that how we understand ourselves is constituted by our practices, the narratives of our lives, and what matters most to us. The postmodern self recognizes the need for narrative identity, shared community, and a shared sense of meaning with an other.[28] The postmodern self recognizes the other and also their need for the other. Furthermore, the postmodern self is constitutively oriented by both common goods shared with others, and common practices that we do with and for others.

But Raimon Panikkar recognizes the importance of understanding and identifying with the other and argues that we must not only become aware of otherness, as in the otherness of the other, but relate with the other as other in a way that allows the other to be other without negating, possessing, or doing violence to the other in subverting the other to our own image of sameness.[29] To recognize the otherness of the other as other implies the active relationality of an everyday life wherein I share with an other my life with a participatory consciousness;[30] the other is required to be there for me to be. The postmodern recognition of the other sparks an understanding of reality that reintroduces a sense of meaning that is not dependent upon social atomism. The postmodern recognition of the other re-introduces us to participating with others, with our culture and society, and even within the political arena: each of these levels of participating with, in, and for the other constitutes our identity as human agents and persons participating within the contexts of an other greater than ourselves. The postmodern mind recognizes the need for relationality and recognizes the constitutive nature of relationships to and for my self-identity.

A postmodern *relational* ontology recognizes the need for relationality, constitutive meaning, and the embeddedness of existence by being-with, caring-for, and belonging-to others, our culture, the world, and/or God in our everyday existence. It sees the faults of social atomism and modern autonomous reason. It sees the constitutive need of/for relationship as a formative dimension of self-identity. The meaning of being is grounded in existential relationships, not in a representational epistemology, because we can only know who we are by the exposure of self through relationships with others, with the world, and/or with God. By participating-in the dimensions of human, cosmic, and divine reality there is an exposure to meaning, an exposure to self-knowledge as constituted through and by everyday relationships.

This section has critiqued the autonomous self of modernity and articulated the ontological need for relationality felt by the postmodern self through the advocation for the renewal of a participatory self-knowledge and the relationship with the other as constitutive to the meaning of being. The secular

The Problems and Promises of a Postmodern Ontology 97

autonomy of existence is lost to relationality and constitutive meaning because its emphasis on individualism entails the (possible) negation of the other in the extremes of social atomism. What a postmodern ontology recognizes is the need for meaning, the understanding that what we know about ourselves is not the limit of the self but rather that the self is constituted meaningfully through a relational ontology that participates with others in ways that opens one to an other as constitutive of my own self-identity. And yet the problem of alterity poses significant challenges in a postmodern ontology—in ways that generates both the question of whether Christian and advaitic critiques of modernity can offer alternate answers to the problems and promises of a postmodern ontology.

THE PROBLEM OF ALTERITY

David Bentley Hart sets out to engage the postmodern ontological problem of whether violence or peace is primordial.[31] He engages "the difference between two narratives: one that finds the grammar of violence inscribed upon the foundation stone of every institution and hidden within the syntax of every rhetoric, and another that claims that within history a way of reconciliation has been opened up that leads beyond, and ultimately overcomes all violence" (*BI*, 2). While David Bentley Hart sees this second ontology of peace as ushered in through the incarnation of the Son of God through Christ (*BI*, 129–32), what would Panikkar's advaitic anthropology offer as an answer to the problem of alterity? Before analyzing Panikkar's contributions, it is worthwhile to address how Bentley Hart and Emmanuel Levinas address the problem of alterity.

Analyzing John Milbank's critique of a postmodern ontology of violence, Bentley Hart argues how the postmodern offers not the denial of metaphysics, but an inversion of the Parmenidean metaphysics for its polar opposite—a Heraclitan metaphysics (*BI*, 37–38). Bentley Hart critiques Milbank's charge of postmodern philosophy as presupposing an ontology of violence because Milbank is not nuancing the differencing between them enough (*BI*, 35–37, 128). And yet Bentley Hart agrees with Milbank and sets out to nuance what Milbank did not. Starting with Kant's account of the sublime (*BI*, 43–52) as the backdrop of a postmodern ontology of violence, Bentley Hart then offers analyses of four different kinds of postmodern ontology and shows how each fall into the trap of an ontology of violence: Lyotard's differential sublime (*BI*, 52–56), Deleuze's cosmological sublime (*BI*, 56–72), Jean-Luc Nancy's ontological sublime (*BI*, 72–75), and Levinas's ethical sublime and Derrida's critique of it (*BI*, 75–90). In particular, David Bentley Hart argues that because Levinas's ethics fails to successfully imagine alterity, Levinas's

98 Chapter 5

philosophy implies an absolute negation in the totalization of otherness where God and the self become infinite totalities separated and sealed off from one another (*BI*, 85). The problem Bentley Hart identifies with a postmodern ontology of violence is the problem of difference and its dialectical implications of the negation of reality if it is the primordial origin of creation (*BI*, 91). By contrast, Bentley Hart is also not arguing for the collapse into the same. Rather he is emphasizing that an ontology of peace adheres to the analogy of being because it allows the difference between transcendence and immanence without collapsing them into the same. Here it is worthwhile to engage Levinas's understanding of alterity, totality, and infinity as a central theme of a postmodern ontology.

In *Totality and Infinity*,[32] Emmanuel Levinas argues how alterity confronts the self with the ethical face of the other. Levinas uses the term "totality" to refer to the denial of alterity and its collapse into the same. The dilemma Levinas poses is whether it is possible to articulate otherness in ways that are not subsumed into the same. Totality implies not just totalization, but for Levinas in particular, totality refers to the denial of difference insofar as difference is subsumed and collapsed into the same. This is a central problem for Levinas because the ethical problem it poses is whether difference is possible when identity collapses and subsumes all difference into the identity of the same. Levinas's solution in particular is to posit "infinity" to refer to the ethical confrontation by transcendence. While totality collapses difference into the same, infinity holds open the space for the ethical confrontation and encounter with a transcendent other that cannot be subsumed into the same. Here being exposed to the alterity of transcendence confronts the human person with an other that transcends the self in ways that implies not peace with God, but the irreducible alterity between God and Self.

In Levinas' *Otherwise than Being* he continues his analysis of alterity, where Alphonso Lingis argues that "in the exposedness to alterity in the face of another" for Levinas there is an "original form of openness" that is shaped not by the vulnerability of death, "but by a relationship with alterity."[33] Lingis states that for Levinas, "The relationship with the other in his alterity consists in being appealed to, and contested, by the other."[34] Furthermore, "alterity comes to me from without, and comes by exceeding my capacities . . . and whose very reality as infinity is in this exceeding of any capacity."[35] This means that for Levinas, alterity presupposes the idea of proximity, which is marked by the immediacy of a closeness without distance that remains *there*, presented before me and to which I must face as an other that takes a stand before me just as I take a stand before him/her.[36] Furthermore, "alterity is irreducible in not being interchangeable with me."[37] Rather its irreducibility is found in the relationship with an other that is not me and cannot be reduced to me. This is what Levinas calls Illeity, the irreducible "there is" before us of an Other. "Illeity is that by which the you is not the simple reverse of the I."[38] Levinas argues that the problem of transcendence and of God goes together with the problem of an irreducible subjectivity into an essential immanence.[39]

And yet, David Bentley Hart "subverts" Levinas's language of totality and infinity to refer to the openness of totality at its border or limit to infinity. According to Bentley Hart, totality refers to an immanent reality "sufficient for itself" that grasps "all things and values . . . within the confines of this immanentism" (*BI*, 14). Infinity for Hart means "what one desires when one seeks to see the totality as the gift of true transcendence, granting the totality its essences, its existence, its values, and its transcendental properties from beyond itself, by the grace of participation and under the 'rule' of analogy" (*BI*, 14). Bentley Hart defines analogy not as identity because to understand analogy as reductive reveals how that "is always also a reduction of the same to 'another other'" (*BI*, 85). By contrast analogy "elevates selves . . . above their isolation, while preserving their differences. To acknowledge a shared participation within a way of being . . . [i]s to be born forth from a false sense of sufficiency into the illuminating strangeness of that to which one belongs before one belongs to oneself" (*BI*, 85). Particularly, Bentley Hart uses the phrase "analogy of being" to refer to a Christian metaphysics outworked across the patristic and medieval Christian tradition in that it unites a participatory metaphysics with "the biblical doctrine of creation," and a trinitarian dogma that allows us "to contemplate both the utter difference of being from beings and the nature of true transcendence" (*BI*, 241).

Clearly what is at issue for David Bentley Hart in his critique of a postmodern ontology is not only the question of alterity, but of how to reconcile transcendence and immanence. While Bentley Hart will offer a distinct Christian metaphysical solution to a postmodern ontology found throughout his theological analyses of the Trinity, creation, salvation, and the eschaton (*BI*, 153–411), a problem that may be posed is whether the question of alterity and the reconciliation between transcendence and immanence only finds solutions in Christian theology. The question here is whether Panikkar's advaitic anthropology offers another answer.

PANIKKAR'S ADVAITIC ANTHROPOLOGY

Panikkar argues that the modern world is governed by autonomous structures of thought that emphasize the individuality and independence of every human being. Furthermore, Panikkar argues that this problem comes in both monistic and dualistic forms as two ends of the same spectrum, while arguing for an advaitic solution that escapes the problems of both. Panikkar's understanding

100   *Chapter 5*

of monism reveals the problem of difference if all of reality is one. Monism denies difference and collapses it into the same. From a dualistic standpoint there is no sense of unity and difference always divides and defers the unity of the self of its ability to engage with alterity as a never-ending differentiation. Here we see that Panikkar has similar concerns to Levinas and Bentley Hart in his critique of modernity.

Another problem Panikkar highlights alongside Levinas and Bentley Hart is the difference between transcendence and immanence. And yet Panikkar's emphasis lies with the problem of how to mediate a conception of transcendence that has been rejected by secular modernity. More significantly Panikkar's problem with modernity is that there is no place for the sacred because of the individualistic belief that we can identify ourselves as separate and independent from all other beings. This reductionistic mindset about what it means to be human assumes the individuation and differentiation of human beings in ways that affirms both the ideas that the individual is the center of reality and that they are differentiated from all other individuals. This atomistic and reductive view of humanity affirms both sameness and difference, and yet can both subsume difference into the same as well as oppose the difference of others in ways that does violence to their difference as a same that cannot be subsumed into our own individuality. Hence individuation and differentiation are both byproducts of the modern violence against the other in the affirmation of the individuated self.

This is because, if we assume the individuated self, when confronted with otherness that cannot be subsumed into that self, we oppose ourselves to everything that differentiates itself from us. In Levinas this is a central thesis that points us to the infinite: in our concern for the "Same" as the universal, we are too constrained to recognize what the Illeity of the "Other" offers to us. By seeing the "other" as a necessary alterity to my individuated identity, in a way the "Other" poses to me the question of my existence as distinctly individual and yet one as fundamentally ethical and relational.[40] This is where transcendence comes into play because when we realize that there is something other than us and that yet transcends us, beyond us yet confronting us, we encounter a wonder and horror when we realize that this transcendent other cannot be reduced to us. A major problem of a postmodern ontology is that we believe that the divine is a being transcendent to us and has no placement in an autonomous world where the individuated autonomous self is sovereign. What is more prevalent in the modern world is not the transcendence of God, but rather the lack of the immanence of God in the autonomy of the modern world where the human individual is the center of reality.

By contrast to modernity and its anthropological fragmentation, Jyri Komulainen states that Panikkar's theological anthropology "dispenses with Western individualism and represents an intrinsically extensive and relational

The Problems and Promises of a Postmodern Ontology 101

understanding of personhood."[41] Komulainen states that Panikkar's view of the human person is not an autonomous individual, but rather a person qua person through his/her participation and co-constitution in and through their surroundings. The human person not only participates in reality, but also is cosmotheandrically permeated by it.[42] Komulainen states that:

> Man's role is not restricted to that of passively reflecting reality, however, since Panikkar's emphasizes the significance of man in the fate of the whole universe. Man plays a part in the cosmic adventure not only as a "spectator" or an "actor," but even as a "co-author." He participates in cosmic rhythms, and correspondingly, these cosmic rhythms are transformed through his participation. The spiritual development of man goes hand in hand with the transformation of reality since . . . Panikkar understands that the person has an intrinsic ontological connection with reality.[43]

While Panikkar's cosmotheandric vision of reality presupposes and emphasizes the lack of an ontological distinction between God and creation, his advaitic insight into the harmony and co-constitution of a cosmotheandric reality offers particular solutions alongside Bentley Hart's understanding of the incarnation as a primordial foundation for an ontology of peace. Through the openness to differentiation in a postmodern ontology, a non-dual understanding of transcendence and immanence implies an intrinsic relation in which the sacred, the cosmic, and the human are co-constitutive via their ontonomic inter-in-dependency. This implies that transcendence and immanence are understood non-dualistically—in harmony, relationally, according to the dynamic rhythms of a cosmotheandric reality. In a religious conception of a cosmotheandric understanding of reality, the confrontation with the otherness of transcendence becomes a participatory co-constitutive experience of its imminence in an advaitic experience of reality. This means that an advaitic experience of reality is ontonomic rather than autonomous and that faith becomes the foundation in which the religious experience of divine immanence can be defined in terms of our ontonomic co-participation in it. It is to this question of faith that we now turn.

AN ONTOLOGICAL FAITH?

Participation in a cosmotheandric reality invokes the ontonomic constitution of everyday existence as necessarily including the idea of faith. Panikkar understands faith as the ground on which we believe and belief as the exposition of faith.[44] The priority of existential, expressed, and lived belief implies the ontological reality of an authentic faith. It is the ontological question that

102   *Chapter 5*

Panikkar argues is the source toward which we experience and know the meaning of our being. Within this context, Panikkar defines the ontological question not only relationally, but also as theologically constitutive through the lens of faith in God. At its heart, for Panikkar faith implies questioning into the unknown to discover the ground and *mythos* found in the questioning—the ontological condition about God and Man. And yet this question always falls short of what it seeks after because it is asking after the infinite.[45]

For Panikkar to question the meaning of being evokes an authentic questioning of human existence into relationship with God. That is, to question the meaning of being is not a mere questioning for an answer about self-knowledge or self-identity. Rather, it is a questioning into the meaning of human relationship with God. Ontological belief implies that through the questioning of the meaning of being, the very relationship we have with God is embedded within the very questioning of his existence. This means that an ontological relationship with God is constitutive of self-identity when we actually question who we are in relation to when we participate with and in the Being of God.

For Panikkar, the question of belief in God is the ontological question that truly reveals who we are and what it means to be truly human in relationship with God. Moreover, God remains ontically present to human existence. Ontic existence for Panikkar, as for the early Heidegger, is just the surface of the ontological questioning of the meaning of being. But for Panikkar our questioning into the meaning of being is a questioning into God's existence in a way that moves beyond the ontic and implicit relationship God has *to* us and becomes an ontological questioning of the existence of God *with* us. Questioning the meaning of being is a questioning into the *mythos* of faith that can only ultimately be fulfilled via the divine as the source of our identity, and as a source and orienting horizon of life. Panikkar argues that this relationship is defined by faith and that by faith we can ontologically understand who we are.[46] Panikkar states that the primary essence of faith is to move humans toward their fullness, a fullness open to fulfillment and perfection found in what we are not yet.[47] Thus, the *mythos* of faith is understood as a constant life of becoming, wherein our relationship with God is a constant unfolding of our perfection. This perfection of the meaning of being is embedded in the active life oriented toward relationship with God through the horizon of faith. Panikkar's notion of a religious *mythos* is ontologically constituted by faith, and that our faith is ontically lived in an ontologically meaningful way as we relate *with* God.

Moreover, the openness of faith is not only an opening or openness to transcendence. Rather it is also an openness to experience and embodies faith as constitutive to what it means to be human. Panikkar says that, "faith cannot be equated with belief, but faith always needs a belief to be faith. Belief is

The Problems and Promises of a Postmodern Ontology   103

not faith, but it must convey faith. A disembodied faith is not faith."[48] Faith must be expressed by the content of lived belief; faith is contextualized, lived, and practiced as the expression of belief. Panikkar states, "faith is not only necessary in order to understand, but also to reach full humanity, to be. In other words, faith is a constitutive human dimension. By faith Man is distinguished from other beings. But precisely because of this, faith is a human characteristic that unites mankind."[49] Panikkar goes on to state that what it means to be a creature is to be in relation to God, and what characterizes humanity as a creature is a faith that connects human be-ing to God through the relationship that ontologically constitutes what it means to be human.[50] It is the reality of faith that implies the truest sense of who we are because faith implies the embodiment of what matters most to us in our everyday lives. Faith is the fundamental openness to finding the meaning of being in, with, to, and through an ultimate other. Panikkar states that, "we could describe faith as existential openness toward transcendence or, if this seems too loaded, more simply as an existential openness. This openness implies a bottomless capacity to be filled without closing."[51] Panikkar's notion of faith is grounded most fundamentally in a position of openness to an other. He states that this openness is a capacious openness "to what one has not yet become . . . [an] openness to Being" where humans become receptive to the infinite in their finitude, and through this receptivity to the infinite, humans begin to become "*in*-finitude" what we are not yet, aiming at our completion in the telos of the transcendent.[52]

The crux of this argument is that faith represents an ontological grounding in the truth, meaning, and reality of God's in-finitude that reflects an ethos and praxis of living where the symbol of God is implied in the sense of its appearance: "as it expresses itself as it manifests itself."[53] Our self-identity in and with God must be understood as implying God as the symbol of our ontological reality. Our self-identity in God implies that our ontological existentiality is not limited by our subjective (self)-consciousness. A subjective interpretation of an ontological reality includes objectivity: it does not include only subjective experience, but also implies the objective reality of our existence in our experience of God through lived faith. Panikkar states that, "faith itself is looking for understanding both of its own nature and of what faith believes."[54] The questioning of the meaning of being indicates the openness to God in the relationship between who we are and God. This relationship connects and constitutes our self-identity to the symbol of our being—God.

If the divine is a constitutively relational good with which we can relate to, it implies the immanence of God-with-us in everyday experience. It is through faith that the relational participation of divine immanence in human embodied action and of human action with the reality of God that one could speak of a Panikkarean relational ontology. Panikkar states, "truth is self-identity . . . ontologically it is the manifestation of self-identity, and epistemologically, truth is the intellectual formulation of self-identity . . . truth is the being itself . . . truth can only be the bond of a thing with itself, its self-identity."[55] We must self-identify with our faith in the active living and praxis of faith for it to be presented as a truth to others, to be shared as an opening of faith that is ontologically constitutive of the meaning of being. Each person has faith in the opening to an other. Whether this is trust in the other as a reliable and faithful human being, or even of faith in God, the relational opening to an other implies some level of vulnerability and trust in what the other opens me to (whether this is myself, learning to know another person, or trust in God). The questioning of the meaning of being is essentially an ontological openness to trust and faith in an other who reveals to me who I am.

CONCLUSION

By examining the problems and promises of a postmodern ontology, this chapter demonstrated several critiques of modernity that offered answers to the problems of autonomy, individuality, and alterity. Furthermore, the answer offered was Panikkar's understanding of an ontology of faith that drew out the ontological and theological implications of the constitutive relationality of the ontological question. This chapter argued for a critique of modern anthropology and dialogues Panikkar with philosophers and theologians who have also offered answers to the problems of a postmodern ontology. Furthermore, it has argued that Panikkar's advaitic critique of modernity opens up a postmodern ontology to the cosmotheandric dimensions of a lived experience of an ontological faith as constitutively a theological question. If Panikkar's advaitic critique of modernity is to provide an answer to the problems of a postmodern ontology, then it must confront the ontological problems of a postmodern ontology with an ontological faith. In this ontological questioning into the immanent experience of God, there is an opening after closure to the possibility of faith. This is an opening that comes through the ontological questioning of who we are in relation not just to an other, but to the ultimate Other who is always already present to and with us. Divine immanence is found in the transformation of what it means to be human. Moreover, the divine is revealed as a co-constitutive dimension of reality through the questioning of the meaning of being. Faith is an ontological openness to an other that transforms what it means to be human insofar as it allows us to live with and participate in the reality of God in our cosmotheandric experience of reality.

The Problems and Promises of a Postmodern Ontology   105

While this chapter has addressed the problems and promises of a postmodern ontology through several critiques of modernity with an emphasis on the problems of a modern anthropology, the following chapter will continue the analysis of a postmodern ontology with a more explicit turn to the limits of a postmodern ontology and will offer a robust analysis of Panikkar in dialogue with Charles Taylor and the Radical Orthodoxy Movement to articulate how they may be read together in their critiques and solutions to modern anthropology. In particular the next chapter offers the most robust analysis of the notion of an advaitic modernity after examining a postmodern ontology at the limits of modernity.

NOTES

1. C.f. Stanley Grenz, *The Social God and the Relational Self: A Trinitarian Theology of the Imago Dei* (Louisville, KY: Westminster John Knox Press, 2001), 53–137; Anthony C. Thistleton, *Interpreting God and the Postmodern Self: On Meaning, Manipulation, and Promise* (Grand Rapids, MI: Eerdmans, 1995); Stanley Grenz, *A Primer of Postmodernism* (Grand Rapids, MI: Eerdmans, 1996); James K. A. Smith, *Who's Afraid of Postmodernism?: Taking Derrida, Lyotard, and Foucault to Church* (Grand Rapids, MI: Baker Academic, 2004).

2. Charles Taylor, *A Secular Age* (Cambridge, MA: The Belknap Press of Harvard University Press, 2007), 302–307; James K. A. Smith, *How (Not) to Be Secular: Reading Charles Taylor* (Grand Rapids, MI: William B. Eerdmans Publishing Co., 2014), 26, 54; Charles Taylor, *Dilemmas and Connections* (Cambridge, MA: Harvard University Press, 2011), 220.

3. C.f. Taylor, *A Secular Age*, 299–422; James K.A. Smith, *How (Not) to be Secular*, 60–78; Charles Taylor, *The Malaise of Modernity: The CBC Massey Lectures* (Toronto: House of Anansi Press, 1991); Charles Taylor, *Sources of the Self: The Making of the Modern Identity* (Cambridge, MA: the Belknap Press of Harvard University Press, 1989); Ruth Abbey, "A Secular Age: The Missing Question Mark," in *The Taylor Effect: Responding to a Secular Age*, ed. Ian Leask et al. (Newcastle Upon Tyne: Cambridge Scholars Publishing, 2010), 8–25, 11.

4. C.f. D. A. Carson, *Telling the Truth: Evangelizing Postmoderns* (Grand Rapids, MI: Zondervan, 2000); and John Piper and Justin Taylor, *The Supremacy of Christ in a Postmodern World* (Wheaton, IL: Crossway Books, 2007), 21–49.

5. Charles Taylor is correct when he argues that the Protestant Reformation's emphasis on the affirmation of ordinary life is a contributing factor to the process of immanentization and secularization. Where we are now, as the Radical Orthodoxy Movement affirms, is the culmination of modernity in a certain nihilistic outworking of the Middle Ages where the nominal turn to will in Ockham and the univocal turn in Scotus distanced God from creation while allowing it a sense of gifted autonomy apart from God, eventually collapsing into the ontic realm devoid of any depth or participation in Being itself. C.f. Conor Cunningham, *Genealogy of Nihilism* (New

106 *Chapter 5*

York and London: Routledge, 2002); John Milbank, Catherine Pickstock, and Graham Ward, eds., *Radical Orthodoxy: A New Theology* (New York and London: Routledge, 1999); Catherine Pickstock, "Duns Scotus: His Historical and Contemporary Significance," *Modern Theology* 21, no. 4 (2005): 543–74; Catherine Pickstock, "Postmodern Scholasticism: Critique of Postmodern Univocity," *Telos* 33, no. 4 (2003): 3–24; John Milbank, "Scholasticism, Modernism, and Modernity," *Modern Theology* 22, no. 4 (2006): 651–71; James K. A. Smith, *Introducing Radical Orthodoxy: Mapping a Post-Secular Theology* (Grand Rapids, MI: Baker Academic, 2004), 87–89; Charles Taylor, *A Secular Age*; Charles Taylor, *Sources of the Self*; Ruth Abbey, *Philosophy Now: Charles Taylor* (Princeton, NJ: Princeton University Press, 2000); Ruth Abbey, ed., *Charles Taylor* (Cambridge, UK: Cambridge University Press, 2004).

6. C.f. Søren Kierkegaard, *The Sickness Unto Death*, trans. Howard Hong and Edna Hong (Princeton, NJ: Princeton University Press, 1983), 11–28; Jean-Paul Sartre, *Being and Nothingness* (New York: Washington Square Press, 1993); Albert Camus, *The Stranger* (New York: Vintage Books, 1989); Charles Taylor, *A Secular Age,* 583.

7. Grenz, *The Social God and the Relational Self*, 120–37.

8. C.f Graham Ward, *Cities of God* (London and New York: Routledge, 2000), 60–62, 249–52; Jean Baudrillard, *Simulations*, trans. Paul Foss, Paul Patton, and Philip Beitchman (USA: Semiotext[e], 1983), 11–12; Steven Shakespeare, *Radical Orthodoxy: A Critical Introduction* (London: SPCK, 2007), 135–36; Jean Baudrillard, *Simulacra and Simulation*, trans. Sheila Faria Glaser, 14th Printing Edition (Ann Arbor, MI: University of Michigan Press, 1994).

9. For an insightful analysis of Heidegger, Levinas, and Derrida's account of Death, c.f. Catherine Pickstock, *After Writing: On the Liturgical Consummation of Philosophy* (Malden, MA: Blackwell Publishing, 1998), 101–18.

10. C.f. Martin Heidegger, *Being and Time*, trans. John MacQuarrie and Edward Robinson (New York: Harper Collins Publishers, 2008); Paul Tillich, *The Courage to Be*, Second Edition (New Haven, CT: Yale University Press, 1952).

11. Here I would extend the logic of Nihilism according to Conor Cunningham in *Genealogy of Nihilism* with a postmodern ontology: (1) Something is rendered nothing; (2) Nothing affirms itself as something; (3) Nothing is still nothing; (4) and therefore we embrace nothing. (5) But does it *have to be* nothing? (5a) If yes, we return to point 3; (5b) if no, we must affirm it not only as something, but as always having been something with ontological value and depth in being gifted existence in love by the creator. C.f. Cunningham, *Genealogy of Nihilism*.

12. Abbey, *Philosophy Now: Charles Taylor*, 79–93.

13. Thistleton, *Interpreting God and the Postmodern Self*.

14. Jean-Francois Lyotard, *The Postmodern Condition: A Report on Knowledge*, Theory and History of Literature 10 (Minneapolis: University of Minnesota Press, 1984).

15. Strange that Enlightenment and modern advocates for autonomy would result not in the integrity of the human person/self by advocating its inalienable rights but rather is its devaluation insofar as it negates a relational character of human nature oriented by love as an ontology of peace. C.f. John Milbank, *Theology and Social Theory*, Second Edition (Malden, MA: Blackwell Publishing, 2006); John Zizioulas,

The Problems and Promises of a Postmodern Ontology   107

"On Being Other," in *Communion and Otherness*, ed. Paul McPartlan (New York: T & T Clark, 2006), 13–98; John Zizioulas, "Human Capacity and Human Incapacity: A Theological Exploration of Personhood," in *Communion and Otherness*, ed. Paul McPartlan (New York: T & T Clark, 2006), 206–49.

16. C.f. Simon Oliver, "Introducing Radical Orthodoxy: From Participation to Late Modernity," in *The Radical Orthodoxy Reader*, eds., John Milbank and Simon Oliver (New York and London: Routledge, 2009), 3–27, 21–24; Charles Taylor, *A Secular Age*; Nicholas H. Smith, *Charles Taylor: Meaning, Morals, and Modernity* (Malden, MA: Polity Press, 2002), 227; John Montag, SJ, "Revelation: The False Legacy of Suárez," in *Radical Orthodoxy: A New Theology*, eds., John Milbank, Catherine Pickstock, and Graham Ward (New York: Routledge, 1999), 38–63.

17. Conor Cunningham, "Language: Wittgenstein after Theology," in *Radical Orthodoxy: A New Theology*, eds., John Milbank, Catherine Pickstock, and Graham Ward (New York and London: Routledge, 1999), 64–90, 82.

18. Taylor, *Dilemmas and Connections*, 217–30.

19. C.f. Charles Taylor, "Modes of Secularism," in *Secularism and Its Critics*, ed. Rajeev Bhargava (Delhi: Oxford University Press, 1998), 31–53; Charles Taylor, *Modern Social Imaginaries* (Durham, NC: Duke University Press, 2004), 49–162.

20. C.f. Bruce Ward, "Transcendence and Immanence in a Subtler Language: The Presence of Dostoevsky in Charles Taylor's Account of Secularity," in *Aspiring to Fullness in a Secular Age: Essays on Religion and Theology in the Work of Charles Taylor*, eds., Carlos Colorado and Justin Klassen (Notre-Dame, IN: University of Notre-Dame Press, 2014), 262–90, 166–67.

21. Understood as ectypically derivative from and dependent on the archetypical image of an infinitely personal and creating God in the person of Christ.

22. Taylor, *Sources of the Self*, 50–51.

23. Adrian Pabst probably offers the most concise and best organizational examination of the metaphysics of the ancient Greeks. C.f. Adrian Pabst, *Metaphysics: The Creation of Hierarchy* (Grand Rapids, MI: William B. Eerdmans, 2012), 5–18.

24. Hence the perennial question of "why is there something instead of nothing?" For a concise account of twenty-three philosophers who asked this question C.f. Leszek Kolakowski, *Why Is There Something Rather Than Nothing?*, trans. Agnieszka Kolakowska (New York: Basic Books, 2007).

25. C.f. Charles Taylor, *Sources of the Self*, 127–76. Taylor's account, though the standard norm, is contested by Michael Hanby who critiques Taylor's continuity between Augustine and Descartes by articulating the discontinuity between the two because of the Pelagian-Stoic resurgence during the intervening 1200 years. C.f. Michael Hanby, *Augustine and Descartes* (New York and London: Routledge, 2003).

26. C.f. John Milbank, *Beyond Secular Order* (Malden, MA: Blackwell Publishing, 2013), 29–31, 50–57; Charles Taylor, *Human Agency and Language*, Philosophical Papers 1 (Cambridge, UK: Cambridge University Press, 1985); Charles Taylor, *Philosophical Arguments* (Cambridge, MA: Harvard University Press, 1995).

27. This in fact is Heidegger's critique of modern representational metaphysics: We are always already existing *in* the world, not as neutral observers *disconnected from* the world. C.f. Heidegger, *Being and Time*; Martin Heidegger, *The Basic Problems of*

Phenomenology, trans. Albert Hofstadter, Revised Edition (Bloomington, IN: Indiana University Press, 1982).

28. Grenz, *A Primer on Postmodernism*, 7, 14. On narrative identity C.f. Charles Taylor, *The Language Animal* (Cambridge, MA: The Belknap Press of Harvard University Press, 2016), 291–319; Abbey, *Philosophy Now: Charles Taylor*, 37–40. This implies not only the postmodern recognition of the need for community, common narrative identities in which we participate (what Taylor calls itineraries), but most centrally to belonging.

29. Raimon Panikkar, "The Myth of Pluralism: The Tower of Babel-A Meditation on Nonviolence," in *Cultures and Religions in Dialogue: Pluralism and Interculturality*, ed. Milena Carrara Pavan, Vol. VI.1, XII vols., Opera Omnia (Maryknoll, NY: Orbis Books, 2018), 3–25, 18.

30. While Panikkar's use of the "other" as a "thou" and participatory consciousness is used primarily by him in interreligious dialogue I would argue that his intuitions into inter-religious dialogue are also represented in ontological dialogue. For Panikkar's participatory consciousness see Raimon Panikkar, *Mysticism and Spirituality: Mysticism, The Fullness of Life*, ed. Milena Carrara Pavan, Vol. I.1, XII vols., Opera Omnia (Maryknoll, NY: Orbis Books, 2014), 143–44. For Panikkar's understanding of the necessity of the other in inter-religious dialogue see also, Raimon Panikkar, *The Intra-Religious Dialogue* (New York and Ramsey, NJ: Paulist Press, 1999), 23–40.

31. David Bentley Hart, *The Beauty of the Infinite: The Aesthetics of Christian Truth* (Grand Rapids, MI: William B. Eerdmans, 2003), 1–2. Henceforth in text as *BI*.

32. Emmanuel Levinas, *Totality and Infinity: An Essay on Exteriority*, trans. Alphonso Lingis (Pittsburgh, PA: Duquesne University Press, 1969).

33. Alphonso Lingis, "Translator's Introduction," in *Otherwise than Being, or Beyond Essence* (Pittsburgh, PA: Duquesne University Press, 1998), xvii–xlv, xxii.

34. Lingis, "Translator's Introduction," xxiii.

35. Lingis, "Translator's Introduction," xxiii.

36. Lingis, "Translator's Introduction," xxv.

37. Lingis, "Translator's Introduction," xxxix.

38. Lingis, "Translator's Introduction," xxxix.

39. Emmanuel Levinas, *Otherwise than Being, or Beyond Essence*, trans. Alphonso Lingis (Pittsburgh, PA: Duquesne University Press, 1998), 17.

40. C.f. Emmanuel Levinas, *Basic Philosophical Writings*, ed. Adrian Peperzak, Simon Critchley, and Robert Bernasconi (Bloomington, IN: Indiana University Press, 1996).

41. Jyri Komulainen, *An Emerging Cosmotheandric Religion? Raimon Panikkar's Pluralistic Theology of Religions* (Leiden and Boston: Brill, 2005), 180.

42. Komulainen, *An Emerging Cosmotheandric Religion?*, 201.

43. Komulainen, *An Emerging Cosmotheandric Religion?*, 202.

44. Panikkar, *The Intra-Religious Dialogue*, 55.

45. Raimon Panikkar, *Myth, Faith, and Hermeneutics: Cross Cultural Studies* (New York: Paulist Press, 1979), 211.

46. Panikkar, *Myth, Faith, and Hermeneutics*, 190–91.

47. Panikkar, *Myth, Faith, and Hermeneutics*, 202.

48. Panikkar, *The Intra-Religious Dialogue*, 55.

49. Panikkar, *Myth, Faith, and Hermeneutics*, 190.

50. Panikkar, *Myth, Faith, and Hermeneutics*, 190.

51. Panikkar, *Myth, Faith, and Hermeneutics*, 207–8.

52. Panikkar, *Myth, Faith, and Hermeneutics*, 208.

53. Raimon Panikkar, *Worship and Secular Man* (Maryknoll, NY: Orbis Books, 1973), 20.

54. Raimon Panikkar, *The Rhythm of Being: The Unbroken Trinity* (Maryknoll, NY: Orbis Books, 2010), 131.

55. Raimon Panikkar, "A Self-Critical Dialogue," in *The Intercultural Challenge of Raimon Panikkar*, ed. Joseph Prabhu (Maryknoll, NY: Orbis Books, 1996), 227–91, 260.

Chapter 6

Postmodern Ontology at the Limits of Modernity

Three Genealogies of Modernity

At the limits of modernity, this chapter argues that a postmodern recovery of meaning is necessary for the theological, religious, and moral renewal of modernity. This postmodern ontology is developed through a threefold genealogical and kairological reading of history and a Romantic-Heideggerian resourcement that opens the space for the renewal of meaning at the limits of modernity. This Romantic-Heideggerian resourcement does so by recovering the linguistic, expressivist, and constitutive nature of meaning. In turn, this retrieval of meaning constitutes the turn to a postmodern ontology that includes John Milbank and the Radical Orthodoxy Movement's participatory ontology, Charles Taylor's moral ontology, and Raimon Panikkar's relational ontology. Throughout the analysis below, what we find are three correlative genealogies of modernity that critique, resource, and offer elements of a postmodern ontology that answers problems at the limits of modernity. While it is clear that Milbank and Taylor have much in common, what is key to the analysis below is how Panikkar's critique of modernity may correlate and overlay Milbank and Taylor's genealogies in ways that opens us to an advaitic critique of modernity. This chapter posits the possibility of an advaitic modernity, or rather, how to make sense of divine immanence at the limits of modernity's ability to make sense of what it means to be human.

THREE CRITIQUES OF MODERNITY

Raimon Panikkar offers ideas that are in a complex relationship with the promises and failures of modernity. He recognized the promise and threat of science and technology and warned against scientism and the worship of

112   *Chapter 6*

what science and technology provide for humanity.[1] And he also recognized modernity's failure because it neglects the immanence of the sacred. He argued that modernity overemphasized divine transcendence at the expense of divine immanence. While Panikkar approaches the limits of modernity from an advaitic, pluralistic, and inter-religious perspective (as well as theological, philosophical, and scientific!), we also see similar critiques of the limits of modernity within the thought of Charles Taylor and John Milbank and the Radical Orthodoxy Movement. This chapter demonstrates a correlation between these three figures and movements in their genealogies of modernity. It does so by developing: (a) a kairological critique of modernity and its limits; (b) a late modern Romantic-Heideggerian resourcement of meaning; and (c) an advaitic, postmodern ontology that integrates participatory, moral, and relational ontologies.

Underlying a postmodern ontology is an integral concern for what it means to be human in terms of openness to God. That is, a postmodern ontology is fundamentally theological, moral, and religious precisely when it is open to and dis-encloses transcendental truth, the good, and experience. For Milbank, the notion of *mathexis* (participation) constitutes a theological openness to truth counterpoised to secular conceptions and disavowals of theological truth. For Taylor, the good is constituted linguistically by the evaluation of moral concerns. And Panikkar seeks to articulate a recovery of a cosmotheandric religious metaphysics of divine immanence that constitutes the religious experience of transcendence. This chapter paints Panikkar as an Indian postmodern theologian and philosopher at the intersection of John Milbank and the Radical Orthodoxy Movement's postmodern theology and Charles Taylor's late modern Catholic philosophy. While Milbank certainly stands within the Christian tradition, and Taylor positions himself philosophically as sympathetic to the Christian tradition, Panikkar offers an advaitic genealogy of modernity that emphasizes the immanence of God as an important retrieval necessary for the future of modernity.

A KAIROLOGICAL GENEALOGY OF MODERNITY

This section develops a critique of modernity through three turns in a kairological genealogy of modernity. These three turns are the univocal, the representational, and the anthropocentric turns of modernity. If Milbank and the Radical Orthodoxy Movement offer a theological critique of modernity as heresy, they argue that it is intimated within the univocal turn often associated with John Duns Scotus.[2] Moreover, developed alongside Taylor, representational epistemology and instrumental reasoning are charged as the second kairological turn in modernity. Finally, Panikkar offers a third kairological turn with modernity as a move to anthropocentrism that alienates us from meaning via modern autonomy and its separation and fragmentation of reality. This section unpacks each of these kairological moments as a genealogical reading of modernity to argue how the limits of modernity lies in its inability to articulate meaning.

The Univocal Turn

The univocal turn of Duns Scotus according to the Radical Orthodoxy Movement is one of the most contested claims in its postmodern theology. While it is beyond the purposes of this chapter to examine substantially those critiques, it is pertinent to articulate its genealogical explanation and implications. Duns Scotus is claimed by the Radical Orthodoxy Movement as a central figure in what went wrong in the shifts toward modernity and the secularization of Christianity.[3] The process of the secularization of Christianity is marked by the collapse or "flattening" of a hierarchical universe over a span of centuries. It is marked by the unhooking of sciences, society, economics, and politics from theology and their theological orientation and participation in God.[4] Simon Oliver claims that Milbank's point "is that the secular is not simply the rolling back of a theological consensus to reveal a neutral territory where we all become equal players, but the replacement of a certain view of God and creation with a different view which still makes theological claims, that is, claims about origins, purpose and transcendence . . . Secularism is . . . an ideological distortion of theology."[5]

The secular is deemed a heresy by John Milbank precisely because it claims an assessment of knowledge and being as autonomously unhooked from their participation in God.[6] The secular is a heresy because it entails a sphere of knowing and being that is not dependent upon God. Milbank argues that "the secular as a domain had to be instituted or imagined, both in theory and in practice" through the secularization of Christianity.[7] The secular for Milbank is imagined from its inception as removing the "sacral allure from the cosmos and men, [and] inevitably, from the political, [the] social, the economic, the artistic—the human itself."[8]

The Radical Orthodoxy Movement claims that the univocal turn in Duns Scotus's thought produced the stage by which God could be infinitized and protected from the fallenness of creation, protecting His sacrality and holiness, thus resulting in a split between a graced nature and an autonomous nature separated from divine grace.[9] This split allowed, according to the Radical Orthodoxy Movement, creation its own autonomy to produce out of itself its own being unhooked from God.[10] Simon Oliver states that

114   *Chapter 6*

> Scotus conceives God and creatures as falling under a common concept of "being." This "being" applies to finite and infinite in the same way. Hence Scotus calls this concept univocal between God and creatures. . . . [In contrast to Aquinas's understanding of the ontological difference between creator and creatures] for Scotus . . . this "difference" between finite and infinite is rethought. God now has a more intense and infinite being which is possessed to a lesser extent, but in essentially the same way, by creatures.[11]

But the claim that Duns Scotus's univocity produced a staggering shift or turn in ontology has been critiqued extensively. Daniel Horan argues that the Radical Orthodoxy Movement mis-construes and misinterprets the Duns Scotus story. Through analyses and surveys of the Duns Scotus story within principal thinkers, Horan examines the critiques by scholars of Duns Scotus and builds on them, communicating the central ideas and theological, logical, and metaphysical implications of Duns Scotus's univocal *language* of being. Horan's analysis of Duns Scotus's concept of univocity surveys what he means by "univocity" to articulate how it posits a univocal *concept* of being that analogously communicates a univocal *logic*—not metaphysics—of how God can be insufficiently spoken of. This position advocates not just for apophatic language but importantly of kataphatic language—and analogously by the quidditative, formal distinction between the perfect, simple, univocal concept of God's Being.[12]

By using the concept of univocity, we are able to make a formal distinction between the Being of God and the being of creatures analogously because in their quidditative *haecceities* (this-ness) there is the uniqueness of created being and the simplicity and perfection of God. Horan debunks the Duns Scouts story that posits how he metaphysically infinitizes God and gives autonomy to creation—the postmodern narrative that blames Duns Scotus for inaugurating the heresy of secularism. Horan does this by articulating how Duns Scotus is dealing with conceptual epistemology and logic (how we speak of God and how he relates to us), not metaphysics and ontology, as against an interpretation of Scotus which separates God and creation—one influenced by a Deleuzean metaphysical reading of Duns Scotus.[13]

Despite this, arguably the univocal logic still implies *essentially* the same thing—a *quantified* difference between God and creatures. The problem lies not necessarily in univocity per se, but rather univocal logic that posits a *quantified haecceities* that does not *qualitatively* differentiate between God and creatures. Conor Cunningham argues that the quantitative difference does not allow any real ontological difference between God and creatures.[14] The quantitative problem of the ontological distinction remains, and implies that univocal logic fails to qualitatively differentiate creatures from creator. The qualitative distinction is the key to Milbank's and the Radical Orthodoxy Movement's critique of their critics.

Indeed, Catherine Pickstock draws this out insofar as she not only highlights how Scotus's univocity set the stage for representational epistemology, but also the semantic problem of difference in theology. Pickstock links the onto-theological shift in Duns Scotus on finitude and its qualitative intensity into infinity as advocating a shift from participation of finitude in infinitude to a univocal commensurability between ontological finitude and theological infinitude. Pickstock questions the theological implications of univocity, arguing that it neglects the embodied mediation and mystical participation between finitude and infinitude, God and creature through Christ and the sacraments of the church, while she advocates for, but recognizes the limitations of, analogy.[15]

The Representational Turn

If the Radical Orthodoxy thinkers articulate a retrieval of analogy and a critique of univocity, they also demonstrate their alliance with Charles Taylor's critique of representational epistemology. Most notably, Pickstock locates the middle of modernity with Descartes as a primary initiator of representational epistemology and its orientation toward *mathesis* and disembodiment.[16] The spatialization of modernity, according to Pickstock, is characterized by its separation not just between mind and body in Descartes, but also by the theological separation between the spheres of knowing and embodiment, as in writing and orality.[17] Pickstock argues for a theological retrieval of participation and embodiment in ways that correct the spatialized separation between being and knowledge.

It is in the representational turn to disembodied epistemology unhooked from a participatory ontology that we find the second kairological turn away from theology. The representational turn is marked by the rationalistic explanation, grasp, and creation of an abstract, objective reality. Charles Taylor states that the Greek understanding of theoretical contemplation "consists in the fact that a theoretical understanding aims at a disengaged perspective. We are not trying to understand things merely as they impinge upon us, or are relevant to the purposes we are pursuing, but rather grasp them as they are, outside the immediate perspective of our goals and desires and activities."[18] The representational turn claims a metaphysical explanation in terms of human reasoning and rationality in ways produced by its disengagement because it posits things in themselves as having their own integrity. Indeed, Taylor argues that rationality is the telos of humanity: "To say that man is a rational animal is to say that this is his telos, the goal he implicitly is directed towards by nature."[19]

116 *Chapter 6*

Furthermore, if rationality is a dynamic central to representational epistemology, it is also marked by the subject-object dichotomy in which human personhood is not defined in practical-moral terms, but more so in scientific explanations of human behavior. The Enlightenment notion of the subject is marked by an individual consciousness who has "a power to frame representations of things."[20] This power to frame the representation of things points beyond themselves and signifies the frameworks by which we construct the world. Part of Taylor's critique of modernity's representationalist turn is a critique of naturalism which is itself, he argues, influenced by a spiritual stance that strips nature of its sacrality and meaning through its advocacy for instrumental reasoning.[21]

Taylor defines a representation as referring to an independent reality that we try to make sense of in a basic sense—an objective reality on which we *impose* meaning, relevance, and importance.[22] Moreover, he links representational epistemology and naturalistic insights to a designative theory of truth as something that depicts independent realities, coded by information that makes them understandable and knowable. The representationalist epistemology and designative theory of truth brings things about, ordering them, and creating meaning in them.[23]

Moreover, Taylor argues that the representational epistemology implies three connected notions: the subject is rationally disengaged and free to distinguish itself from others; it treats others and the world instrumentally for the betterment of self and other; and it implies a social atomism of individualism where the individual, not the community, determines purpose and the purposes of one's life.[24] Taylor argues that this social atomism inherited a vision of society from social contract theory of the Enlightenment, where the fulfillment of ends is constituted primarily by the individual.[25] This orientation to individuation marks the representational turn as ordered by an autonomous ontology of what it means to be human.

The representational turn away from ontology toward epistemology is one marked by a new ontology—one governed and determined by autonomy. If the univocal turn potentially initiated a theological shift in the relation between God and creatures—whether their quantitative sameness and/or qualitative difference—the representational turn opens the way to understanding nature as something designated and determined and controlled by human rationality—and this results in the human alienation from themselves, God, and nature: precisely the point of Panikkar's anthropocentric critique of modernity.

The Anthropocentric Turn

But Taylor argues that there is a strength and appeal in the modern worldview. He argues it lies in the underlying image of the human, and that this idea of the human advocates for the ideal of disengagement and the images of freedom, dignity, and power which we attach to it. He argues that "the more we are led to interpret ourselves in light of the disengaged picture, to define our identity by this, the more the connected epistemology of naturalism will seem right and proper to us."[26] Taylor articulates that "it is the hold of a particular set of background distinctions of worth, those of the disengaged identity, which leads people to espouse what are ultimately rather implausible epistemological doctrines."[27]

Panikkar's critique of modernity parallels Taylor's critique. Panikkar argues that modernity is marked by fragmentation, alienation, and isolation between a cosmotheandric reality. Panikkar not only argues that modernity fragments reality, but also that modernity reduces reality to mere materiality and consciousness. Furthermore, modernity for Panikkar is marked by the univocal turn which opposes difference and sameness in a dialectical interplay against one another. Modernity's adoption of universal reason and absolute truth is grounded in the human attempt to control and conform reality into its image to the exclusion of the other—whether that is a human other, the natural world, or God. Modernity is marked by the representational turn toward instrumental reasoning and social atomism and its orientation toward the separation, isolation, and fragmentation of reality.

Panikkar's critique of modernity works alongside Milbank and Taylor insofar as he critiques the ontological implications of representational epistemology as producing conceptions of truth through human reason. Panikkar states that, "truth then is not only what we can see with clarity and distinction, but, above all, that about which we can be certain because we monitor the proper functioning of the mind, without unduly transgressing its rules or the fundamental exigencies of empirical data."[28] What results is humanity's estrangement not only from nature through humanity's use of reason, but also from their feelings and history in their turn to idealism. The historical nature of humanity finds itself at the end of modernity in a crisis that cannot be answered by modernity. Modernity has reached its limits. Gerard Hall states that Panikkar's notion of the "end of history" is marked by a "postmodern 'crisis of otherness'" where Western modernity's emphasis on the "infinite power of human reason" is confronted with the cosmological, spatial, and temporal limits of the "one-dimensional" nature of humanity that exploits the earth and pays no attention to the divine.[29] Panikkar articulates that the limits of modernity lie within the end of history: the limitations of humanity as

118   *Chapter 6*

historical beings lie within modernity's inability to offer answers to the most pressing questions of what it means to be human. Panikkar states:

> Once upon a time there "was" a Man. This Man had lived consciously for millennia. He had outlived his history, and had all the data and riches of the world at his disposal, but he seemed to have no hope. . . . Though he was educated and well-fed, millions were starving, victims of injustice. The Man felt troubled, uncertain—a future for him seemed unlikely to be bearable, his present he found quite uninhabitable, and his past he knew to be lost to him irretrievably. . . . He had constructed an entire worldview, which some call ideology. He had thought about everything: he thought all unthinkable things and found the impotence of reason along with his need for it. He could demonstrate the existence of God and could equally invalidate every proof; he could think of life as meaningful, but he could equally find arguments in favor of its meaninglessness. He could imagine technology solving all his problems, and he could by the same token show technology to be the greatest blight ever to affect human existence. He began to surmise that what are called freedom and democracy are nothing but the expressions of the human despair of truth. His head grew tired and his thinking aimless. He began to fear that one thing might do as well as another, provided he never examined the extreme consequences of anything. Then, exhausted, he began to look for an icon, to sing, to dance, to gesticulate, and even something like an inarticulate prayer went up from his body. Soon enough he went to sleep, or died, or was annihilated by forces beyond his control. Nobody remarked his passing. And yet something had happened.[30]

The limits of modernity, of the end of history, of historical humanity, lies within the question of meaning. Hall argues how modernity is marked by an anthropological disunity. This anthropological disunity is marked by three losses: of God, self, and cosmic rhythm.[31] Hall argues that Panikkar's critique of modernity is marked by a conscious and unconscious "dislocation" and absence of harmony that produces an experience of anxiety and dis-ease. Moreover, Hall indicates that technology and modern science have fragmented reality and caused disharmony with cosmic rhythm. Panikkar realizes that classical Christianity and modern humanism both fail to address the problems of modernity.[32] What has been eclipsed in the turn to the secularization of Christianity into instrumental reasoning is the meaning of humanity: what it means to be human, what it means to have purpose and to make sense of reality, meaning, self, nature, and God. The limits of modernity show that the quest for meaning is central to what it means to be human. And a late modern critique of modernity finds resources in the Romantics and Martin Heidegger to address this problem at the limits of modernity.

LATE MODERN ROMANTIC-
HEIDEGGERIAN RESOURCEMENT

If Milbank, Taylor, and Panikkar all offer critiques of modernity, what we also find in each is a late modern Romantic resourcement instigated by Martin Heidegger's ontological questioning of the meaning of Being. This section articulates how Milbank, Taylor, and Panikkar offer a Romantic-Heideggerian resourcement for the retrieval of meaning in postmodern ontology. The quest for meaning initiates a religious or theological turn back to God in understanding what it means to be human. This section orients the retrieval of ontology developed below as geared toward making sense of what it means to be human.

Heidegger's ontological question is inescapable when it comes to trying to understand meaning. And yet it also initiates an opening to a religious or theological critique of modernity. Taylor argues that the questioning of the meaning of being is something that marks the individual person with an engaged and embodied agency.[33] Taylor argues that Heidegger revolutionizes and critiques modern philosophy with his critique of disengaged agency in favor of an engaged agency. Engaged agency entails that the content-context of embodied experience confers intelligibility of our world within and through the conditions and possibilities of our engagement with and in it. Taylor argues that engaged agency helps us situate ourselves and our actions within the world and makes sense of our world through the know-how of existence in the world. To have engaged agency means to know not what it means to be human, but how to be human through the situated experience of being-in-the-world.

John Milbank is also indebted to the onto-theological tradition initiated by Heidegger. Milbank's critique of phenomenology is marked by a theological resourcement that goes back beyond Duns Scotus and Henry of Ghent to the Neo-Platonism of Augustine.[34] Building on Milbank's thesis, Conor Cunningham takes issue with the phenomenological reduction of being to "meontotheology"—the nothingness of Being or the Being of Non-Being.[35] The onto-theological tradition—stemming from Husserl to Heidegger, Levinas, and Marion—is marked according to Milbank by the givenness of being's Being in its phenomenal disclosure. And yet the givenness of being's Being discloses the otherness of God in ways that points to the presence of its absence. It is in the presence of God's absence that onto-theology posits the givenness of being. This space opens us to God in ways that points us beyond ourselves to the gift of Being.[36] Rather Milbank argues that only a theology of the gift can overcome phenomenology and the problem of onto-theology, because a theology of the gift is the giving, not givenness, and receiving of love from Being to beings.[37]

If Milbank and Taylor find resourcement in Heidegger, so also does Panikkar. Panikkar's theological spin on Heidegger's fundamental ontology leads to a theological immanence that is marked by a fundamental openness to God through awareness of our presuppositions to believing. Just as Milbank argues that theology overcomes metaphysics through the giving and receiving of divine love, Panikkar argues that fundamental theology is marked by the awareness of our presuppositions that inform and justify our faith. Panikkar argues that "fundamental theology is the effort to understand the actual theological situation in any given context," and is marked not by the content of faith but rather its intelligibility.[38] The intelligibility of believing is marked by the opening to, and openness of, faith to make sense of life in light of who God is. Panikkar is clear that a fundamental theology is not marked by the dualism of divine transcendence and divine immanence, nor of creator and created, Being and beings. Rather it is marked by a dis-enclosure to lived, embodied faith where God becomes intelligible through the excesses of a lived faith.

It is in this dis-enclosure, or opening to and of faith, that points us beyond Heidegger's fundamental ontology—which questions the meaning of being as we exist in-the-world—to a metatheology which questions the conditions and presuppositions of believing within the situated contexts of a life marked by pluralism and cross-cultural mediations of belief. Panikkar's metatheology is oriented not *a priori*, but rather *a posteriori* in the experience of the other and it is in this experience that faith finds its life and intelligibility. Panikkar's cross-cultural hermeneutics opens fundamental theology to the metatheological experience of the religious other in ways that authentically allows one to love and experience the other as other.

In connection to late modern Heideggerian resourcement, the question of meaning is something Taylor develops, most notably in his advocacy of the Romantic emphasis on expressivism. Romantic expressivism entails the linguistic constitution of self and reality. It is where the individual self is expressed through its linguistic and symbolic communication. What it means to be an individual is not only self and relationally constituted, but it expresses its identity through the means of its communication. According to Taylor, Romantic-expressivism marks our own search for meaning in ways that open us authentically to others and ourselves precisely because we come to know ourselves in the context of how we express ourselves in the situated conditions of life as embodied and engaged agents. Taylor argues that expressivism entails the expression of making something manifest through its embodied presence.[39]

Contrasting expressivism with Enlightenment designative theories of self, Taylor argues that even the designative dimension is an expression manifesting meaning. That is, Taylor's Romantic resourcement of meaning points out that even designative theories of meaning are expressions of who we are as human persons. Even the expressivist turn to language implies that there is a medium for and of expression that is manifest in the very contours of language. Following Hamann and Herder, Taylor states "that language is not just a set of words which designate things; it is the vehicle of this kind of reflective awareness. This reflection is a capacity we only realize in speech. Speaking is not only the expression of this capacity, but also its realization."[40] The manifestation of meaning expresses itself through language: who we are is expressed through the mediums and significations that mediate meaning.[41] The fundamentality of expressive notions of self implies the linguistic constitution of who we are.

Taylor argues that human persons are constitutive and constituting agents of meaning. We are constituted by others just as much as we constitute the beings of others through our relationships and situated experiences. Taylor argues that meaning-making is constituted by our experience. Or rather, experience produces meaning and importance in the context of the situatedness of our experiences as embodied agents in the world. Building on the Romantics, Taylor opens us to the reality that emotion "involves making explicit the import-ascription, a judgement which is not thereby affirmed, it is true, but experienced as holding the sense of the situation which it incorporates."[42] Moreover, a person finds their self-dignity, worth, and identity through their self-referencing in the contexts of their relationships and the constitutive meaning-making processes of evaluating what we deem good. For Taylor, meaning is marked by the significance of goals and the aspirations and purposes of being virtuous.[43]

Like Taylor, Hall argues that the Romantic expressive notion of sentiment found in Jacobi influenced Panikkar's anthropology insofar as it did not reduce meaning-making to the ability to will or reason, but rather advocated the centering of human meaning-making in our sentiments as a synthesizing faculty of knowledge. Sentiments, according to Hall for Panikkar, "are the transcendental link between earth and heaven. Embedded in the soul, sentiments orient humans to supernatural faith and divine life."[44] The Romantic conception of reality, according to Taylor, is one in which "God embodies his ideas and makes them manifest. But unlike God, man needs his expression in order to make his ideas manifest to himself."[45] Tying into this, Milbank argues that for Hamann and Jacobi, "we can never have an abstract faith in God as author of nature, sustaining the reality of things, without *reading* these things in their specific, revealed and always *historical* contingency as the primary divine language."[46]

Milbank argues that according to Hamann, it is in the depths of historical contingency that we see the creative power of God. Milbank argues that Herder reworked Christian allegorical interpretations of history to prophecy how our past situates our existence into the "typological projection of the future."[47] The religious disclosure of God as the real is found, according to Milbank's reading of Hamann, in the natural unseen depth of things.[48] It is in the contingency of history that God reveals himself through Christ and in his absence that we wait for his presence to disclose in faith the restoration of all things through Christ. Milbank argues that for the Romantics such as Jacobi and Hamann, "the idea that the natural human response to the world in faith is a reading of the world as a language emanating from a mysterious source directs faith . . . already in a somewhat contingent, historical direction, especially when the necessary mediation by culturally specific human language is allowed for."[49] Hamann and Herder assert that metaphorical language expresses the depths of human, natural, and cultural difference.[50] Milbank argues that Hamann's critique of modern philosophy is one oriented toward trusting in the hidden depth of things and points one in faith to trust in the depth of God present in the historical contingency of creation as speaking beyond itself to the truth of God and hope for restoration through Christ.[51]

The Romantic-Heideggerian resourcement of Panikkar, Taylor, and Milbank is characterized by the linguistic resourcement of meaning because language expresses the constitutive identity of humanity in ways that concretizes the situated contexts of their engaged human agency and embodiment in the world. Taylor argues that language is "a pattern of activity by which we express/realize a certain way of being in the world, that which defines the linguistic dimension; but the pattern can be deployed only against a background we can never fully dominate."[52] We can reshape according to our language and it is by language that we are both makers and made.[53] Language according to Taylor opens us to a new awareness, which Panikkar points out through the synthesis of sentiment and the affections, of something more. The linguistic resourcement of meaning implies a sense of self-awareness in the light of God or an Other in ways that opens us through our experience of God or the Other to the dis-enclosure of faith. That is, the linguistic resourcement of meaning opens us not only to theological reflection on God, but to the linguistic constitution of meaning in the contexts of our experience as living by faith, open to giving and receiving love to and from God and others.

CONSTRUCTING A POSTMODERN ONTOLOGY

At the limits of modernity lies its inability to meaningfully articulate what it means to be human. This chapter has shown how Milbank et al., Taylor, and

Panikkar saw problems with the univocal, representational, and anthropocentric turns of modernity. All of these turns are a turn away from theology and towards human autonomy. And yet, this chapter argued that at the limits of modernity, human autonomy is marked by the problem of meaning. In a turn toward a late modern Romantic-Heideggerian resourcement of meaning, this chapter showed how a linguistic model for meaning, heavily indebted to Taylor and supported by Milbank and Panikkar, posits initial answers to modernity. But a mere linguistic resourcement of meaning is not enough. This section develops a postmodern ontology that seeks to retrieve theologically, morally, and relationally from Milbank et al.'s, Taylor's, and Panikkar's ontological visions a corrective to the modern collapse of meaning. Furthermore, by describing Milbank's participatory ontology, Taylor's moral ontology, and Panikkar's relational ontology, this chapter argues that not only may modernity be renewed ontologically, but that it may be done through its orientation to transcendental Good, Truth, and Experience.

Radical Orthodoxy's Participatory Ontology

Milbank and the Radical Orthodoxy Movement offer a postmodern theology that critiques modernity by resourcing pre-modern theology. They argue for a postmodern recovery of a Neo-Platonic participation of creation and human ways of being as dependent upon the Being of God. And this Neo-Platonic participation is grounded in a trinitarian panentheism that advocates for an asymmetry between God, world, and humanity, wherein humanity and the cosmos are dependent upon God for their being—suspended from and dependent upon God—while God remains not dependent upon creation but rather is its source from which their being is derived.[54] The Neo-Platonic spin on postmodernity entails that creation and humanity are not autonomous or unhooked from God. This implies that the being of creation is derived from the Being of God as a gift of His gratuity.[55] Milbank's pneumatological account of the second difference within the Trinity opens creation to the analogical gift of difference precisely because the Trinity is not only the model for unity-in-difference, but allows the gift of difference-as-participation-in-unity through the church's participation in the Spirit's atoning work through Christ, its historical fulfillment of salvation history through the economic Trinity, and its interplay and perichoretic dance with the *Logos*.[56]

Christian theology in Aquinas and Augustine according to Milbank et al. sparks a reimagining of what it means to be human and created in light of their dependence upon and suspension from the Being of God. Simon Oliver states "that creation has no self-subsisting autonomy but only exists by God's gift of participation in his own substantiality."[57] The onto-theological critique according to Milbank does not stand in this participatory worldview because

124   *Chapter 6*

it denies the participatory theological vision. A participatory ontology holds together the essence of God as Being itself as suspending all beings from it. In their suspension from God as Being itself, beings participate within a graced nature that is not separated from God.[58] Heidegger's onto-theology neglects the participatory ontology of Milbank's Aquinas, and thereby separates God from Being, and thus beings from their gratuity of being from God.

Furthermore, Milbank's pre-modern resourcement not only genealogically critiques the sources and implications of modernity, but it also offers a theological spin on postmodern thought. If Milbank and the Radical Orthodoxy Movement argue for a pre-and-post-modern critique of modernity, they do so genealogically through a theological resourcement that seeks to out-narrate modern secularism.[59] Milbank's notion of out-narration not only intimates that Christian theological tradition—particularly Augustinian Neoplatonism and Thomistic Aristotelianism—offers better answers than modernity. It also intimates a genealogical reading of history. If Augustine's *The City of God* is reversed by Nietzsche's *Genealogy of Morals*, then Milbank's *Theology and Social Theory* does half of a reversal back to Augustine's position after Nietzsche's critique. Augustine traces a theology of history that runs from paganism to Christianity. Nietzsche reverses this with a genealogical history from Christianity to Paganism. In turn Milbank brings us back to the cusp of Christianity from secularism.

This partial return to Christianity from secularism is marked by a theological vision that encompasses every discipline because without it, it would be grounded in nothing.[60] The Radical Orthodoxy Movement's vision of the theological encompassment of human discourses is not so much about reforming secular discourses with theological content. Rather, more fundamentally, "theology could be about anything, because everything is fundamentally related to God" because it is created and participates in his Being. Just as all things are created and participate in the Being of God, theology in turn includes all non-theological discourse because they "point beyond themselves to the transcendent."[61] Oliver makes a qualified attempt to address the magnanimity of this statement: "In so far as the subject matters of non-theological discourses are fundamentally related to God the creator, so those non-theological subject matters will be related to theology itself. The nature of that relation would require very careful and sophisticated articulation, but the central point for Radical Orthodoxy is that no discourse which seeks truth can count itself as wholly autonomous from issues of transcendent origin and purpose."[62]

The Radical Orthodoxy Movement denies autonomy to secular, non-theological discourse precisely because, "just as the metaphysics of participation points to the proper existence of creation which yet owes its created being at every moment to that which is Being itself (God), so too the peculiar character of non-theological discourses must be maintained while denying that those discourses are self-standing and autonomous from, or indifferent to, theological considerations."[63] Milbank and the Radical Orthodoxy Movement make an attempt to point us not to theological isolation, but to its integration and engagement with non-theological discourses and their reformation, resourcement, and orientations toward transcendental truth. The Radical Orthodoxy Movement's theology is not an ivory tower theology. Rather it is one that points the non-theological back to the theological resources of the Christian tradition to make theological sense of life and reality in secular modernity.

Milbank and the Radical Orthodoxy Movement's attempt to out-narrate modernity and resource its problems with a pre- and otherwise-than-modern theological vision are primarily done through their articulation of a participatory ontology.[64] Participation (*mathexis*) is key to the Radical Orthodoxy Movement's Christian resourcement of modernity. *Mathexis* indicates an integrated worldview. It integrates the social, cultural, political, and economic world into a theological vision of reality embodied ideally by the church and their interactions with and in the world. Josef Bengtson articulates Milbank's vision with apt awareness that his theological metaphysics entails the ecclesial transformation of the world and dynamics of human life and discourse through its incorporation into and transformation as the church.[65] But this also hearkens us to the reality that for Milbank, a participatory ontology implies a return to Christendom reimagined after modernity. Milbank's theological vision of the church entails the transformation of the world and its re-orientation to God through the church. In Milbank's vision the medieval saeculum is no longer separated as in modernity. Rather modern discourses are mediated back to God through the church in ways that are ideally redemptive and restorative.

The Protestant notion of being in the world but not of it subtly integrates the dynamics, interactions, and influences of human life into its vision of a redeemed and redeeming Church. James K. A. Smith's third volume of his cultural liturgies series points to the political reformation of how Americans should reform their politics in light of awaiting the King as agents of restoration and reform rather than that of withdrawal or imposition.[66] Smith's vision of discipleship and worship demonstrate a keen awareness that seems missing in Milbank: the brokenness and negative habitus of the world and its residual effects upon the church. Smith advocates for an awareness of the implicit things of the world in the church and calls for the reformation of our affections and habits.[67]

Smith argues via Taylor and Bourdieu that our background frameworks implicitly shape our beliefs insofar that our beliefs are embodied in cultural habitus' and social imaginaries that are practiced throughout everyday life.

This implies an implicit understanding of what matters most to us—what we deem our ultimate concerns. Smith argues that our social imaginaries and cultural habitus embody through everyday rituals—both secular and religious—the formative practices of belief of what matters most to us. He argues that these embodied beliefs are habitually practiced and articulate who we are (identity) and what we believe (belief).[68]

Practices are formative and constitutive of identity and belief, just as they form us to believe based on embodied experiences of what matters most to us in our everyday lifeworld. Our beliefs are constituted by practices which in turn are informed by beliefs and ultimate concerns. Smith advocates for an "affective, embodied anthropology, which recognizes the central role of the pre-cognitive and its embodied formation through ritual. Once we make that move, then even much that claims to be 'secular' will be seen as religious—not in the sense that it is covertly concerned with transcendence or the gods or the afterlife, but insofar as we can discern secular rituals and practices, which have an affective, formative power, that shape how practitioners construe 'what ultimately matters.'"[69] Smith calls these "secular liturgies" formative practices of what we believe and how we conceive of ourselves and our world.

For Smith, the shape of the world permeates our understanding of worship, discipleship, and politics in ways that must be reformed because of the counter-formative practices and habitus of secular liturgies.[70] And Smith argues this through his Augustinian understanding of human beings as desiring creatures: our desires implicitly shape what matters most to us. Smith draws us into awareness of what the world pulls us to desire: the world tells us what to love. It is in the very contours of Christian discipleship, Smith argues, that we must reform the church and what it means to participate in and be reformed by the church.[71] Smith's Reformed spin on Radical Orthodoxy demonstrates the necessary awareness of sin and its latent and implicit presence within the church.

If the Radical Orthodoxy Movement indicates elements of a postmodern ontology that offers religious or theological answers at the limits of modernity, it does so through its complex articulations and engagements with Western philosophy, theology, and other non-theological discourses. The religious or theological resourcement of a participatory ontology raises questions of theological integration and engagement and the extent and promise of ecclesial reformations of modernity in ways that opens us theologically to meaning in the midst of modernity. If Milbank et al. opens us theologically to an ontological retrieval of participation, Charles Taylor opens us morally to the retrieval of ontology at the limits of modernity.

Charles Taylor's Moral Ontology

The Romantic-Heideggerian resourcement of meaning is not merely oriented toward meaning and making sense of who we are. It is also oriented fundamentally toward making sense of meaning in light of God and evaluating the worthiness and dignity of moral concerns. Taylor's articulation of a moral ontology re-orients us to God in ways that opens us beyond naturalistic reductions of humanity and nature by representational epistemology. It opens us to God and the Other in ways that open a life of faith to the situated conditions of human life as embodied, relational agents making sense and expressing who we are as moral, human agents in the constitutive contexts of situated existence. Taylor's Romantic resourcement is marked by constitutive self-understandings in light of the Other and the situated conditions of life. But furthermore, it is marked by a moral ontology that makes sense of the world in light of moral sources and common goods.

According to Taylor, a moral ontology is one marked by the Romantic expressivist views on language. Taylor argues that language constitutes the conditions for three things. First, "in language we formulate things. Through language we can bring to explicit awareness what we formerly had only an implicit sense of. Through formulating some matter, we bring it to fuller and clearer consciousness."[72] That is, language allows us to express and articulate what we know. Second, language opens the space for community, communication, belonging, and participation in a common meaning in public space. Third, language mediates concerns for right and wrong (that shapes societal and cultural) expressions of moral concerns. In doing so it shapes common goods and things that are significant and meaningful for people who act toward a good. Taylor states that there are three things language does: it articulates and brings "about explicit awareness; put[s] things in public space, thereby constituting public space; and [makes] the discriminations which are foundational to human concerns" by opening us to the judgements of what is right or wrong in these potential common concerns.[73] Language as such builds rapport, discloses, and constitutes meaning.[74]

Language implies an expressive and constitutive morality according to Taylor. He states, "morality requires some recognition that there are higher demands than one, and hence the recognition of some distinction between kinds of goal."[75] That is, morality demands evaluation of what is good, in determining the Good. Taylor argues this evaluation may be strong or weak. Weak evaluation is inauthentic insofar as we have not evaluated the demands and promises of what we deem "good." Weak evaluation entails the unquestioning of goods, and especially not ranking which is better than others. Strong evaluations by contrast evaluate levels and layers of constitutive goods that are evaluated authentically because they make judgements

128 *Chapter 6*

on which goods are superior or move us to act virtuously in light of what we deem the good. Strong evaluations move us to do and be good and authentically constitute who we are because of our judgements on what the good *is*. The link between language and morality however also implies an ontology of the person as a human agent. Taylor defines a person as

> an agent who has a sense of self, of his/her own life, who can evaluate it, and make choices about it. This is the basis of the respect we owe persons . . . the central importance of all of this for our moral thinking is reflected in the fact that these capacities form an important part of what we should respect and nourish in human beings. To make someone less capable of understanding himself, evaluating and choosing is to deny totally the injunction that we should respect him as a person.[76]

Taylor argues that the constitutive nature of human persons lies not only in their evaluations but also their practical ends: to what end shall I act? This implies that human agency is done by a being who acts, who has "goals, and endeavors to fulfill them."[77] A human person is also a human agent with the ability to evaluate what matters to them, making judgments of importance, and articulate what is meaningful to them in ways that draws us into common concerns of activity.

Taylor's moral ontology demands the evaluation of goods and the constitutive-expressive dynamics of human language in ways that open us to what it means to be human alongside other humans, God, and the natural world. Each of these may become a moral source for evaluating what the good is and how we may act in response to or alongside others in what we deem the good. Moral ontology entails not merely the expression of meaning, but makes meaning manifest with its moral concerns for and evaluations of the good. Moral ontology points us beyond ourselves and constitutes our identity in light of what we deem the good. It points us to act in light of the good. Moral ontology entails human agency and embodiment as central to what it means to be human.

If the Radical Orthodoxy Movement's participatory ontology points to the theological and ecclesial engagement, resourcement, baptism, and reform of non-theological discourses in light of their participation in God as created things that point to transcendental truth, then Charles Taylor's moral ontology points to the linguistic-expressive-constitutive evaluations of what we deem the good and how to authentically both act and be virtuous in light of the good. Both Milbank et al.'s participatory ontology and Taylor's moral ontology baptize meaning morally and theologically, drawing us into the third realm of the religious baptism of meaning in the cosmotheandric vision of Raimon Panikkar. A postmodern ontology includes the moral, theological, *and* religious baptism of meaning. It is to Panikkar's religious baptism of meaning of a postmodern ontology that we now turn to with an analysis of his relational ontology.

Raimon Panikkar's Relational Ontology

Much work in recent years has sought to unpack Panikkar's relational ontology.[78] A common theme drawn out of these accounts is the primacy of a relational ontology grounded in Panikkar's theories of cosmotheandrism and ontonomy wherein each of the three dimensions of reality co-constitute reality perichoretically through a mutual inter-in-dependence upon and with and in one another. Panikkar's understanding of a relational ontology is grounded in a cosmotheandric ontonomy. Panikkar's idea of a cosmotheandric ontonomy implies that we are a cosmotheandric being intrinsically constituted by three dimensions of reality that we advaitically experience as a *pars pro toto*; that we are cosmotheandrically experiencing reality both as a cosmotheandric person (a part that expresses the whole) *and* as we participate within a whole cosmotheandric reality (as embodied, material human creatures participating in the divine). Cosmotheandric reality permeates through every person as an intrinsic relationality; each person expresses a knot of relations that relates to every other person and to all of reality as we are cosmotheandrically constituted. The person is a conjunction to the affect that he is *aware* of his own inter-independence within reality.

Crucially, Panikkar's conception of a person is grounded in the idea of relationality or relativity as constitutive of the self. In this context a self is constituted as real ontonomically insofar as the person participates within reality as both part of it and constituted by it. This is what Panikkar calls the radical relativity of reality and what has been developed also as the *pars pro toto* effect wherein each part reflects the whole within every part.[79] Young-chan Ro has argued that Panikkar's conception of relativity:

> Is a notion emphasizing the nature of inter-dependence of every being. This affirms that each being is in need of the other in the sense that no single being can exist on its own independently. Relativity is an ontological constitution of all beings. Relativity is a way of recognizing the intrinsic relatedness of each being. Relativity in this sense . . . describes the relationship found in all beings. Every being is in relationship with other beings to become its own being . . . Relativity is . . . an "intrinsic relation" of every being. Every being exists in relation to other beings. In this sense, relativity is nothing but the affirmation of the relatedness of every being to other beings in an intrinsic way. Relationship is not to be understood as an external string binding one being to another being, but it expresses the idea of the intrinsic relatedness of one being [with] another being.

130 *Chapter 6*

In this respect, relationship is the foundation that allows each being to be found in existence with other being[s], both epistemologically and ontologically.[80]

Within this context the relationship becomes the constitutive link to and of reality and the self in such a way that constituted within the person is the relativity of his or her being insofar as he or she participates in reality because he or she is constituted by and as a part of this reality. Here the cosmotheandric reality finds its best expression in that what is real is constitutively composed of world, God, and Man in a way that allows each to express itself holistically and ontonomically, each in its own way as itself participating within a reality that finds itself in the relationships that constitute it. Here the law of ontonomy, often called by Panikkar as radical relativity, the Buddhist *pratityatsamudpada*, and the Christian *perichoresis*, is of utmost importance to understanding what constitutes the real *as real*; the relation. For Panikkar the relations *themselves* constitute the real: every person, the Trinity, Christ, and the material world that Panikkar proposes as real are real insofar as they ontonomically manifest *as real* in their intrinsic, relational constitution.

Tied to this relational ontology is that relationality replaces the substantiality of reality as fundamentally constituted through relations that mutually co-inhere, vivify, permeate, and sustain the reality of each dimension of reality with and in one another as Real through the embeddedness of experience within reality. Anselm Min has argued that for Panikkar, the relation, not substance, becomes constitutive of reality and the self:

> Central to Panikkar's cosmotheandric vision, then, is the ontological primacy of relation over the substantiality of things. . . . The alternative, however, is not to deny the real differences among things but to locate such differences and identities on the more primordial level of constitutive relations. It is relations that constitute each in its distinctive reality yet also relate them to one another. On this view reality is neither one because many things do exist, nor many because they do not exist in their absolute independence but only in a mutually intrinsic, constitutive relationship. What is ultimate is not substantiality but relationship, which is neither one nor two. This, then, is the heart of the advaitic insight that sees reality in a non-dualistic way. Applied to the relationship between humanity, nature, and the divine, this means that the three are not reducible to one another yet constitute a whole in which each is connected to one another in a mutually constitutive relationship.[81]

For Panikkar the basis of reality and self as governed by a cosmotheandric ontonomy characterized by a constitutive relationality serves to show how reality is not substantial, but rather relationally constituted through the inter-in-dependence of reality. Underlying Panikkar's relational ontology are several inter-religious resourcements that tap into the cosmotheandric intuition into the nature of reality. If reality is inter-relationally co-constituted by world, God, and humanity, it is underpinned metaphysically by a relational ontology grounded in various religious, theological, and philosophical insights. From the advaitic insight into the absence of duality and the Christian insight of dependent co-origination to the Christian notion of *perichoresis*, Panikkar's relational ontology is at once religious, philosophical, and theological.

Panikkar's relational ontology demonstrates a cross cultural awareness of the human attempt to mediate unity and difference without collapsing or reducing them into one another. Panikkar's cosmotheandric ontonomy articulates a metaphysical vision of reality that collapses the ontological distinction between God and created things. And yet it also advocates for an advaitic mediation of unity and difference by recognizing the mutual incommensurability and irreducibility of reality to one sphere of the real. The relational constitution of reality implies a religious vision of reality that remains open not only to God, but to the religious other, without reducing them to nature and materiality, to their inability to recognize truth in the experience of the other, to the reduction of transcendence to finitude, or to the infinitization of God's transcendence without recognizing divine immanence in creation's participation in the Being of God.

Panikkar's relational ontology and cosmotheandric ontonomy offers an integral vision that seeks to draw from both classical Christian theology and modern humanism without falling into their failures. From classical Christian thought, mediated through the *Nouvelle Theologie* Movement, Panikkar advocates for the integration of grace and nature through his appeals to divine immanence in a theology of history that is teleologically oriented by the Christic principle. Furthermore, from modern humanism, Panikkar advocates for the constitutive human dimension of meaning-making and reason, without reducing humanity to mere rationalism or irrational spirituality.[82]

Panikkar integrates the possibility and intelligibility of God through religious experience and synthesis for modern man as a way of guarding against the reduction of humanity to instrumental reasoning or mere materiality. Panikkar's relational ontology offers an integral ontology that is both theological and philosophical, rational and religious. It is in his integral vision of reality that he realizes we cannot reduce reality. Rather Reality is mutually constituted by irreducible dimensions of the real that in turn constitute reality as real. Panikkar's relational ontology opens us religiously to the integral possibility and intelligibility of believing and meaning in the midst of the situated contexts and conditions of existence and experience.

AN ADVAITIC MODERNITY? PANIKKAR'S POSTMODERN ONTOLOGY

If the Radical Orthodoxy Movement's theological resourcement of a participatory ontology and Charles Taylor's moral ontology articulate the theological and moral baptism of meaning, then Panikkar's cosmotheandric ontonomy articulates a relational ontology that constitutes reality both metaphysically and (inter-)religiously. The religious resourcement of Panikkar's relational ontology advocates for the importance of unity and difference. It also demonstrates how his metaphysics sees three dimensions of reality as irreducible to one another through the advaitic lens of radical relativity, opening reality to the constitution of its reality as real through the inter-in-dependency of what it means to be real.

This implies that Panikkar's religious resourcement radically articulates a seemingly heterodox theology wherein Milbank's asymmetrical relation between God and creatures and creation is absent. Without the asymmetrical relation between God and creation, this implies, for Panikkar, God's dependence upon creation and humanity to be, and for humanity and creation's dependence upon God to be. For without the Being of God, humanity and creation would not be a full expression of creation in God's eyes, but so also, more controversially, would this imply that without creation and creatures, God could not be God. God is understood to exist as God from the human perspective as God precisely because of the created dependence upon God. But equally so, Panikkar's relational ontology and cosmotheandric ontonomy implies that God could not truly be God without his dependence on creation to be, participate in, and to love him.[83]

The controversy of Panikkar's theological ideas embodied in his cosmotheandric ontonomy certainly lies within his advaitic spin on God the creator as in ontonomic relation with creation and humanity. Panikkar is distinctively influenced by his long-standing exposure and dwelling within Indian philosophy and theology, which posits both the eternity and timelessness of creation and creation as a manifestation of divine substance, essence, or being. In Panikkar, the Hindu notion of creation as a manifestation of a divine cosmic essence is combined with Buddhist and Jain understandings of the eternal becoming of time and being.

But Panikkar's turn to Indian conceptions of creation and its lack of ontological distinction with a Creator lies fundamentally in a failure he sees of modern, Western theology. Gerard Hall argues that Panikkar's "argument is that Western thought has been so preoccupied with its mission of safeguarding the unity of reality and the transcendence of God that it has sacrificed awareness of the multiplicity of reality and the immanence of God."[84] Hall argues, rather, that Panikkar's "focus is not on divine transcendence but on divine immanence as it is manifested in human reality and earthly life. The world is read theologically and teleologically, that is, as originating from, participating in, and returning to its divine origin, sustenance and goal."[85] In this Panikkar remains remarkably Catholic, marked by his intimate awareness of and advaitic spin upon *Nouvelle Theologie*.[86]

Panikkar critiques Western philosophy and theology's reduction of God to mere transcendence at the expense of God's immanence. This reduction of God to mere transcendence has several implications. First, it neglects the constitutive asymmetrical relationship and dependence between God's immanence to humanity and the cosmos. Second, it neglects any role God may have in human life in the human affirmation of autonomy. Third it neglects the human role in shaping creation and culture in harmonious ways. This also implies that the human role in the cosmos is reduced to controlling, determining, and understanding nature through instrumental reasoning. The limits of modernity are found within its abandonment of a theologically informed ontology and in its affirmation of instrumental reason and representational epistemology.

By contrast, Panikkar's relational ontology is underpinned by a participatory ontology that emphasizes divine immanence in creation. If Milbank's panentheism implies the asymmetrical relation between God and creation, this asymmetrical relation is lacking in Panikkar's panentheism. Indeed, Panikkar's critique of modern theology is not only advaitically resourced in Indian theology, but it plays with conceptions of being and becoming, time and eternity, in ways that produces staggering reformations of the idea of participation. Panikkar's participatory and relational theology, ontology, and metaphysics is marked by a panentheism wherein Being and God are imagined in terms of the becoming and perduring of creation.[87]

In turn, Panikkar's relational ontology recognizes the importance of experience and human agency, engagement, and embodiment found within the constitutive meaning-making of Taylor's moral ontology. The Romantic resourcement of meaning through a linguistic turn in modernity is found also in Panikkar's understanding of fundamental theology and his appropriation of Jacobi's sentiment. But if it is conceived that Panikkar fails to appropriate a moral ontology found in Taylor, it is crucial to point out his long-term advocacy for inter-religious dialogue and cross-cultural hermeneutics which are grounded in his pluralistic experience of a multi-religious identity. Furthermore, Panikkar can be resourced with Taylor's moral ontology in terms of ecological reformations as well as his concern for justice and openness to the mystery and incommensurability of the religious other.

134   *Chapter 6*

***

The constitution of meaning in Panikkar's postmodern ontology is one marked not necessarily by Taylor's moral ontology, though may include it, but it is certainly marked by an advaitic spin upon the Radical Orthodoxy Movement's participatory ontology. The linguistic-expressivist-constitution of meaning at the limits of modernity is marked by a threefold postmodern ontological critique of modernity. Each of these ontological critiques of modernity implies their irreducibility to one another, but also their mutual interpenetration with one another. They constitute an inter-in-dependent critique of modernity in their retrieval of ontology at the limits of modernity. They are inter-in-dependent because we can learn from each of them constitutive elements of what it means to be human in light of their participatory, moral, and relational ontologies on their own terms as well as in their mutual affinities with one another without reducing them to one another.

From this we can see that each is supported by and supports in their own way a late modern resourcement of a Romantic-expressivist-linguistics mediated to us through their postmodern engagement with Martin Heidegger's ontology. In the kairological genealogy offered above, we see three moods or consciousnesses as they developed across modernity through three turns—univocal, representational, and anthropocentric—that imply the end of history and the limits of modernity: the problem of meaning. At the heart of a postmodern ontology is not only the search for and articulation of meaning. At the heart of a postmodern ontology is also the retrieval of ontology in its theological, moral, and religious reformations of what it means to be human in light of a transcendent truth, good, and experience that finds its resources in the complex space, place, and time of an advaitic modernity.

NOTES

1. Raimon Panikkar, *Ontonomia de La Ciencia* [Ontonomy of Science] (Madrid: Gredos, 1961).

2. For critiques of the Scotus story as adopted by Milbank and the Radical Orthodoxy Movement, c.f. Daniel P. Horan, *Postmodernity and Univocity: A Critical Account of Radical Orthodoxy and John Duns Scotus* (Minneapolis, MN: Fortress Press, 2014); Richard Cross, "Duns Scotus and Suárez at the Origins of Modernity," in *Deconstructing Radical Orthodoxy*, eds., Wayne J. Hankey and Douglas Hedley (Burlington, VT: Ashgate, 2005), 85–102; Richard Cross, "'Where Angels Fear to Tread': Duns Scouts and Radical Orthodoxy," *Antonianum* 76 (2001): 7–41; Thomas Williams, "The Doctrine of Univocity Is True and Salutary," *Modern Theology* 21, no. 4 (2005): 575–85.

Postmodern Ontology at the Limits of Modernity

3. C.f. John Milbank, *Theology and Social Theory*, Second Edition (Malden, MA: Blackwell Publishing, 2006), xxv–xxvi; John Milbank, *Beyond Secular Order* (Malden, MA: Blackwell Publishing, 2013), 29–31, 50–57; Conor Cunningham, *Genealogy of Nihilism* (New York and London: Routledge, 2002), 16–32; Catherine Pickstock, *After Writing: On the Liturgical Consummation of Philosophy* (Malden, MA: Blackwell Publishing, 1998), 121–35; Adrian Pabst, *Metaphysics: The Creation of Hierarchy* (Grand Rapids, MI: William B. Eerdmans, 2012), 277–86; Derrick Peterson, "No True Scotsman: On the Presence, Character, and Origin of the 'Scotus Story' in Radical Orthodoxy and Beyond," *A Greater Courage* (blog), July 23, 2016, http://agreatercourage.blogspot.com/2016/07/no-true-scotsman-on-presence -character.html; http://agreatercourage.blogspot.com/2016/07/no-true-scotsman-part -two-scotus-story.html.

4. Simon Oliver, "Introducing Radical Orthodoxy: From Participation to Late Modernity," in *The Radical Orthodoxy Reader*, eds., John Milbank and Simon Oliver (New York and London: Routledge, 2009), 3–27, 3–12.

5. Oliver, "Introducing Radical Orthodoxy," 6.

6. Milbank, *Theology and Social Theory*, 3.

7. John Milbank, "Political Theology and the New Science of Politics," in *The Radical Orthodoxy Reader*, eds., John Milbank and Simon Oliver (New York and London: Routledge, 2009), 178–96, 178.

8. Milbank, "Political Theology and the New Science of Politics," 178.

9. C.f. Guido Vanheeswijck, "The End of Secularization?," in *Rethinking Secularization: Philosophy and the Prophecy of a Secular Age*, eds., Herbert De Vriese and Gary Gabor (Newcastle Upon Tyne: Cambridge Scholars Publishing, 2009), 1–26.

10. Oliver, "Introducing Radical Orthodoxy," 21–24.

11. Oliver, "Introducing Radical Orthodoxy," 22.

12. Horan, *Postmodernity and Univocity*.

13. C.f. Horan, *Postmodernity and Univocity*.

14. Cunningham, *Genealogy of Nihilism*, 30.

15. Catherine Pickstock, "Duns Scotus: His Historical and Contemporary Significance," *Modern Theology* 21, no. 4 (2005): 543–74.

16. Pickstock, *After Writing*, 47–100.

17. Pickstock, *After Writing*, 3–46; Michel De Certeau, *The Practice of Everyday Life*, trans. Steven Randall (Berkeley, CA: University of California Press, 1984), 154–76.

18. Charles Taylor, "Rationality," in *Philosophy and Human Sciences*, Philosophical Papers 2 (Cambridge, MA: Harvard University Press, 1985), 134–51, 136.

19. Taylor, "Rationality," 142.

20. Charles Taylor, "The Concept of a Person," in *Human Agency and Language*, Philosophical Papers 1 (Cambridge, MA: Harvard University Press, 1985), 97–114, 98.

21. Taylor, "The Concept of a Person," 112–13; C.f. Charles Taylor, *Sources of the Self: The Making of the Modern Identity* (Cambridge, MA: The Belknap Press of Harvard University Press, 1989), 1–104.

136   *Chapter 6*

22. Charles Taylor, "Theories of Meaning," in *Human Agency and Language*, Philosophical Papers 1 (Cambridge, MA: Harvard University Press, 1985), 248–92, 249.

23. Taylor, "Theories of Meaning," 252–53.

24. Charles Taylor, "Overcoming Epistemology," in *Philosophical Arguments* (Cambridge, MA: Harvard University Press, 1995), 1–19, 7.

25. Charles Taylor, "Atomism," in *Philosophy and Human Sciences*, Philosophical Papers 2 (Cambridge, MA: Harvard University Press, 1985), 187–210, 187.

26. Charles Taylor, "Introduction," in *Human Agency and Language*, Philosophical Papers 1 (Cambridge, MA: Harvard University Press, 1985), 1–12, 6.

27. Taylor, "Introduction," 6.

28. Raimon Panikkar, *The Cosmotheandric Experience: Emerging Religious Consciousness*, ed. Scott Eastham (Maryknoll, NY: Orbis Books, 1993), 35.

29. Gerard Hall, "Anthropology: Being Human," in *Raimon Panikkar: A Companion to His Life and Thought*, eds., Peter Phan and Young-Chan Ro (Cambridge, UK: James Clarke and Co., 2018), 194–216, 207–8.

30. Raimon Panikkar, "Man as a Ritual Being," *Chicago Studies* 15, no. 1 (1977): 5–28, 5ff.

31. Hall, "Anthropology: Being Human," 196.

32. Hall, "Anthropology: Being Human," 197.

33. Charles Taylor, "Engaged Agency and Background in Heidegger," in *The Cambridge Companion to Heidegger*, ed. Charles Guignon, Second Edition (Cambridge, UK: Cambridge University Press, 2006), 202–21.

34. John Milbank, "Only Theology Overcomes Metaphysics," in *The Word Made Strange: Theology, Language, and Culture* (Malden, MA: Blackwell, 1997), 36–52, 41.

35. Cunningham, *Genealogy of Nihilism*, xiii.

36. Milbank, "Only Theology Overcomes Metaphysics," 41–42.

37. Milbank, "Only Theology Overcomes Metaphysics," 49.

38. Raimon Panikkar, *Myth, Faith, and Hermeneutics: Cross Cultural Studies* (New York: Paulist Press, 1979), 327.

39. Charles Taylor, "Language and Human Nature," in *Human Agency and Language*, Philosophical Papers 1 (Cambridge, MA: Harvard University Press, 1985), 215–47, 219.

40. Taylor, "Language and Human Nature," 228–29.

41. Taylor, "Language and Human Nature," 220–21.

42. Charles Taylor, "Self-Interpreting Animals," in *Human Agency and Language*, Philosophical Papers 1 (Cambridge, MA: Cambridge University Press, 1985), 45–76, 50.

43. Taylor, "Language and Human Nature," 218.

44. Hall, "Anthropology: Being Human," 199–201; Raimon Panikkar, *F. H. Jacobi y La Filosofía Del Sentimiento [F. H. Jacobi and the Philosophy of Sentiment]* (Buenos Aires: Sapientia, 1948).

45. Taylor, "Language and Human Nature," 229.

46. John Milbank, "Knowledge: The Theological Critique of Philosophy in Hamann and Jacobi," in *Radical Orthodoxy: A New Theology*, eds., John Milbank,

Catherine Pickstock, and Graham Ward (New York and London: Routledge, 1999), 21–37, 27.

47. John Milbank, "The Linguistic Turn as a Theological Turn," in *The Word Made Strange: Theology, Language, and Culture* (Malden, MA: Blackwell, 1997), 84–120, 107.

48. Milbank, "Knowledge: The Theological Critique of Philosophy in Hamann and Jacobi," 27.

49. Milbank, "Knowledge: The Theological Critique of Philosophy in Hamann and Jacobi," 28.

50. Milbank, "The Linguistic Turn as a Theological Turn," 106–107.

51. Milbank, "Knowledge: The Theological Critique of Philosophy in Hamann and Jacobi," 28–32.

52. Charles Taylor, "The Importance of Herder," in *Philosophical Arguments* (Cambridge, MA: Harvard University Press, 1995), 79–99, 97.

53. Taylor, "The Importance of Herder," 97.

54. C.f. Amene Mir, "A Panentheist Reading of John Milbank," *Modern Theology* 28, no. 3 (2012): 526–60.

55. Oliver, "Introducing Radical Orthodoxy," 18.

56. John Milbank, "The Second Difference," in *The Word Made Strange: Theology, Language, and Culture* (Malden, MA: Blackwell, 1997), 171–93.

57. Oliver, "Introducing Radical Orthodoxy," 18.

58. Milbank, "Only Theology Overcomes Metaphysics," 47.

59. James K. A. Smith, *Introducing Radical Orthodoxy: Mapping a Post-Secular Theology* (Grand Rapids, MI: Baker Academic, 2004), 87–89.

60. John Milbank, Catherine Pickstock, and Graham Ward, "Introduction: Suspending the Material: The Turn of Radical Orthodoxy," in *Radical Orthodoxy: A New Theology* (New York and London: Routledge, 1999), 1–20, 3.

61. Oliver, "Introducing Radical Orthodoxy," 19.

62. Oliver, "Introducing Radical Orthodoxy," 19.

63. Oliver, "Introducing Radical Orthodoxy," 19–20.

64. Smith, *Introducing Radical Orthodoxy*, 87–89.

65. Josef Bengtson, *Explorations in Post-Secular Metaphysics* (New York: Palgrave Macmillan, 2016), 53–74.

66. James K. A. Smith, *Awaiting the King: Reforming Public Theology*, Vol. 3, 3 vols., Cultural Liturgies (Grand Rapids, MI: Baker Academic, 2017); Rod Dreher, *The Benedict Option: A Strategy for Christians in a Post-Christian Nation* (New York: Sentinel, 2017).

67. James K. A. Smith, *Desiring the Kingdom: Worship, Worldview, and Cultural Formation*, Vol. 1, 3 vols., Cultural Liturgies (Grand Rapids, MI: Baker Academic, 2009); James K. A. Smith, *Imagining the Kingdom: How Worship Works*, Vol. 2, 3 vols., Cultural Liturgies (Grand Rapids, MI: Baker Academic, 2013); James K. A. Smith, *You Are What You Love: The Spiritual Power of Habit* (Grand Rapids, MI: Brazos Press, 2016).

68. James K. A. Smith, "Secular Liturgies and the Prospects for a 'Post-Secular' Sociology of Religion," in *The Post-Secular in Question: Religion in Contemporary*

138   *Chapter 6*

Society, ed. Philip S. Gorski et al. (New York and London: New York University Press and Social Science Research Council, 2012), 159–84.

69. Smith, "Secular Liturgies and the Prospects for a 'Post-Secular' Sociology of Religion," 176.

70. Smith, *Awaiting the King*; Smith, *Desiring the Kingdom*; Smith, *Imagining the Kingdom*.

71. C.f. Smith, *You Are What You Love*; Smith, *Desiring the Kingdom*.

72. Taylor, "Theories of Meaning," 256–57.

73. Taylor, "Theories of Meaning," 263.

74. Taylor, "Theories of Meaning," 263–73; C.f. Taylor, "The Importance of Herder," 92.

75. Taylor, "The Concept of a Person," 102.

76. Taylor, "The Concept of a Person," 103.

77. Taylor, "The Concept of a Person," 103.

78. C.f. Francis X. D'Sa, "Time, History, and Christophany," in *Raimon Panikkar: A Companion to His Life and Thought*, eds., Peter Phan and Young-Chan Ro (Cambridge, UK: James Clarke and Co., 2018), 171–93; Anselm Min, "The Trinity and the Cosmotheandric Vision: Reflections on Panikkar's Intercultural Theology," in *Raimon Panikkar: A Companion to His Life and Thought*, eds., Peter Phan and Young-Chan Ro (Maryknoll, NY: Orbis Books, 2018), 152–70; Gerard Hall, "Anthropology: Being Human," 194–216; Veli-Matti Kärkkäinen, *Trinity and Religious Pluralism: The Doctrine of the Trinity in Christian Theology of Religions* (Burlington, VT: Ashgate, 2004), 119–33; Veli-Matti Kärkkäinen, *Trinity and Revelation*, Vol. 2, 5 vols., A Constructive Theology for the Pluralistic World (Grand Rapids, MI: William B. Eerdmans, 2014), 347–52.

79. Raimon Panikkar, *Mysticism and Spirituality: Mysticism, The Fullness of Life*, ed. Milena Carrara Pavan, Vol. I.1, XII vols., Opera Omnia (Maryknoll, NY: Orbis Books, 2014), 20; Young-Chan Ro, "Relativism, Universalism, and Pluralism in an Age of Globalization," *CIRPIT Review* 3 (2012): 91–101.

80. Young-Chan Ro, "Relativism, Universalism, and Pluralism in an Age of Globalization," *CIRPIT Review* 3 (2012): 91–101, 98.

81. Anselm Min, "Panikkar's Radical Trinitarianism: Reflections on Panikkar's Transformation of the Christian Trinity into Cosmotheandrism," *CIRPIT Review* 6 (2015): 75–100, 77; C.f. Raimon Panikkar, *The Rhythm of Being: The Unbroken Trinity* (Maryknoll, NY: Orbis Books, 2010), 53, 60, 218–19.

82. Hall, "Anthropology: Being Human," 196, 198.

83. Christians, raise your shackles at this: God exists in and of himself as a communion of three persons subsisting relationally as love. While what we can know of God is only mediated by how he acts in the economy of salvation, the intimations of God's immanent existence as an eternal communion of love without creation is something to challenge Panikkar on. Panikkar's theology implicates the idea, while not necessarily the reality, that there could be no God eternally without creation, implicating the eternity of creation.

84. Gerard Vincent Hall, "Raimon Panikkar's Hermeneutics of Religious Pluralism," Catholic University of America (Ann Arbor, MI: UMI Dissertation Services, 1994), 67.

85. Hall, "Raimon Panikkar's Hermeneutics of Religious Pluralism," 69.

86. Hall, "Anthropology: Being Human," 196–99.

87. C.f. Peter Phan, "Raimon Panikkar's 'Eschatology': The Unpublished Chapter," in *Raimon Panikkar: A Companion to His Life and Thought*, eds., Peter Phan and Young-Chan Ro (Cambridge, UK: James Clarke and Co., 2018), 242–57.

Chapter 7

Panikkar's Postsecular Vision

A Panikkarean Reading of Charles Taylor

The question of the postsecular is about the place of religion in the secular. While much ink has been spilled on the political parameters of postsecularism, this chapter argues that another approach to postsecularism may come through the thought of Raimon Panikkar. Raimon Panikkar's postsecular vision is one that re-reads secularization through a kairological reading of history, critiques secularism on the basis of his cosmotheandric experience, and seeks to re-sacralize ordinary life through his notion of sacred secularity. The work of Raimon Panikkar offers key resources in rethinking postsecularism as geared toward the re-enchantment of secular experience. This chapter analyzes and develops Panikkar's postsecular vision and overlays it onto the thought of Charles Taylor. This chapter argues that Taylor is an ally to Panikkar, who questions the modern processes of secularization, the ideology of secularism, and seeks to understand the phenomenon of religion in the midst of late modernity. Panikkar and Taylor articulate (post)secular visions in differing ways, but they both ask a central question: what does it mean to be religious in the midst of the secular? This chapter analyzes the postsecular visions of Taylor and Panikkar and articulates how they conceive of what it means to be religious alongside or in the midst of secular, everyday experience.

For Taylor, secularity articulates the complex space of the religious within the cross pressures of a secular, immanent frame. Secularity for Taylor is marked by the cross pressures between believing, unbelieving, and non-believing in ways that produces the lived and constitutive tensions between religion and secularity in daily life. This middle condition between belief, unbelief, and non-belief marks the lived reality and phenomenon of Taylor's postsecular religiosity. For Panikkar, secularity is inherently

142   *Chapter 7*

religious. That is, Panikkar's notion of secularity is one in which humans religiously exist in secular life as liturgical beings marked by temporality, materiality, and spatiality. Panikkar's account of sacred secularity, kairological readings of human consciousness, and his cosmotheandric experience each offer resources for Panikkar's postsecular critique.

Between Fred Dallmayr's work on Charles Taylor and Raimon Panikkar and Gerard Hall's work on Panikkar's pluralistic hermeneutics, a gap follows between the correlation between Taylor and Panikkar on the problem of secularization and secular re-enchantment.[1] Whereas Dallmayr draws out the fundamental distinction between Taylor's and Panikkar's understandings of transcendence and immanence in modern secularity, and whereas Hall draws out Panikkar's pluralistic interpretation of the secular, this chapter extends their analyses to argue how Panikkar critiques and offers answers to the problems of modernity. It develops Panikkar's postsecular vision and critique of the secular. But it also does so through an analysis and description of Charles Taylor's accounts of the secular. What lacks in Dallmayr is a substantial engagement with Taylor's corpus, and what lacks in Hall is a substantial engagement with secularization and secularism. This chapter offers a substantial engagement with Taylor's account of the secular in hopes of deepening the conclusions and implications of Panikkar's postsecular vision.

This chapter analyzes Taylor and Panikkar's accounts of secularization, secularism, and secularity. It offers a thick description of both Taylor and Panikkar's postsecular readings of secularization, their critiques of secularism as an ideology, and their advocation for secularity. Moreover, it argues for a pluralistic and correlative overlay of Panikkar onto Taylor to demonstrate how they are postsecular allies that can learn from and mutually enhance one another in their critiques of modernity. In doing so this chapter argues that Panikkar's kairological reading of history and his idea of sacred secularity embody Panikkar's postsecular vision of reality.

WHAT IS THE SECULAR? RESOURCES FROM TAYLOR

Taylor's *A Secular Age* charts roughly 500 years of Western secularization—but in a way that defies the normal secularization thesis that the more modern we become the less religious we become.[2] Taylor articulates a metaphor of a house to explain the development of the secular and the process of secularization. If the basement of the house is political secularism—marked by the privatization of religion in the public sphere—the ground floor is marked by sociological secularism—the decline of religious practice and belonging to religious institutions. The upper floor for Taylor is phenomenological secularism, which is marked by the lived experience of living between the options of living a religious or secular life.[3] Within this metaphor, we can also see the process of secularization. When the basement (political sphere) is no longer marked by the religious, the second stage develops (the decline of religious practice) because religious institutions are no longer dominating structuring structures to society and culture. Tone Svetelj summarizes Taylor's account of secularism and secularization through three points: (1) secularism as a retreat of religion from public life;[4] (2) secularism as decline in belief and practices; and (3) secularity as changed conditions for belief.[5] However, while the saeculum is no longer hooked to religion as the structuring structure of modern society, culture, and politics, religion still explodes in its variety, combinations, and plurality of options within what Taylor calls the Nova Effect. Taylor's account of secularity, Tone Svetelj argues:

> should not be seen as the time where belief and religious practices will finally decline; it is rather a time that undermines earlier forms and creates space for new ones. Once the traditional ways of expressing belief and actualizing religious practices become insufficient—that is, to provide convincing answers— people should start looking for new, creative practices and belief systems, hoping that [they] will provide meaningful answers.[6]

Thus, the second story of the house of secularity is marked by the lived tension between the optionality of religious life and secularity—the complex space between religious belief, unbelief, and non-belief. The experience of secularity is marked by Taylor's understanding of living in a secular age between the cross pressures of belief. Within these cross pressures of belief, we are pulled in differing directions of *what* to believe and *whether* to believe.

By following a cultural historical approach to modernity Taylor argues that religion adapts to new historical contexts and is marked by discontinuity and continuity via adaptation and adoption to a re-embedding of religious belief and practices within new historical frameworks and contexts. But what is clear in Taylor's account of secularization is a transition between a pre-modern hierarchical universe marked by the dominating powers of religion over society and politics, to a modern direct access society, marked by the flattening of the vertical relationship with God through the church into the horizontal structures of immediacy. If the pre-modern saeculum mediated God to society through the church, the modern saeculum no longer sees the church as necessary, and the political sphere and the market economy in turn allow the immediacy of access along a horizontal plane.[7]

For Taylor, there is a shift in the processes of secularization grounded in the historical development of an impersonal moral order, rather than the cosmic chain of being. This process is marked by disenchantment via providential deism, the creation of a nation-state, and a focus on the market economy in

144   *Chapter 7*

providing material wealth and prosperity through industry, science, contract, and technology. These developments link the process of disenchantment to a development of exclusive humanism and its emphasis on human flourishing, dignity, freedom, and benevolence. It is through these factors that religious belief and practice have declined in modern secular society. Furthermore, Pádraig Hogan highlights five shifts in Taylor's understanding of the decline of the sacred in modern society:

> [First,] the yielding of the notion of cosmos (the Great Chain of Being with its inherent hierarchies) to that of a natural universe; [second,] the demise of enchantment within the experience of religious belief, both socially and individually; [third,] the decline of invocations or evocation of God in public society; [fourth,] the decline of a capability to hold tensions in some equilibrium (e.g. between observance of religious authority, on the [one] hand, and "festivals of un-rule," such as carnival, on the other); [fifth,] the waning of a common understanding of time, especially sacred time.[8]

According to Paul Janz, three features of pre-modernity vanish in modern secular society: (1) The natural world no longer points to or "testifies to divine purposes or action"; (2) God is no longer "implicated in the very existence of society"; and (3) the enchanted world disappears.[9] Svetelj offers a coherent account of the hallmarks of enchantment and what was lost in disenchantment.[10]

In an ordered cosmos, not only was it teleologically and hierarchically understood, but it was understood as enchanted: open to spirits and transcendence as having a causal effect on the world and human beings, ordering and disordering the created world in its orientation to the good. This ordered cosmos was concerned with a social and political hierarchical order suspended from God in a two-tiered conception of higher and lower time and vocations.[11] For the medieval world, "even the perception of time was split into two: the sacred and the not-sacred, i.e., secular time. There were sacred periods of intense dedication to rituals, celebrations, prayers, and the periods of ordinary time. The sacred moments regulated perception of the time-horizon."[12]

Highlighting three characteristics of a medieval social imaginary—social cohesion, the distinction between higher time and secular time, and the enchanted dependency of human beings suspended from God—there is a teleological order to the cosmos in a participatory social imaginary as the work and will of God in ordering us toward the Good. An enchanted worldview implies the openness not only to experiencing transcendence, but also the openness of being ordered toward the good. Here the Medieval social imaginary has an end, and that end is not only the good, but it finds its completion in God. The changed conditions for belief and the loci of the fifteenth and sixteenth centuries for Taylor imply that Christians before the sixteenth century imagined themselves as participating in a hierarchical and ordered cosmos that teleologically functioned toward the good (as God) as the natural end of the cosmos.

In the context of late modernity, religion has transformed and has done so in several senses: (1) with the changed conditions for belief, religion is now optional in our pluralistic late modern society; (2) through the modernizing process of the disembedding of belief and disenchantment, and the "drive to reform," religion is now a contested position in secular modernity; and (3) late modern re-enchantment marks the creation of new religions, religious beliefs, and practices—in ways that have often transgressed, and offer alternative options to, traditional religions—that help us cope and live with the stark, dark, empty ennui of meaninglessness, despair, and nihilism. Within the context of nihilism and meaninglessness, the search for meaning finds its place as a search for authenticity and wholeness or fullness, where secular modernity has become fragmented, fragilized, alienated, isolated, and fractured within itself in the creation of both a modern moral order and the creation of new possibilities of living in a technocratic society. The new possibilities of a technocratic society are marked by the use of efficient instrumental reason which has eclipsed the possibilities of its ends in the creation of a society that lacks the moral clarity of a substantial telos toward which it is aimed. Within this framework, transcendence or God may be seen as absent or dead, but it has certainly been displaced and replaced by an immanent frame that may or may not be open to transcendence.

PANIKKAR'S POSTSECULAR CRITIQUE

It is in the postsecular space of the immanent frame, that may be open or closed to various extents, that the problem of alienation, fragmentation, meaninglessness, and isolation is given answers to by Raimon Panikkar. Raimon Panikkar offers (religious) answers to the problems of modernity in his postsecular re-readings of human history. The following describes Panikkar's postsecular critique through an account of his analyses of secularization, secularism, and especially secularity. Then it analyzes his kairological reading of history, and finally ends with a conceptual overlay of Panikkar's account of the secular onto Taylor's account of the secular. Each of these sections underscore the religious re-enchantment of modernity as central to Panikkar's postsecular vision.

146 *Chapter 7*

Secularization, Secularism, and Secularity

Panikkar clearly prefers to talk of secularity as a more fruitful term than secularization or secularism. Secularization for Panikkar refers to the historical processes and conditions by which the saeculum has been unhooked from institutional religion through various movements found within modern history: reason, science, technology, industrialization, the Protestant Reformation, etc.[13] In this sense, Panikkar is in fundamental agreement with Taylor's account of secularization. Panikkar's position on secularism also fundamentally agrees with Taylor. Secularism for Panikkar is a modern ideology that advocates for and explains the decline of religion in an enlightened modernity. For Panikkar, it implies a dualism between the sacred and the profane, a dualism introduced by the secularizing processes that stem at least to the Protestant Reformation. Secularism tries to say that there is only this world, a secular profane one, in which the vertical relationship to an imagined God has collapsed into a horizontal-only reality.[14] Gerard Hall states that for Panikkar:

> Although representing secularization as "the progression from the sacred to the secular," Panikkar suggests a further distinction between secularism that may "still be tolerant of the sacred and its rights" and secularity that is equated with "the intolerant destruction of any sacred order."[15] Consequently, secularization as such is perceived as a new experience of space and time, or a new mode of being in the world, through which fundamental human and religious symbols are not annihilated, but transformed.[16]

In contrast to, and building upon, secularization and secularism, Panikkar's notion of secularity implies the lived experience of time, matter, and space. This triad according to Panikkar is one that marks secularity.[17] Panikkar argues that the metaphysics of secularity is one characterized by the temporal structure of the world.[18] He argues that just as time is marked by temporality, secularity is marked by time, space, and materiality in ways that structure our world.[19] If secularism reduces reality to the space/time/matter triad, God clearly has no place in the structures of secularity. But secularity for Panikkar is the lived experience of temporality—and it is one that does not absolutize the secular triad of space/time/matter.[20] Rather it sees the secular triad as the place in which God enters into lived experience. Hall states that:

> Secular consciousness does not necessarily deny the reality of the sacred. However, it no longer allows the sacred (in the sense of the non-secular) to assume prior rights over the secular "reality" of the world. In fact, "secularization is the process of the penetration of reality into the world, the process of making the world real."[21] In a somewhat different formulation, we may say

that Panikkar perceives secularization as the process in which the world, matter, space and time become definitive and, in a sense, sacred (that is, ultimate) realities.[22]

Panikkar states that, "sacred secularity will say therefore that the secular is real and that its degree of reality is primordial. The notion of secularity derives from the experience that the life of the world (the matter/space/time triad) belongs to the ultimate condition of Being—and is therefore sacred. The *saeculum* itself, and not only that which it can bring or indicate, is 'real,' that is to say, sacred."[23] Panikkar's understanding of the saeculum is one in which we experience the sacred, temporal nature of Being. God enters into the saeculum for Panikkar because God is not totally transcendent. Rather, Panikkar advocated for a divine immanence within the temporal structures of lived existence in the saeculum. Secularity for Panikkar is one in which we experience the sacred. It is not marked by either the dualism between the sacred and the profane, nor its collapse into the monism of religion or the secular. Secularity is about the advaitic space in which we experience the sacred through, and within, the temporal structures of secular life.

Panikkar's Kairological Readings of History

This section articulates Raimon Panikkar's account of the kairological moments of human consciousness. This section argues that Panikkar's kairological reading of history assumes a correlation with Charles Taylor's accounts of secularization and intentionally overlays Panikkar onto Taylor's accounts of secularization. Panikkar advocated for a renewal of secular experience through his three kairological moments of human consciousness as historical shifts in human religiosity and ritual action that intentionally affirms the re-sacralization of secularization (but not its de-secularization). Panikkar argues that there are three kairological moments—pre-historical (or non-historical), historical, and trans-historical—characterized by shifts in human consciousness and ways of being human. Much literature has summarized Panikkar's kairological readings of history. It is worth working with Francis D'Sa and Gerard Hall's accounts to draw out Panikkar's understanding of kairological moments in history. Francis D'Sa states that time-consciousness for Panikkar is directed to the past (pre-/non-historical consciousness), oriented toward the future (historical consciousness), and centered in the present (trans-historical consciousness) and that they are "human modes of being-in-the-world" that "can exist simultaneously in a way where one dominates the other two."[24]

These three kairological moments as such are not chronological. Rather they emphasize the quality of religious consciousness across time and place. Gerard Hall states categorically that if the pre-(non-)historical consciousness is cosmocentric, and the historical consciousness is anthropocentric,[25] then the trans-historical consciousness is cosmotheandric. Cosmocentrism is marked by living in harmony with nature in a hierarchical, heteronomic universe and is oriented toward the past.[26] It is also marked by orality and memory. Anthropocentrism arrives when humans become self-aware and begin to dominate reality. Anthropocentrism is marked by the desacralization of reality and emphasizes history and future.[27] Francis D'Sa states that for the historical consciousness, "truth is dependent on history and historical evidence. This mode of consciousness is pervaded by history, and is at home in the myth of history. . . . Progress (a sacred word in the world of history) is spelled in terms of more, not better, and consists in multiplying the possibilities at [humanity's] disposal."[28] The historical consciousness looks to the destiny of humanity which eclipses God, who largely becomes irrelevant. D'Sa states that, "the search for knowledge is motivated by the will to power, that is, how to control things. Historical consciousness is constructed on an autonomous principle that God has left the world to the strivings of men."[29] The focus on the end of history for the historical consciousness implies the emergence of humans as historical beings.[30] But it also splinters reality in the human drive to dominate it: fragmentation, alienation, and the reduction of reality to mere matter are all results of the failed project envisioned by the anthropocentricism of modern progress and autonomy.[31]

By contrast, the trans-historical consciousness is marked by Panikkar's notion of ontonomy. It implies the lived experience of "the irreducible character of the divine, human and cosmic, realities that are differentiated but interconnected."[32] The cosmotheandric, trans-historical consciousness is marked by the experience of advaitic harmony-in-tension, the diversity-in-unity, and the sacredness of the secular. The trans-historical consciousness lives in the present between the past and the future. It draws upon the past for living in the present. It looks to the future not as longing to become, but rather the future is seen from the contentment and presence of lived experience. D'Sa states that "Panikkar asserts that the present is the most important factor of reality because only the present has full ontological weight, because its tempiternal core as consciousness holds being and time together."[33] Hall argues that the trans-historical cosmotheandric consciousness is Panikkar's

> answer to both the modern crisis of history and the postmodern crisis of otherness. In his foundational period, Panikkar spoke of the unfolding of Western consciousness in terms of three distinct human attitudes–heteronomy, autonomy, and ontonomy–which correlate with his notions of cosmocentric, anthropocentric, and cosmotheandric consciousness, but now applied universally.[34]

Panikkar's Postsecular Vision 149

Panikkar's kairological reading of history highlights not only the transitions of centricity—from cosmic to anthropic, and then to cosmotheandric—but also via D'Sa their orientation to time. It is in the experience of a cosmotheandric reality that Panikkar locates the promise and answer to the problems of modernity without reverting to pre-modern heteronomy. It is the space of being between the past and the future, of living in the tensions of the present with a certain irreducible depth, that we can find the resources that may help us to live within renewed hope, faith, and love in the midst of brokenness and disharmony. The integration of reality for Panikkar lies within the very experience of the real—of God in the midst of human experience found within the cosmos. Cosmotheandric experience is the experience of the presence of God in the temporal structures of secularity. Cosmotheandric experience is the experience of God within and through the temporality, materiality, and spatiality of secular life. It is a tempiternal experience of living between the sacred and the secular, of experiencing the sacredness of the secular and the secularity of the sacred.[35]

Reading Panikkar and Taylor Together

If we compare Panikkar's kairological readings of history to Taylor's accounts of the secular, we find several correlations that may overlay one over the other for mutual fecundation. Panikkar's pre-historical consciousness is similar to what Charles Taylor calls the enchanted worldview characteristic of pre-modern societies and cultures. Taylor's pre-modern imaginary and Panikkar's pre-historical consciousness entails the ritualistic human participation in higher life as symbolically linked to religious belief insofar as what we do and experience reflects a symbolic participation in a sacred cosmos.[36] The liturgical dimension displays the idea that our actions are somehow linked to a higher conception of time and experience insofar as its symbolic power is inherent in its teleological order toward completion in the Good (and God).[37] Hall argues that for Panikkar "the universe [is] already on the way to its completion, fulfillment, perfection, redemption or resurrection in Christ. As interpreted by Panikkar, this Christic confidence is always in the context of human responsibility for—and collaboration with—the entire creation."[38] If the pre-historical kairological moment of human consciousness entails a participatory cosmotheandric experience of a *sacramentum mundi* in a teleologically ordered cosmos, human identity is embedded within a sacralized conception of the cosmos.

However what happens during Panikkar's second kairological moment—historical consciousness—is Taylor's sense of the disembedding of belief through the formation of secular structures that lead to the disenchantment of the world.[39] In the turn to autonomic conceptions of human experience

150   *Chapter 7*

and individuation, the fragmentation of medieval cosmology resulted in the separation of integral human experience where the individual person becomes the arbiter of reality in two senses: God and transcendence are displaced and replaced by transcendentals and the immanent frame; and the cosmos, now understood as nature,[40] is subject to human domination and control.[41] Autonomy for Panikkar refers to the modern movement toward the fragmentation of human experience, the infinitization of divine transcendence, the virtual collapse of divine immanence into the suppression and disenchantment of human religiosity, and the rejection of heteronomic experience of participating as a microcosmic symbol of a macrocosmic universe reflecting divine providence.[42]

Autonomy in the historical kairological moment fundamentally states that humanity becomes the master of themselves through their use of reason to the extent that humanity alienates themselves from nature, God, and other human beings; including a fragmentation within themselves. Panikkar characterizes this moment in history as a stage where humanity forgets and rejects the integration of the cosmic and theological dimensions with the human, and elevates the human dimension at the cost of the fragmentation and separation of reality, cosmotheandric consciousness, and human participation in the divine.[43] Autonomy implies the separation of human identity from not just its participation in the cosmos and God but from others and ourselves, fracturing human relationships with the heightened concern of autonomy and individuation.

Despite this, for Panikkar, the historical kairological moment also entails a positive appraisal of individual autonomy and the use of reason and science as important advancements in human society. And yet, Panikkar issues a critical warning of modernity's emphasis on scientism, naturalism, and the destructive capability of human reason insofar as we may become blind to its limits, abuse the environment,[44] worship technology,[45] and succumb to the pride and elevation of human rationality as the arbiter of reality. This results in the individuation, fragmentation, and disembedding of human identity from its participation in the cosmos.

In turn, Panikkar's trans-historical consciousness includes the idea of ontonomy, the law of being, and seeks to recover the participatory character of human beings in the cosmos while preserving individuality for the sake of wholeness and harmony. In the attempt to restore a fragmented reality, Panikkar proposes an ontonomic conception of reality that integrates with rhythmic quality the space for every being its own wholeness via its participation as a part in the whole.[46] Panikkar's ontonomy is a "postmodern" conception of human religiosity that includes the individualistic tendencies of modern autonomy, but sees individualism not as fragmented or fractured because every person is seen as participating in the whole of reality, thus revitalizing human autonomy as participating harmoniously in the cosmos and with the divine without the fragmentation of the whole person. Fred Dallmayr states in sum: "Where 'heteronomy' designates a worldview relying on a hierarchical structure of reality regulating behavior from above, whereas 'autonomy' insists on radical human self-reliance and self-determination; 'ontonomy' finally refers to a perspective shunning both internal and external constitution and accentuating instead a web of (ontological) relationships."[47]

Panikkar does not advocate for a simplistic return to a pre-modern society, nor for the fragmented, fractured, and disembedded self of modernity that lacks its link to transcendence and its neglect of participating in nature. Rather Panikkar nuances ontonomy as maintaining a participatory ontology of human be-ing by participating as individual beings in the whole of reality. Panikkar calls this the trans-historical moment where the tension between both unity and distinction is maintained, that is, where wholeness is recaptured. It entails the recovery of the pre-historical (pre-modern) wholistic and constitutively relational experience of nature and the divine dimension in human experience while also maintaining the historical (modern) emphasis on the autonomy of the individual. Whereas the pre-historical lacks distinction and the historical lacks wholeness, the trans-historical consciousness seeks to recover an ontonomic difference/distinction-in-unity/wholeness and allow human beings to authentically live out in secular life the sacrality of ordinary life.

SACRED SECULARITY: THE SACRALIZATION OF ORDINARY LIFE

This section articulates Panikkar's notion of sacred secularity and demonstrates how it re-sacralizes ordinary life. It does so by articulating human beings as ritual beings. If humans are ritual beings, then it entails that they are in some sense religious beings. We can see this by developing Panikkar's theory of transmythicization and the mapping of human experience across history. By emphasizing the need in secular experience for liturgy in ordinary life,[48] Panikkar argues for the re-enchantment of secular experience and ordinary life through his idea of sacred secularity. Panikkar's postsecular vision is one that re-enchants and moves to re-sacralize ordinary life in ways that produces the sacred dimensions of ordinary life. But if Taylor sees the Protestant affirmation of ordinary life as a step in the process of secularization, Panikkar by contrast sees ordinary life as the space and place of its sacralization and trans/re-mythicization.

Taylor argues that the affirmation of the ordinary life has its roots in the Protestant Reformation's sacralization of ordinary life where daily vocations

152   *Chapter 7*

were given meaning, significance, and worth: "The original form of this affirmation was theological, and it involved a positive vision of ordinary life as hallowed by God, and this is what is seen as having a higher significance conferred on it by God and this life itself grounds the affirmation."[49] Tied to disenchantment was also the leveling of higher forms of life as glorifying God into secular vocations.[50] Ironically, the Protestant Reformation not only affirmed ordinary life as sacred, but, as Taylor argues, served as a starting point in the process of secularization. For Taylor, the affirmation of ordinary life unhooked from sacred time continued the process of secularization insofar as ordinary life was unhooked from its participation in transcendence through a univocal collapse of the necessity of sacred vocations into ordinary life in the process of reform.[51] Ruth Abbey argues that by affirming ordinary life, the Protestant Reformers believed "that a significant part of one's identity is expressed in the realms of work and family life, and that what happens in these domains makes a substantial contribution to one's sense of the value or meaning of life."[52]

The move of sacralizing ordinary life and human vocations as for the glory of God in the Protestant Reformation indicates for Taylor a crucial move that lead not only to the desacralization of ordinary life insofar as it became unhooked from the liturgical and participatory nature of time and vocation, but also to the disembedding of identity from its vertical axis insofar as it is negated for a horizontal immanence that lacks substantially the *quiddity* of its participation in something "more" and "other" than us—eclipsing and emptying ordinary life of anything greater or other than it insofar as we must now create and elevate immanent goods as of ultimate value.

For Panikkar, however, it is at the precise point of what went wrong for Taylor since the Protestant Reformation—the inverted secularization of ordinary life—that Panikkar's postsecular vision seeks to re-enchant human religiosity. For Panikkar the Protestant affirmation of ordinary life is correlated with the sacralization of work as the transmythicization of pre-modern, pre-historical worship as sacrifice. In Panikkar's account of historical consciousness, Hall argues that there is a transition in the historical consciousness from a theocosmic worldview to an anthropocosmic one. There is a

> movement towards human interiority and independence. In line with the secular insight into the ultimacy of time and history, Panikkar says that the most important ritual actions are those associated with secular activity and human work. In fact, "work is worship." It is also "heir to the traditional sacrifice" since work transforms temporal actions through meaningful participation in the world's destiny.[53]

Panikkar's Postsecular Vision
153

With the turn from sacrifice to work as worship between the pre-historical to historical consciousness there is a fundamental shift in understanding the notion of worship. Hall states that "Panikkar suggests that the transition from sacred to secular consciousness does not destroy but transmythicizes sacrificial ritual."[54] Panikkar states that

> Modern work claims to liberate Man from the strictures of time and to allow him both to rescue his life from the chains of a time-bound existence and to justify his life by allowing him to collaborate in the "salvation" of the World. All the traditional motives of sacrifice have been preserved in the process of being transplanted into another horizon. We have here a typical example of transmythicization.[55]

Panikkar's transmythicization of worship from sacrifice to work as a means to salvation implies that the shift in human consciousness between heteronomy to autonomy does not secularize worship, but rather transforms its function and how it functions. Work transforms worship's function insofar as our ordinary vocations symbolically reflect their sacralization and affirmation as worthy through their participation in the whole of reality. Likewise, *how* worship functions is symbolically transformed by reflecting our ultimate concern: what matters most to us and what we have faith in.[56]

Panikkar's notion of ontonomy furthers the re-sacralization of ordinary life insofar as it "has the ability to integrate the essential insights of both traditional religious rites and modern secular rituals. [Cosmo]theandric ontonomy, he says, forges a new relationship between the heavenly kingdom and the earthly city creating therein 'a possibility of regeneration without alienation.' This transformation of secular consciousness perceives in the 'temporal' flux of life a 'sacred' dimension."[57] Thus, Hall argues that Panikkar's ontonomic interpretation of "secularization represents the regaining of the sacramental structure of existence, the new awareness that the real full human life is worship, because it is the very expression of the mystery of existence."[58]

Panikkar's account of participation in the sacramental character of reality implies that secular action is transformed into worship insofar as it experiences a harmony between the three dimensions of reality. In turn, secular action is seen as worship, becomes sacralized, and transforms secular experience through his idea of sacred secularity. Panikkar's challenge to secularization is real. He advocates for a renewal of human experience insofar as it participates in the dynamism of reality. However, he is also aware of the dangers of both the secularization of worship and the worship of secularization. Dallmayr states that, "in the encounter of worship and the world, [Panikkar] notes, a mutual 'total risk' emerges: namely, that worship may wish to 'eliminate or anathematize secularization, as being the main evil confronting man,'

154   *Chapter 7*

while secularism may try to 'get rid of worship as being a remnant of an age dead and gone.'"[59]

By linking secular experience to human ritualistic action Panikkar renews secular experience by re-sacralizing human work as an act of worship. Hall states that "in a generic sense, worship and sacrifice are described as symbolic acts, arising from particular beliefs, and oriented towards human transcendence."[60] If in Panikkar, as Dallmayr argues, secularization is positively evaluated to display the sacred dimension of human action, this transforms the secular insofar as every action symbolically reflects the nature of being.[61] Here Panikkar argues for a sacred secularity wherein human action liturgically sacralizes the saeculum insofar as human beings participate with and in a cosmotheandric reality, and reflect ontonomously the inter-in-dependence of each dimension to reality.

Panikkar's kairological account of secularization implies that the experience of sacred secularity can be described by the mutual constitutiveness of a trinitarian experience of an integrally and relationally constituted reality. Thus "cosmotheandrism" implies secular experience as transformed by humanity's participation in reality as *homo liturgicus*. In human action not only is secular experience transformed by its participation in the divine, but material matter is inspirited and sanctified through its participation in God, while God is materially enpresented through human action.

Hall states for Panikkar "secular activity is considered to be sacred action insofar as it fulfills the criteria of ritual behavior."[62] For Panikkar sacred secularity entails the enpresenting of divine immanence in and through human action as we live in the cosmos. The secular does not lack transcendence because, rather than lacking vertical transcendence as in Taylor, Panikkar sees transcendence as immanent within human action, transforming it, sacralizing it as it participates harmoniously with divine ordering of the cosmos. Furthermore, "sacred secularity in Panikkar's thought implies the presence of the sacred in human worship mediating [and transforming] the secular with the presence of the sacred in [and through] human action."[63]

Panikkar's understanding of the divine is relationally constitutive to the reality of both human be-ing and is permeated in the cosmos precisely through his emphasis on its immanence to created reality. It entails a sacramental reality wherein human action participates in a sacred cosmos that finds itself relationally constituted by its dependency upon divine reality. Undergirding Panikkar's understanding of sacred secularity is a cosmotheandric reality that sees each of the three tripartite dimensions of reality as co-constitutive to reality in and through their participatory relationality with and in one another. Within a sacramental framework for secular life and action, not only are its ritual dynamics and habits constitutive of its orientation toward the divine as worship, but they entail that humans are inherently liturgical in such a way that ordinary life becomes re-sacralized.

If the modern worldview dis-enchants the world through an anthropocentric dominance over the natural world at the rejection of the divine, this entails that a secular world not only rejects transcendence but also its immanence in human action and ordinary life as an act of worship. However, with this disenchantment, Panikkar is key to hone in on the importance of divine immanence with, in, and to the world. If divine immanence is emphasized within the world, not only does the world become a sacramental reality where God's presence is experienced and known intimately, but it becomes intrinsic within a cosmotheandric conception of reality where the world and humanity are elevated to a level of ultimacy precisely through their constituted and constitutive relationship with the divine reality.

CONCLUSION: IMPLICATIONS OF PANIKKAR'S POSTSECULAR VISION

Gerard Hall argues that Panikkar advocates a "hermeneutics of secularization in terms of its impact on human consciousness and religious experience. This involves a description of his critiques of both traditional religion and contemporary secularization."[64] Panikkar's cosmotheandric vision for an ontonomically constituted reality finds in its sacramental reflection of reality, through human work and ritual, not only the re-mythicization of classical resourcement, but more properly the re-enchantment of secularity. Panikkar's kairological readings of history speak of a transmythicization of the cosmotheandric *mythos* which transforms how we perceive reality—as inherently sacred. It also emphasizes the constitutive relationships of cosmotheandric experience as the model by which the secular is renewed and re-enchanted. Sacred secularity for Panikkar implies the transformation of human religiosity in ways that finds ordinary life as inherently religious precisely within its liturgical expression of a sacramental reality.

This chapter has argued that Panikkar's postsecular vision is one inherently geared towards the re-enchantment, re-sacralization, and transformation of lived experience. Panikkar's postsecular vision sees human religiosity as enacted through human actions and the transformation of work and worship in the ordinary experiences of secular life. Panikkar's sacred secularity entails the transformation of lived experience in the saeculum. It is a religious transformation of everyday experience where what it means to be human means to be inherently religious in the very actions of human life and being. The tempiternal meeting between the sacred and the secular lies within the very experience of a cosmotheandric reality, and it is here that humanity

156 Chapter 7

is transformed: where the sacred and the secular meet in the very experience of life.

NOTES

1. Gerard Vincent Hall, "Raimon Panikkar's Hermeneutics of Religious Pluralism," Catholic University of America (Ann Arbor, MI: UMI Dissertation Services, 1994); Fred Dallmayr, "Rethinking Secularism (with Raimon Panikkar)," *The Review of Politics* 61, no. 4 (1999): 715–35; Fred Dallmayr, "A Secular Age?: Reflections on Taylor and Panikkar," *International Journal of the Philosophy of Religion* 71, no. 3 (2012): 189–204.

2. C.f. Peter Berger, *The Sacred Canopy: Elements of a Sociological Theory of Religion* (New York: Anchor Books, 1969); Thomas Luckmann, *The Invisible Religion* (New York: Macmillan Company, 1967); Charles Taylor, *A Secular Age* (Cambridge, MA: The Belknap Press of Harvard University Press, 2007), 15–17.

3. Taylor, *A Secular Age*, 431–33.

4. This is contested by José Casanova, *Public Religions in the Modern World* (Chicago, IL: The University of Chicago Press, 1994).

5. Tone Svetelj, "Rereading Modernity—Charles Taylor on Its Genesis and Prospects" (Chestnut Hill, MA: Boston College, 2012), 449.

6. Svetelj, "Rereading Modernity," 455–56.

7. Charles Taylor, "Modes of Secularism," in *Secularism and Its Critics*, ed. Rajeev Bhargava (Delhi: Oxford University Press, 1998), 31–53.

8. Pádraig Hogan, "Religious Inheritances of Learning and the 'Unquiet Frontiers of Modernity,'" in *The Taylor Effect: Responding to a Secular Age*, ed. Ian Leask et al. (Newcastle upon Tyne: Cambridge Scholars Publishing, 2010), 134–45, 134–35.

9. Paul D. Janz, "Transcendence, 'Spin,' and the Jamesian Open Space," in *Aspiring to Fullness in a Secular Age: Essays on Religion and Theology in the Work of Charles Taylor*, eds., Carlos Colorado and Justin Klassen (Notre-Dame, IN: University of Notre-Dame Press, 2014), 39–70, 50; Taylor, *A Secular Age*, 25–26.

10. Svetelj, "Rereading Modernity," 395.

11. Ruth Abbey, *Philosophy Now: Charles Taylor* (Princeton, NJ: Princeton University Press, 2000), 200–205.

12. Svetelj, "Rereading Modernity," 395–96.

13. Raimon Panikkar, *Sacred Secularity*, ed. Milena Carrara Pavan, Vol. XI, XII vols., Opera Omnia (Maryknoll, NY: Orbis Books, 2022), 4–7.

14. Panikkar, *Sacred Secularity*, 6.

15. Raimon Panikkar, *Worship and Secular Man* (Maryknoll, NY: Orbis Books, 1973), 54.

16. Hall, "Raimon Panikkar's Hermeneutics of Religious Pluralism," 162.

17. Panikkar, *Sacred Secularity*, 7, 9, 18.

18. Panikkar, *Sacred Secularity*, 9–10.

19. Panikkar, *Sacred Secularity*, 9.

20. Panikkar, *Sacred Secularity*, 9–10.

21. Panikkar, *Worship and Secular Man*, 13.

22. Hall, "Raimon Panikkar's Hermeneutics of Religious Pluralism," 162.

23. Panikkar, *Sacred Secularity*, 18.

24. Francis X. D'Sa, "Time, History, and Christophany," in *Raimon Panikkar: A Companion to His Life and Thought*, eds., Peter Phan and Young-Chan Ro (Cambridge, UK: James Clarke and Co., 2018), 171–93, 181; Raimon Panikkar, *The Cosmotheandric Experience: Emerging Religious Consciousness*, ed. Scott Eastham (Maryknoll, NY: Orbis Books, 1993), 80–82.

25. Panikkar, *The Cosmotheandric Experience*, 36.

26. Panikkar, *The Cosmotheandric Experience,* 90.

27. Panikkar, *The Cosmotheandric Experience*, 103.

28. D'Sa, "Time, History, and Christophany," 182f.

29. Panikkar, *The Cosmotheandric Experience*, 106; D'Sa, "Time, History, and Christophany," 182f.

30. Panikkar, *The Cosmotheandric Experience*, 109; D'Sa, "Time, History, and Christophany," 183f.

31. Panikkar, *The Cosmotheandric Experience*, 115, 118.

32. Gerard Hall, "Anthropology: Being Human," in *Raimon Panikkar: A Companion to His Life and Thought*, eds., Peter Phan and Young-Chan Ro (Cambridge, UK: James Clarke and Co., 2018), 194–216, 209–10.

33. Panikkar, *The Cosmotheandric Experience*, 91; D'Sa, "Time, History, and Christophany," 183.

34. Hall, "Anthropology: Being Human," 209–10.

35. Panikkar, *Sacred Secularity*, 32–33.

36. Charles Taylor, *Dilemmas and Connections* (Cambridge, MA: Harvard University Press, 2011), 217ff.

37. C.f. Charles Taylor, *Modern Social Imaginaries* (Durham: Duke University Press, 2004), 49–67; Charles Taylor, *A Secular Age*, 159–211; Taylor, *Dilemmas and Connections*, 217–29; Ruth Abbey, *Philosophy Now: Charles Taylor*, 204.

38. Hall, "Raimon Panikkar's Hermeneutics of Religious Pluralism," 66.

39. Taylor, *Modern Social Imaginaries*, 49–67.

40. On the transition from physis to natura C.f. John Montag, SJ, "Revelation: The False Legacy of Suárez," in *Radical Orthodoxy: A New Theology*, eds., John Milbank, Catherine Pickstock, and Graham Ward (New York: Routledge, 1999), 38–63, 45.

41. The domination and control of physical reality, though argued to have roots in Christianity is something postmodern philosophy and theology contests. John Milbank would call this an "ontology of violence." C.f. John Milbank, *Theology and Social Theory*, Second Edition (Malden, MA: Blackwell Publishing, 2006), 278–326.

42. Panikkar, *The Cosmotheandric Experience*.

43. Panikkar, *The Cosmotheandric Experience*, 32–46.

44. Anthony Savari Raj, *Ecosophical Justice* (Bangalore: Capuchin Publication Trust, 2010); Anthony Savari Raj, *A New Hermeneutic of Reality: Raimon Panikkar's Cosmotheandric Vision* (New York: Peter Lang, 1998), 117–32.

45. Raimon Panikkar, *The Rhythm of Being: The Unbroken Trinity* (Maryknoll, NY: Orbis Books, 2010), 368–404.

46. Panikkar, *The Rhythm of Being*, 53.

47. Dallmayr, "Rethinking Secularism (with Raimon Panikkar)," 725.

48. Panikkar, *Worship and Secular Man*, 59–62.

49. Charles Taylor, *Sources of the Self: The Making of the Modern Identity* (Cambridge, MA: The Belknap Press of Harvard University Press, 1989), 104.

50. Abbey, *Philosophy Now: Charles Taylor*, 204–5.

51. Abbey, *Philosophy Now: Charles Taylor*, 89–90.

52. Abbey, *Philosophy Now: Charles Taylor*, 89; C.f. Charles Taylor, *Human Agency and Language*, Philosophical Papers 1 (Cambridge, UK: Cambridge University Press, 1985), 155, 255; Charles Taylor, *The Malaise of Modernity: The CBC Massey Lectures* (Toronto: House of Anansi Press, 1991), 45, 49–50.

53. Hall, "Raimon Panikkar's Hermeneutics of Religious Pluralism," 172.

54. Hall, "Raimon Panikkar's Hermeneutics of Religious Pluralism," 172.

55. Raimon Panikkar, "Time and Sacrifice: The Sacrifice of Time and the Ritual of Modernity," in *Proceedings of the III Conference of the International Society for the Study of Time*, eds., J. T. Fraser, N. Lawrence, and D. Park, vol. 3, The Study of Time (New York, Heidelberg, and Berlin: Springer-Verlag, 1978), 683–725, 706f.

56. Paul Tillich, *The Dynamics of Faith* (New York: Perennial Classics, 2001).

57. Hall, "Raimon Panikkar's Hermeneutics of Religious Pluralism," 175.

58. Panikkar, *Worship and Secular Man*, 92.

59. Dallmayr, "Rethinking Secularism (with Raimon Panikkar)," 723.

60. Hall, "Raimon Panikkar's Hermeneutics of Religious Pluralism," 173.

61. Dallmayr, "Rethinking Secularism (with Raimon Panikkar)," 723–24; Hall, "Raimon Panikkar's Hermeneutics of Religious Pluralism," 162–81.

62. Hall, "Raimon Panikkar's Hermeneutics of Religious Pluralism," 171.

63. Andrew D. Thrasher, "A Glossary of Panikkarean Terms," in *Raimon Panikkar: A Companion to His Life and Thought*, eds., Peter Phan and Young-Chan Ro (Cambridge, UK: James Clarke and Co., 2018), 271–81, 280.

64. Hall, "Raimon Panikkar's Hermeneutics of Religious Pluralism," 5–6.

Conclusion

An Advaitic Modernity?

At the outset of this book, it asked the question, "What does Panikkar have to do with postmodern philosophical theology?" Throughout the book, it has argued that Panikkar offers an Indic spin to postmodern philosophical theology, particularly through an advaitic interpretation of modernity. It has done so through analyses of four organizing themes—cosmotheandrism (chapters one and two), advaitic metaphysics (chapters three and four), postmodern ontology (chapters five and six), and sacred secularity (chapter seven). Furthermore, it has implicitly addressed several problems that have been raised throughout this book around the philosophical discourses of metaphysics, ontology, and anthropology, particularly the problems of being and time, meaning, individualism, and alterity through the lens of advaita. Not the least, it has also implicitly articulated an advaitic theological resolution to the ontological distinction between God and creation throughout its analyses of transcendence and immanence, infinitude and finitude, and eternity and time. This concluding chapter seeks to explicitly address each of these themes, problems, and issues through a constructive articulation of an advaitic critique of modernity.

ORGANIZING THEMES

This book was organized around four central themes that are either Panikkar's own terms or were interpreted from Panikkar in dialogue with other philosophers and theologians. First, chapters one and two particularly addressed Panikkar's understanding of cosmotheandrism, laying out not only how it is cross-culturally influenced and articulated, but also how it is implicitly shaped by a relational ontology that presupposes both the trinitarian structure of reality as cosmic/material, human, and divine and the rejection of an ontological distinction between God and creation. Panikkar's understanding of cosmotheandric metaphysics is at once both intrinsically inter-related and can serve as a cross-cultural metaphysics through which particular religious theologies may be articulated. Second, chapters three and four addressed Panikkar's advaitic metaphysics in relationship to the ontology and metaphysics of Martin Heidegger and William Desmond. While the analyses in chapter three addressed both Panikkar's indebtedness to Heidegger as well as Panikkar's tempiternal solutions to Heidegger's onto-theological problems of Being and time, chapter four offered a more comparative analysis of how Panikkar's understanding of advaita and William Desmond's idea of *metaxu* articulate two examples of contemporary metaphysics that create the space and articulations by which immanence may be metaphysically imagined as open to transcendence.

Third, chapters five and six addressed an interpretation of postmodern ontology and argued how Panikkar's own philosophy and theology finds resonances with contemporary philosophical theology. Chapter five in particular addressed the problems and promises of a postmodern ontology through a critique of modernity's overemphasis on individualism and autonomy and how this creates an ontological crisis of meaning and authenticity that can be overcome through a return in ontological faith to God as the ground of what it means to be. Likewise, chapter six addressed the notion of a postmodern ontology, but aimed in particular at the question of the recovery of meaning through a genealogical analysis of modernity that read Raimon Panikkar alongside the contributions of both Charles Taylor and the Radical Orthodoxy Movement.

Fourth, chapter seven in turn analyzed Panikkar's postsecular vision through a dialogue with the postsecular contributions of Charles Taylor and argued how Panikkar's idea of sacred secularity offers postsecular revisionings of modernity in its ability to resacralize modernity without desecularizing it. This means that Panikkar's postsecular contributions are firmly situated in his notions of sacred secularity and they offer helpful ways of rethinking the relationship between the sacred and the secular in late modernity. While chapter seven focuses on Panikkar's reformulations of Taylor's postsecular contributions, the reader should note that the sociological and theological implications and contributions of Charles Taylor were the focus of the author's doctoral dissertation. This book should be seen as an advaitic approach to modernity, while my doctoral dissertation should be seen as a more thorough engagement with postsecularism and the work of Charles Taylor around the idea of incarnation.

Conclusion

THE PROBLEMS OF MEANING, INDIVIDUALISM, ALTERITY

This book has also raised questions around the problems of meaning, individualism, and alterity. The question of the meaning of being—the ontological question—remains a central concern developed across this book and it is the hinge by which the problems of meaning, individualism, and alterity are examined. The problem of meaning entails the questions of authenticity, depth, and faith. Authenticity becomes a problem when there is a lack of ontological depth, or a ground on which one's existence may be deemed meaningful. In turn, this book has argued how religious faith provides that ground of meaning, depth, and authenticity. The problem of individualism is also shaped by the problem of meaning, but in particular is linked to the genealogical development of modernity and secularization where the autonomy of the human person—or rather anthropocentrism, instrumental reasoning and representation epistemology, and the unhooking of the being of creation from its dependency upon God—allows the space for an understanding of reality in which the transcendence of God is eclipsed and becomes irrelevant and inaccessible.

While there are theological shifts that contribute to this developed by those found in the *Nouvelle Theologie* movement, there are also modern shifts that lead to this possibility related to the Protestant Reformation, European Enlightenment, modern secularization, and postmodern culture that have dislocated the legitimacy of the religious over modern society and have questioned the value of religious and theological answers to the problems of modernity. In turn the problem of alterity plays a central role throughout this book because of the problem it poses of *difference*. Alterity exposes us to another that is not reducible to us—it exposes us to difference in ways that cannot be subsumed into the same. The problem alterity generated however, is how to make sense of difference in ways that opens the space for the participation in transcendence and how transcendence confronts us with the otherness of not only other human beings, but also of the cosmos and God in ways that are not reducible to human individuals. Alterity confronts us with the reality of non-reductive relationality and asks us to be relationally, meaningfully, and morally constituted by and constitutive of what it means to be as a cosmotheandric person who microcosmically reflects a macrocosmic reality.

162   *Conclusion*

METAPHYSICS, ONTOLOGY, ANTHROPOLOGY

Philosophically, this book has also engaged with at least three philosophical discourses: metaphysics, ontology, and anthropology. In its articulations of a cosmotheandric metaphysics, this book has opened postmodern philosophical theology to the reality that we must begin to engage not only with theological questions about God, but also about how to confront and integrate our theological convictions with the cosmological and anthropological implications of what it means to be material and human. Here Panikkar's background in scientific, philosophical, and theological discourses may prove fruitful grounds for engagement.

In turn, this book has especially emphasized the role of ontology as a central discourse of engagement. Especially working with, building on, and critiquing the fundamental ontology of Martin Heidegger, the continental tradition and its influences on postmodern philosophical theology are inescapable. But this book has also shown how Heidegger is inescapable when discussing the ontological implications and insights of Raimon Panikkar. The question of the meaning of Being for Panikkar, however, is not limited to *Dasein* as it is for Heidegger. Panikkar's questioning of the meaning of being draws us into a cosmotheandric metaphysics that is shaped by his advaitic understanding of reality. Panikkar's advaita in particular rejects the ontological distinction between God and creation and rather sees transcendence and immanence as co-participatory and shaped by a harmonious dynamism of inter-relatedness of the divine, the cosmic, and the human dimensions of reality.

Finally, the anthropological contributions of Panikkar are also of immense important. This book has read Panikkar's high theological anthropology through the lens of both his advaitic critique of modernity as well as in dialogue with western philosophers and theologians. Panikkar has an immensely high view of what it means to be human, and he integrates scientific, philosophical, and theological discourses into his understanding of what it means to be a cosmotheandric human person.

ADVAITIC THEOLOGICAL RECONCILIATIONS

Finally, this book has also offered an advaitic theological reconciliation or resolution to the ontological distinction between God and creation. If indeed modernity is marked by the inaccessibility of divine transcendence through modern discourses—both theological and secular—then it poses a question of how to relate and bridge the divide between God and creation, transcendence and immanence, infinitude and finitude, time and eternity. Panikkar's answer

Conclusion 163

is to posit divine immanence in, with, and to creation. While this is a way in which to address the problem of divine inaccessibility, it may indeed go too far in its rejection of the ontological distinction between God and creation, at least coming from an orthodox Christian theological point of view.[1] And yet, his cosmotheandric understanding of reality, advaitic metaphysics, and tempiternity each generate stimulating ways of rethinking the problem of the divide between transcendence and immanence, theological infinitude and its enpresenting within finite existence, and the temporally co-participatory co-constitution of what it means to be divine, cosmic, and human. The tempiternal relationship between time and eternity and Panikkar's emphasis on divine immanence offer particular ways of imagining the participation of time in eternity and of eternity in time.[2]

CONCLUSIONS AND CONTRIBUTIONS

Throughout this book I have argued that Raimon Panikkar was an Indian postmodern philosophical theologian. He offers advaitic spins upon contemporary Western philosophical theology in ways that not only generates new possibilities for thinking about God, ontology, secularity, modernity, and metaphysics. He also generates unique answers to the problems of modernity by problematizing how divine immanence may transform and re-enchant contemporary Anglo-Catholic philosophical theology. If the problem of modernity lays in its overemphasis on divine transcendence—to the point that the divine is no longer immanent to or in this world—Panikkar's solution to this problem is to rearticulate through an advaitic spin what divine immanence would look like in an advaitic modernity.

The contributions of Raimon Panikkar to philosophical theology are astounding. His plurivocal metaphysics articulates new ways of imagining the relationship not only between religions, but more importantly of the relationship between God and creation and the tempiternal relationship between Being and beings in time. His cosmotheandric ontonomy offers a symbolic and relational ontology that articulates a plurivocity of cosmotheandric theologies that find their source in the metaphysics of a divine mystery that tempiternally reconciles being in time with its experience of divine eternity in the time of becoming.

Furthermore, his postmodern ontology critiques modernity in agonistic ways that also complement Christian critiques of modernity. By reading his postmodern ontology as an opening of/to faith after the closure of faith in modernity alongside Taylor and Milbank et al.'s genealogical critique of modernity, this book has argued how Panikkar offers important resources for rethinking the problems of modernity and the presence of faith and God

164   *Conclusion*

in lived religious experience. His advaitic and cosmotheandric metaphysics allows us to speak of God from immanence in similar ways to William Desmond's metaxological metaphysics of God. Both Panikkar and Desmond speak of transcendence *from immanence*. It is only from our immanent experience that we can speak of God. This means that something about immanence not only echoes transcendence, but more particularly for Panikkar that immanence echoes the divine mystery.

By reading Panikkar with philosophers and theologians like Charles Taylor, Martin Heidegger, William Desmond, and John Milbank and the Radical Orthodoxy Movement, this book has argued that Panikkar has much to contribute to the discourse of postmodern philosophical theology. His pluralistic and advaitic spins on metaphysics, theology, and ontology offer important reformulations to problems in contemporary thought through his theologically inter-religious turn to the possibility of rethinking reality not only without an ontological distinction between God and creation, but more importantly of rethinking the nature of the divine as immanent to and in creation.

Furthermore, by reading Panikkar alongside these thinkers, what we find is an agonistic affinity with them. Certainly, I think, John Milbank would chafe at being compared positively with Panikkar. I think William Desmond would find my arguments for his affinities with Panikkar strange but astonishing. Heidegger's friendship with Panikkar was characterized by Panikkar as shy lovers who intimately shared their minds with one another.[3] And yet, I think Panikkar's theological openness to thinking faith philosophically was probably something Heidegger puzzled over throughout his life. I would like to think that Panikkar opened again to Heidegger the possibility of faith as evidenced in one of Heidegger's last letters: a poem to Panikkar and his students that expresses his anticipation of entering into the silence that his writings echoed since *Being and Time* as his own-most end: Death.[4]

Fred Dallmayr has already addressed the affinities between Panikkar and Charles Taylor, and Dallmayr's point remains the same here: Panikkar is addressing issues from a pluralistic perspective. This book has sought to analyze the implications of Panikkar's pluralistic perspective in contemporary Anglo-Catholic philosophical theology through an analysis of their common critique of modernity. Each of these thinkers are addressing in various ways how to conceive of transcendence after modernity's overemphasis on divine transcendence to its exclusion in a disenchanted natural world. By reading Panikkar's advaitic critique of modernity with these thinkers, this book has demonstrated his worth in rethinking modernity as an Indian postmodern philosophical theologian.

While this book has engaged the question of what Panikkar offers to postmodern philosophical theology, the implications of Raimon Panikkar's

Conclusion 165

philosophical and theological insights cannot be underestimated, even where his ideas may not align with theological orthodoxy. This book has argued that Panikkar offers important insights into rethinking traditionally Western philosophical and theological themes through the lens of advaita, and indeed it has argued how someone who is both Western, Catholic, and Indian can stimulate the postmodern philosophical and theological world. I hope to write two more books on Panikkar, one engaging him with contemporary Christian theology—with attention to contemporary Catholic and Protestant theological discourses alongside the doctrines of Trinity, Christ, Creation, and Eschatology—and another to examine his advaitic confluences with and Indic interpretations of the continental philosophical tradition—in particular with Martin Heidegger, Edmund Husserl, Hans-Georg Gadamer, Emmanuel Levinas, Martin Buber and others around the themes of religious otherness and experience, apophatic silence, personalism, Hindu phenomenology, and inter-religious hermeneutics.

NOTES

1. I plan to pursue this line of thought in another project on Panikkar in dialogue with Christian theology.

2. I have already begun exploring this in a chapter on eschatology from the planned book on Panikkar and Christian theology.

3. Raimon Panikkar, *Philosophical and Theological Thought*, ed. Milena Carrara Pavan, Vol. X.2, XII vols., Opera Omnia (Maryknoll, NY: Orbis Books, 2021), 485–90.

4. Panikkar, *Philosophical and Theological Thought*, 488–90.

Bibliography

Abbey, Ruth. "A Secular Age: The Missing Question Mark." In *The Taylor Effect: Responding to a Secular Age*, edited by Ian Leask, Eoin Cassidy, Alan Kearns, Fainche Ryan, and Mary Shanahan, 8–25. Newcastle Upon Tyne: Cambridge Scholars Publishing, 2010.

———, ed. *Charles Taylor*. Cambridge, UK: Cambridge University Press, 2004.

———. *Philosophy Now: Charles Taylor*. Princeton, NJ: Princeton University Press, 2000.

Baudrillard, Jean. *Simulations*. Translated by Paul Foss, Paul Patton, and Philip Beitchman. Fourteenth. USA: Semiotext[e], 1983.

———. *Simulations and Simulacra*. Translated by Sheila Faria Glaser. Ann Arbor: The University of Michigan Press, 1994.

Bengtson, Josef. *Explorations in Post-Secular Metaphysics*. New York: Palgrave Macmillan, 2016.

Bentley Hart, David. *The Beauty of the Infinite: The Aesthetics of Christian Truth*. Grand Rapids, MI: William B. Eerdmans, 2003.

Berger, Douglas. "Acquiring Emptiness: Interpreting Nagarjuna's MMK 24:18." *Philosophy East and West* 60, no. 1 (2010): 40–64.

Berger, Peter. *The Sacred Canopy: Elements of a Sociological Theory of Religion*. New York: Anchor Books, 1967.

Betz, John R. "Overcoming the Forgetfulness of Metaphysics: The More Original Philosophy of William Desmond." In *William Desmond and Contemporary Theology*, edited by Christopher Ben Simpson and Brenden Thomas Sammon, 57–91. Notre-Dame, IN: University of Notre-Dame Press, 2017.

Burrell, David D. "Creator/Creatures Relation: 'The Distinction' vs. 'Onto-Theology.'" *Faith and Philosophy* 25, no. 2 (2008): 177–89.

Camus, Albert. *The Stranger*. New York: Vintage, 1989.

Carman, Taylor. "The Principle of Phenomenology." In *The Cambridge Companion to Heidegger*, edited by Charles Guignon, Second Edition, 97–119. Cambridge, UK: Cambridge University Press, 2006.

Carson, D. A. *Telling the Truth: Evangelizing Postmoderns*. Grand Rapids, MI: Zondervan, 2000.

168 Bibliography

Casanova, José. *Public Religions in the Modern World*. Chicago, IL: The University of Chicago Press, 1994.

Cousins, Ewert. "Panikkar's Advaitic Trinitarianism." In *The Intercultural Challenge of Raimon Panikkar*, edited by Joseph Prabhu, 119–30. Maryknoll, NY: Orbis Books, 1996.

Cross, Richard. "Duns Scotus and Suarez at the Origins of Modernity." In *Deconstructing Radical Orthodoxy*, edited by Wayne J. Hankey and Douglas Hedley, 85–102. Burlington, VT: Ashgate, 2005.

———. "'Where Angels Fear to Tread': Duns Scouts and Radical Orthodoxy." *Antonianum* 76 (2001): 7–41.

Cunningham, Conor. *Genealogy of Nihilism*. New York: Routledge, 2002.

———. "Language: Wittgenstein after Theology." In *Radical Orthodoxy: A New Theology*, edited by John Milbank, Catherine Pickstock, and Graham Ward, 64–90. New York and London: Routledge, 1999.

Dallmayr, Fred. "A Secular Age?: Reflections on Taylor and Panikkar." *International Journal of the Philosophy of Religion* 71, no. 3 (2012): 189–204.

———. "Rethinking Secularism (with Raimon Panikkar)." *The Review of Politics* 61, no. 4 (1999): 715–35.

De Certeau, Michel. *The Practice of Everyday Life*. Translated by Steven Randall. Vol. 1. 2 vols. Berkeley, CA: University of California Press, 1984.

De Lubac, SJ, Henri. *Augustinianism and Modern Theology*. Translated by Lancelot Sheppard. New York: Crossroads Publishing, 2000.

———. *The Mystery of the Supernatural*. Translated by Rosemary Sheed. New York: Herder and Herder, 2022.

Deleuze, Gilles. *Difference and Repetition*. Translated by Paul Patton. New York: Columbia University Press, 1994.

Deleuze, Gilles, and Felix Guattari. *What Is Philosophy?* Translated by Hugh Tomlinson and Graham Burchell. New York: Columbia University Press, 1994.

Desmond, William. *Being and the Between*. Albany: State University of New York Press, 1995.

———. "Between System and Poetics: On the Practices of Philosophy." In *Between System and Poetics: William Desmond and Philosophy after Dialectic*, edited by Thomas A. F. Kelly, 13–36. London and New York: Routledge, 2007.

———. *Ethics and the Between*. Albany, NY: State University of New York Press, 2001.

———. *God and the Between*. Malden, MA: Blackwell, 2008.

———. "Wording the Between." In *The William Desmond Reader*, edited by Christopher Ben Simpson, 195–227. Albany: State University of New York Press, 2012.

Dostal, Robert J. "Time and Phenomenology in Husserl and Heidegger." In *The Cambridge Companion to Heidegger*, edited by Charles Guignon, Second Edition, 120–48. Cambridge, UK: Cambridge University Press, 2006.

Dreher, Rod. *The Benedict Option: A Strategy for Christians in a Post-Christian Nation*. New York: Sentinel, 2017.

Bibliography

D'Sa, Francis X. "How Trinitarian Is Panikkar's Trinity." *CIRPIT Review* 3 (2012): 33–50.

———. "Time, History, and Christophany." In *Raimon Panikkar: A Companion to His Life and Thought*, edited by Peter Phan and Young-chan Ro, 171–93. Cambridge, UK: James Clarke & Co., 2018.

Frede, Dorothea. "The Question of Being: Heidegger's Project." In *The Cambridge Companion to Heidegger*, edited by Charles Guignon, Second Edition, 42–69. Cambridge, UK: Cambridge University Press, 2006.

Gadamer, Hans-Georg. *Truth and Method*. Translated by Joel Weinsheimer and Donald Marshall. Second Revised Edition. New York: Continuum, 1999.

Gardner, Patrick X. "God Beyond and Between: Desmond, Przywara, and Catholic Metaphysics." In *William Desmond and Contemporary Theology*, edited by Christopher Ben Simpson and Brenden Thomas Sammon, 165–90. Notre-Dame, IN: University of Notre-Dame Press, 2017.

Garfield, Jay. "Dependent Arising and the Emptiness of Emptiness: Why Did Nagarjuna Start with Causation?" *Philosophy East and West* 44, no. 2 (1994): 219–50.

Garfield, Jay, and Graham Priest. "Nagarjuna and the Limits of Thought." *Philosophy East and West* 53, no. 1 (2003): 1–21.

Gelven, Michael. *A Commentary of Heidegger's Being and Time: A Section by Section Interpretation*. New York: Harper and Row, 1970.

Grenz, Stanley. *A Primer on Postmodernism*. Grand Rapids, MI: William B. Eerdmans, 1996.

———. *The Social God and the Relational Self: A Trinitarian Theology of the Imago Dei*. Grand Rapids, MI: William B. Eerdmans, 2001.

Hall, Gerard. "Anthropology: Being Human." In *Raimon Panikkar: A Companion to His Life and Thought*, edited by Peter Phan and Young-chan Ro, 194–216. Cambridge, UK: James Clarke & Co., 2018.

Hall, Gerard Vincent. *Raimon Panikkar's Hermeneutics of Religious Pluralism*. Catholic University of America. Ann Arbor, MI: UMI Dissertation Services, 1994.

Hanby, Michael. *Augustine and Descartes*. London and New York: Routledge, 2003.

Heidegger, Martin. *Being and Time*. Translated by John MacQuarrie and Edward Robinson. New York: HarperCollins, 2008.

———. *Identity and Difference*. Translated by Joan Stambough. Chicago, IL: The University of Chicago Press, 2002.

———. *Introduction to Metaphysics*. Translated by Gregory Fried and Richard Polt. New Haven, CT: Yale University Press, 2014.

———. *On the Way to Language*. New York: HarperOne, 1982.

———. *Poetry, Language, and Thought*. New York: Harper Perennial Modern Classics, 2013.

———. *The Basic Problems of Phenomenology*. Translated by Albert Hofstadter. Revised Edition. Bloomington and Indianapolis: Indiana University Press, 1988.

———. "The Origin of the Work of Art." In *Basic Writings*, translated by David Farrell Krell, 138–212. New York: Harper Collins, 2008.

170 *Bibliography*

Hoffman, Piotr. "Death, Time, History: Division II of *Being and Time*." In *The Cambridge Companion to Heidegger*, edited by Charles Guignon, Second Edition, 222–40. Cambridge, UK: Cambridge University Press, 2006.

Hogan, Pádraig. "Religious Inheritances of Learning and the 'Unquiet Frontiers of Modernity.'" In *The Taylor Effect: Responding to a Secular Age*, edited by Ian Leask, Eoin Cassidy, Alan Kearns, Fainche Ryan, and Mary Shanahan, 134–45. Newcastle upon Tyne: Cambridge Scholars Publishing, 2010.

Horan, Daniel P. *Postmodernity and Univocity: A Critical Account of Radical Orthodoxy and John Duns Scotus*. Lanham, MD: Fortress Press, 2014.

Jager, Colin. "This Detail, This History: Charles Taylor's Romanticism." In *Varieties of Secularism in a Secular Age*, edited by Michael Warner, Jonathan VanAntwerpen, and Craig Calhoun, 166–92. Cambridge, MA: Harvard University Press, 2010.

James, Ian. *The Fragmentary Demand: An Introduction to the Philosophy of Jean-Luc Nancy*. Stanford, CA: Stanford University Press, 2006.

Janz, Paul D. "Transcendence, 'Spin,' and the Jamesian Open Space." In *Aspiring to Fullness in a Secular Age: Essays on Religion and Theology in the Work of Charles Taylor*, edited by Carlos Colorado and Justin Klassen, 39–70. Notre-Dame, IN: University of Notre-Dame Press, 2014.

Jones, Richard. *Nagarjuna: Buddhism's Most Important Philosopher*. Revised and Expanded Edition. New York: Jackson Square Books, 2018.

Kärkkäinen, Veli-Matti. *Trinity and Religious Pluralism: The Doctrine of the Trinity in Christian Theology of Religions*. Burlington, VT: Ashgate, 2004.

———. *Trinity and Revelation*. Vol. 2. 5 vols. A Constructive Theology for the Pluralistic World. Grand Rapids, MI: William B. Eerdmans, 2014.

Kierkegaard, Søren. *The Sickness unto Death*. Translated by Howard Hong and Edna Hong. Princeton, NJ: Princeton University Press, 1983.

Kolakowski, Leszek. *Why Is There Something Rather Than Nothing?* Translated by Agnieszka Kolakowska. New York: Basic Books, 2007.

Komulainen, Jyri. *An Emerging Cosmotheandric Religion? Raimon Panikkar's Pluralistic Theology of Religions*. Leiden and Boston: Brill, 2005.

Laitinen, Arto. "A Critique of Charles Taylor's Notions of Moral Sources and Constitutive Goods." *Acta Philosophica Fennica* 76 (2004): 73–104.

Levinas, Emmanuel. *Basic Philosophical Writings*. Edited by Adrian Peperzak, Simon Critchley, and Robert Bernasconi. Bloomington: Indiana University Press, 1996.

———. *Otherwise than Being, or Beyond Essence*. Translated by Alphonso Lingis. Pittsburgh, PA: Duquesne University Press, 1998.

———. *Totality and Infinity: An Essay on Exteriority*. Translated by Alphonso Lingis. Pittsburgh, PA: Duquesne University Press, 1969.

Lingis, Alphonso. "Translator's Introduction." In *Otherwise than Being, or Beyond Essence*, xvii–xlv. Pittsburgh, PA: Duquesne University Press, 1998.

Luckmann, Thomas. *The Invisible Religion*. New York: Macmillan Company, 1967.

Lyotard, Jean-Francois. *The Postmodern Condition: A Report on Knowledge*. Vol. 10. Theory and History of Literature. Minneapolis: University of Minnesota Press, 1984.

Bibliography

MacIntyre, Alasdair. *After Virtue: A Study of Moral Theory*. Second Edition. Notre-Dame, IN: University of Notre-Dame Press, 1984.

Marsh, James L. "William Desmond's Overcoming of the Overcoming of Metaphysics." In *Between System and Poetics: William Desmond and Philosophy after Dialectic*, edited by Thomas A. F. Kelly, 95–105. London and New York: Routledge, 2007.

McPherson, David. "Re-Enchanting the World: An Examination of Ethics, Religion, and Their Relationship in the Work of Charles Taylor." Milwaukee, WI: Marquette University, 2013.

Merleau-Ponty, Maurice. *Phenomenology of Perception*. New York: Routledge, 2013.

Milbank, John. *Beyond Secular Order*. Malden, MA: Blackwell, 2013.

———. "Knowledge: The Theological Critique of Philosophy in Hamann and Jacobi." In *Radical Orthodoxy: A New Theology*, edited by John Milbank, Catherine Pickstock, and Graham Ward, 21–37. New York and London: Routledge, 1999.

———. "Only Theology Overcomes Metaphysics." In *The Word Made Strange: Theology, Language, and Culture*, 36–52. Malden, MA: Blackwell, 1997.

———. "Political Theology and the New Science of Politics." In *The Radical Orthodoxy Reader*, edited by John Milbank and Simon Oliver, 178–96. New York and London: Routledge, 2009.

———. "Scholasticism, Modernism, and Modernity." *Modern Theology* 22, no. 4 (2006): 651–71.

———. "The Linguistic Turn as a Theological Turn." In *The Word Made Strange: Theology, Language, and Culture*, 84–120. Malden, MA: Blackwell, 1997.

———. "The Second Difference." In *The Word Made Strange: Theology, Language, and Culture*, 171–93. Malden, MA: Blackwell, 1997.

———. *Theology and Social Theory*. Second Edition. Malden, MA: Blackwell, 2006.

Milbank, John, Catherine Pickstock, and Graham Ward, eds. *Radical Orthodoxy: A New Theology*. London and New York: Routledge, 1999.

Milbank, John, Graham Ward, and Catherine Pickstock. "Introduction: Suspending the Material: The Turn of Radical Orthodoxy." In *Radical Orthodoxy: A New Theology*, edited by John Milbank, Graham Ward, and Catherine Pickstock, 1–20. London and New York: Routledge, 1999.

Min, Anselm. "Panikkar's Radical Trinitarianism: Reflections on Panikkar's Transformation of the Christian Trinity into Cosmotheandrism." *CIRPIT Review* 6 (2015): 75–100.

———. "The Trinity and the Cosmotheandric Vision: Reflections on Panikkar's Intercultural Theology." In *Raimon Panikkar: A Companion to His Life and Thought*, edited by Milena Carrara Pavan, 152–70. Cambridge, UK: James Clarke & Co., 2018.

Mir, Amene. "A Panentheist Reading of John Milbank." *Modern Theology* 28, no. 3 (2012): 526–60.

Montag, S. J., John. "Revelation: The False Legacy of Suarez." In *Radical Orthodoxy: A New Theology*, edited by John Milbank, Catherine Pickstock, and Graham Ward, 38–63. London and New York: Routledge, 1999.

172 *Bibliography*

Nagarjuna. *The Fundamental Wisdom of the Middle Way: Nagarjuna's Mulamadhyamikakarika.* Translated by Jay Garfield. New York: Oxford University Press, 1995.

Nancy, Jean-Luc. *Being Singular Plural.* Translated by Robert D. Richardson and Anne E. O'Bryne. Stanford, CA: Stanford University Press, 2000.

———. *The Inoperative Community.* Translated by Peter Connor. Vol. 76. Theory and History of Literature. Minneapolis: University of Minnesota Press, 1991.

———. *The Sense of the World.* Translated by Jeffrey S. Librett. Minneapolis: University of Minnesota Press, 1997.

Oliver, Simon. "Introducing Radical Orthodoxy: From Participation to Late Modernity." In *The Radical Orthodoxy Reader,* edited by John Milbank and Simon Oliver, 3–27. New York and London: Routledge, 2009.

Ortiz, Jared, ed. *With All the Fullness of God: Deification in Christian Tradition.* Lanham, MD: Lexington Press, 2021.

Pabst, Adrian. *Metaphysics: The Creation of Hierarchy.* Grand Rapids, MI: William B. Eerdmans, 2012.

Panikkar, Raimon. "A Self-Critical Dialogue." In *The Intercultural Challenge of Raimon Panikkar,* edited by Joseph Prabhu, 227–91. Maryknoll, NY: Orbis Books, 1996.

———. "Deity." In *Trinitarian and Cosmotheandric Vision.* Edited by Milena Carrara Pavan. Vol. VIII: 5–27. XII vols. Opera Omnia. Maryknoll, NY: Orbis Books, 2019.

———. *F. H. Jacobi y La Filosofía Del Sentimiento [F. H. Jacobi and the Philosophy of Sentiment].* Buenos Aires: Sapientia, 1948.

———. *Hinduism: The Dharma of India.* Edited by Milena Carrara Pavan. Vol. IV.2. XII vols. Opera Omnia. Maryknoll, NY: Orbis Books, 2017.

———. "Introduction." In *Trinitarian and Cosmotheandric Vision.* Edited by Milena Carrara Pavan. Vol. VIII: xiii–xv. XII vols. Opera Omnia. Maryknoll, NY: Orbis Books, 2019.

———. "Man as a Ritual Being." *Chicago Studies* 15, no. 1 (1977): 5–28.

———. "Man—A Trinitarian Mystery." In *Trinitarian and Cosmotheandric Vision.* Edited by Milena Carrara Pavan. Vol. VIII: 93–118. XII vols. Opera Omnia. Maryknoll, NY: Orbis Books, 2019.

———. *Mysticism and Spirituality: Mysticism, The Fullness of Life.* Edited by Milena Carrara Pavan. Vol. I.1. XII vols. Opera Omnia. Maryknoll, NY: Orbis Books, 2014.

———. *Myth, Faith, and Hermeneutics: Cross Cultural Studies.* New York: Paulist Press, 1979.

———. *Ontonomia de La Ciencia [Ontonomy of Science].* Madrid: Gredos, 1961.

———. *Philosophical and Theological Thought.* Edited by Milena Carrara Pavan. Vol. X.2. XII vols. Opera Omnia. Maryknoll, NY: Orbis Books, 2021.

———. *Sacred Secularity.* Edited by Milena Carrara Pavan. Vol. XI. XII vols. Opera Omnia. Maryknoll, NY: Orbis Books, 2022.

———. *The Cosmotheandric Experience: Emerging Religious Consciousness.* Edited by Scott Eastham. Maryknoll, NY: Orbis Books, 1993.

Bibliography

———. *The Intra-Religious Dialogue*. New York, ; Ramsay, NJ: Paulist Press, 1999.

———. "The Law of Karman and the Historical Dimension of Man." *Philosophy East and West* 22, no. 1 (1972): 25–43.

———. "The Myth of Pluralism: The Tower of Babel-A Meditation on Nonviolence." In *Cultures and Religions in Dialogue: Pluralism and Interculturality*. Edited by Milena Carrara Pavan. Vol. VI.1: 3–25. XII vols. Opera Omnia. Maryknoll, NY: Orbis Books, 2018.

———. *The Rhythm of Being: The Unbroken Trinity*. Maryknoll, NY: Orbis Books, 2010.

———. "Time and Sacrifice: The Sacrifice of Time and the Ritual of Modernity." In *Proceedings of the III Conference of the International Society for the Study of Time*. Edited by J. T. Fraser, N. Lawrence, and D. Park. Vol III: 683–725. The Study of Time. New York, Heidelberg, and Berlin: Springer-Verlag, 1978.

———. *Trinity and the Religious Experience of Man*. Maryknoll, NY: Orbis Books, 1973.

———. *Worship and Secular Man*. Maryknoll, NY: Orbis Books, 1973.

Parappally, Jacob. "Panikkar's Vision of Reality and Contextual Theology." *CIRPIT Review* 4 (2013): 217–26.

Peterson, Derrick. "No True Scotsman: On the Presence, Character, and Origin of the 'Scotus Story' in Radical Orthodoxy and Beyond." *A Greater Courage* (blog), July 23, 2016. http://agreatercourage.blogspot.com/2016/07/no-true-scotsman-on -presence-character.html; http://agreatercourage.blogspot.com/2016/07/no-true -scotsman-part-two-scotus-story.html.

Phan, Peter. "Raimon Panikkar's 'Eschatology': The Unpublished Chapter." In *Raimon Panikkar: A Companion to His Life and Thought*, edited by Peter Phan and Young-chan Ro, 242–57. Cambridge, UK: James Clarke & Co., 2018.

Pickstock, Catherine. *After Writing: On the Liturgical Consummation of Philosophy*. Malden, MA: Blackwell, 1998.

———. "Duns Scotus: His Historical and Contemporary Significance." *Modern Theology* 21, no. 4 (2005): 543–74.

———. "Postmodern Scholasticism: Critique of Postmodern Univocity." *Telos* 33, no. 4 (2003): 3–24.

Piper, John, and Justin Taylor. *The Supremacy of Christ in a Postmodern World*. Wheaton, IL: Crossway Books, 2007.

Prabhu, Joseph. "Panikkar's Trinitarianism and His Critique of (Mono) Theism." *CIRPIT Review* 5 (2014): 79–87.

Rambachan, Anantanand. *The Advaita Worldview: God, World, and Humanity*. Albany, NY: State University of New York Press, 2006.

Ro, Young-chan. "Relativism, Universalism, and Pluralism in an Age of Globalization." *CIRPIT Review* 3 (2012): 91–101.

Sammon, Brenden Thomas. "The Reawakening of the Between: William Desmond and Reason's Intimacy with Beauty." In *William Desmond and Contemporary Theology*, edited by Christopher Ben Simpson and Brenden Thomas Sammon, 15–56. Notre-Dame, IN: University of Notre-Dame Press, 2017.

174 *Bibliography*

Sammon, Brenden Thomas, and Christopher Ben Simpson. "Introduction." In *William Desmond and Contemporary Theology*, edited by Christopher Ben Simpson and Brenden Thomas Sammon, 1–13. Notre-Dame, IN: University of Notre-Dame Press, 2017.

Sartre, Jean-Paul. *Being and Nothingness*. New York: Washington Square Press, 1993.

Savari Raj, Anthony. *A New Hermeneutic of Reality: Raimon Panikkar's Cosmotheandric Vision*. New York: Peter Lang, 1998.

———. *Ecosophical Justice*. Bangalore: Capuchin Publication Trust, 2010.

Schindler, D. C. "The Positivity of Philosophy: William Desmond's Contribution to Theology." In *William Desmond and Contemporary Theology*, edited by Christopher Ben Simpson and Brenden Thomas Sammon, 117–37. Notre-Dame, IN: University of Notre-Dame Press, 2017.

Shakespeare, Steven. *Radical Orthodoxy: A Critical Introduction*. London: SPCK, 2007.

Smith, James K. A. *Awaiting the King: Reforming Public Theology*. Vol. 3. 3 vols. Cultural Liturgies. Grand Rapids, MI: Baker Academic, 2017.

———. *Desiring the Kingdom: Worship, Worldview, and Cultural Formation*. Vol. 1. 3 vols. Cultural Liturgies. Grand Rapids, MI: Baker Academic, 2009.

———. *How (Not) to Be Secular: Reading Charles Taylor*. Grand Rapids, MI: William B. Eerdmans, 2014.

———. *Imagining the Kingdom: How Worship Works*. Vol. 2. 3 vols. Cultural Liturgies. Grand Rapids, MI: Baker Academic, 2013.

———. *Introducing Radical Orthodoxy: Mapping a Post-Secular Theology*. Grand Rapids, MI: Baker Academic, 2004.

———. "Secular Liturgies and the Prospects for a 'Post-Secular' Sociology of Religion." In *The Post-Secular in Question: Religion in Contemporary Society*, edited by Philip S. Gorski, David Kyumankim, John Torpey, and Jonathan VanAntwerpen, 159–84. London and New York: New York University Press and Social Science Research Council, 2012.

———. *Who's Afraid of Postmodernism?: Taking Derrida, Lyotard, and Foucault to Church*. Grand Rapids, MI: Baker Academic, 2004.

———. *You Are What You Love: The Spiritual Power of Habit*. Grand Rapids, MI: Brazos Press, 2016.

Smith, Nicholas H. *Charles Taylor: Meaning, Morals, and Modernity*. Malden, MA: Polity Press, 2002.

Svetelj, Tone. "Rereading Modernity—Charles Taylor on Its Genesis and Prospects." Chestnut Hill, MA: Boston College, 2012.

Taylor, Charles. *A Secular Age*. Cambridge, MA: The Belknap Press of Harvard University Press, 2007.

———. "Atomism." In *Philosophy and Human Sciences*, 187–210. Philosophical Papers 2. Cambridge, MA: Harvard University Press, 1985.

———. *Dilemmas and Connections*. Cambridge, MA: Harvard University Press, 2011.

———. "Engaged Agency and Background in Heidegger." In *The Cambridge Companion to Heidegger*, edited by Charles Guignon, Second Edition, 202–21. Cambridge, UK: Cambridge University Press, 2006.

————. *Human Agency and Language*. Philosophical Papers 1. Cambridge, UK: Cambridge University Press, 1985.

————. "Introduction." In *Human Agency and Language*, 1–12. Philosophical Papers 1. Cambridge, MA: Harvard University Press, 1985.

————. "Language and Human Nature." In *Human Agency and Language*, 215–47. Philosophical Papers 1. Cambridge, MA: Harvard University Press, 1985.

————. *Modern Social Imaginaries*. Durham, NC: Duke University Press, 2004.

————. "Modes of Secularism." In *Secularism and Its Critics*, edited by Rajeev Bhargava, 31–53. Delhi: Oxford University Press, 1998.

————. "Overcoming Epistemology." In *Philosophical Arguments*, 1–19. Cambridge, MA: Harvard University Press, 1995.

————. *Philosophical Arguments*. Cambridge, MA: Harvard University Press, 1995.

————. "Rationality." In *Philosophy and Human Sciences*, 134–51. Philosophical Papers 2. Cambridge, MA: Harvard University Press, 1985.

————. "Self-Interpreting Animals." In *Human Agency and Language*, 45–76. Philosophical Papers 1. Cambridge, MA: Harvard University Press, 1985.

————. *Sources of the Self: The Making of the Modern Identity*. Cambridge, MA: The Belknap Press of Harvard University Press, 1989.

————. "The Concept of a Person." In *Human Agency and Language*, 97–114. Philosophical Papers 1. Cambridge, MA: Harvard University Press, 1985.

————. "The Importance of Herder." In *Philosophical Arguments*, 79–99. Cambridge, MA: Harvard University Press, 1995.

————. *The Language Animal*. Cambridge, MA: The Belknap Press of Harvard University Press, 2016.

————. *The Malaise of Modernity: The CBC Massey Lectures*. Toronto: House of Anansi Press, 1991.

————. "Theories of Meaning." In *Human Agency and Language*, 248–92. Philosophical Papers 1. Cambridge, MA: Harvard University Press, 1985.

Thistleton, Anthony C. *Interpreting God and the Postmodern Self: On Meaning, Manipulation, and Promise*. Grand Rapids, MI: William B. Eerdmans, 1995.

Thomson, Ian D. *Heidegger on Ontotheology: Technology and the Politics of Education*. Cambridge, UK: Cambridge University Press, 2005.

————. "Ontotheology." In *Interpreting Heidegger: Critical Essays*, edited by Daniel Dahlstrom, 106–31. Cambridge, UK: Cambridge University Press, 2011.

————. "Ontotheology? Understanding Heidegger's Destruktion of Metaphysics." *International Journal of Philosophical Studies* 8, no. 3 (2000): 297–327.

Thrasher, Andrew D. "A Glossary of Panikkarean Terms." In *Raimon Panikkar: A Companion to His Life and Thought*, edited by Peter Phan and Young-chan Ro, 271–81. Cambridge, UK: James Clarke & Co., 2018.

————. "Fantastic Inter-Religious Resourcement in Robert Jordan and David Eddings." In *Theology, Fantasy, and the Imagination*, edited by Andrew D. Thrasher and Austin M. Freeman, 133–53. Lanham, MD: Rowman & Littlefield, 2023.

Tillich, Paul. *The Courage to Be*. Second Edition. New Haven, CT: Yale University Press, 1952.

————. *The Dynamics of Faith*. New York: Perennial Classics, 2001.

Bibliography

Tonner, Philip. "The Univocity of Being: With Special Reference to the Doctrines of John Duns Scotus and Martin Heidegger." Glasglow: The University of Glasglow, 2006.

Tutewiler, Corey Benjamin. "On the Cause of Metaphysical Indeterminacy and the Origin of Being." In *William Desmond and Contemporary Theology*, edited by Christopher Ben Simpson and Brenden Thomas Sammon, 93–116. Notre-Dame, IN: University of Notre-Dame Press, 2017.

Tuttle, Howard N. *The Crowd Is Untruth: The Existential Critique of Mass Society in the Thought of Kierkegaard, Nietzsche, Heidegger, and Ortega y Gasset*. New York: Peter Lang, 1996.

Vanheeswijck, Guido. "The End of Secularization?" In *Rethinking Secularization: Philosophy and the Prophecy of a Secular Age*, edited by Herbert De Vriese and Gary Gabor, 1–26. Newcastle Upon Tyne: Cambridge Scholars Publishing, 2009.

Ward, Bruce. "Transcendence and Immanence in a Subtler Language: The Presence of Dostoevsky in Charles Taylor's Account of Secularity." In *Aspiring to Fullness in a Secular Age: Essays on Religion and Theology in the Work of Charles Taylor*, edited by Carlos Colorado and Justin Klassen, 262–90. Notre-Dame, IN: University of Notre-Dame Press, 2014.

Ward, Graham. *Cities of God*. London and New York: Routledge, 2000.

Ward, Keith. *Concepts of God: Images of the Divine in Five Religious Traditions*. Oxford: Oneworld, 1998.

———. *Religion and Creation*. Oxford: Clarendon Press, 1996.

———. *Religion and Human Nature*. Oxford: Clarendon Press, 1998.

Wiitala, Michael. "The Metaphysics of Duns Scotus and Onto-Theology." *Philosophy Today* 53 (2009): 158–63.

Williams, Paul. "On the Abhidharma Ontology." *Journal of Indian Philosophy* 9, no. 3 (1981): 227–57.

Williams, Thomas. "The Doctrine of Univocity Is True and Salutary." *Modern Theology* 21, no. 4 (2005): 575–85.

Zizioulas, John. "Human Capacity and Human Incapacity: A Theological Exploration of Personhood." In *Communion and Otherness*, edited by Paul McPartlan, 206–49. New York: T&T Clark, 2006.

———. "On Being Other." In *Communion and Otherness*, edited by Paul McPartlan, 13–98. New York: T&T Clark, 2006.

Index

action, 3, 8, 29, 32–34, 103, 119, 144, 147, 149, 152–55

advaita, 2–17, 21, 24, 26, 34–35, 39–41, 45–46, 49–52, 54–55, 57–59, 61–62, 67–69, 71–73, 83–86, 89, 97, 99–101, 104–5, 111–12, 129–34, 147–50, 159–65

autonomy, 40, 78, 80, 82, 89–92, 94–96, 99–101, 104–5, 113–14, 116, 123–25, 133, 148, 150–51, 153, 160–61

Being, 3, 4, 8, 11, 13, 15, 16, 21–22, 25–43, 45–65, 68, 70–85, 87, 89–107, 113–15, 118–26, 128–33, 136, 138–39, 142–44, 146–51, 153–54, 157, 159–64

Brahman, 18, 20–21, 73

Buddhism, 1, 6, 15, 16, 18, 34, 36–37, 55, 57, 59, 64, 73, 132

Catholic, 1–3, 87, 112, 133, 163–65

Clooney, Francis, 2

Comparative Theology, 2

cosmotheandrism, 2–26, 32–40, 42, 52–53, 57, 59, 67–68, 71, 73, 83–87, 101, 104, 108, 112, 117, 128–32, 136, 138, 141–42, 148–50, 154–55, 157, 159–64

cultural invariant, 11, 16–18, 20–21

Cunningham, Conor, 91–92, 105–7, 114, 119, 135–36

D'Sa, Francis X., 23, 60, 65, 138, 147–48, 157

Dao, 18, 56–57

Dasein, 26–29, 46–49, 54, 162

dependent co-origination, 55, 57, 131

Desmond, William, 1, 2, 4, 62, 67–68, 70, 74–89, 160, 164

dualism, 5, 11–13, 15, 19, 67–68, 72, 81, 84–85, 99, 120, 146–47

equivocity, 18, 25, 52, 72, 76–79, 82, 92

finitude/infinitude, 3, 7, 32, 40–41, 46, 49–51, 53, 68–71, 74, 76, 78–79, 81–86, 92–93, 97–100, 102–3, 108, 113–15, 117, 131, 150, 159, 162–63

fundamental ontology, 4, 25–29, 31, 34, 45, 47–49, 61, 120, 162

God, 3–5, 10–15, 18, 20–22, 25, 29–30, 32–33, 35–37, 40, 45–46, 49–53, 56–61, 68–71, 73–83, 87–88, 90–93, 95–98, 100–106, 112–34, 138, 141–50, 152, 154–55, 159–64

178 *Index*

harmony, 5–7, 9–13, 17–19, 22, 25, 38–40, 67–69, 71–73, 84–86, 101, 118, 133, 148–50, 153–54, 162

Hart, David Bentley, 1–2, 89, 97–101

Heidegger, Martin, 1–4, 25–28, 30–32, 34, 39, 41, 45–57, 59–65, 74, 81–82, 86, 89, 95, 102, 106–7, 111–12, 118–20, 122–24, 127, 134, 160, 162, 164, 165

heteronomy, 78, 148–51, 153

Hinduism, 1, 9, 12–13, 16, 18–21, 23, 34, 57, 59, 64, 73, 132, 165

homeomorphic equivalents, 17–21

immanence, 2–4, 7, 13, 15, 17, 19, 34–36, 46, 49, 53, 56–62, 67–69, 71–86, 92, 98–101, 103–5, 107, 111–12, 120, 131–33, 141–42, 145, 147, 150, 152, 154, 159–60, 162–64

Incarnation, 12, 20–21, 36, 77, 97, 101, 160

incommensurability, 6, 17–18, 20–21, 31, 69, 86, 131, 134

Indian/Indic, 1–2, 4–6, 34, 52, 54–55, 112, 132–33, 159, 163–64

inter-religious dialogue, 1, 6, 9, 108, 133

Karma, 6, 57

Levinas, Emmanuel, 1–2, 75, 89, 97–100, 108, 119, 165

liturgy, 3, 20, 32–33, 92, 125–26, 142, 149, 151–52, 154–55

Lubac, Henri de, 3, 8

mathexis, 112, 125

metaphysics, 2–4, 6–7, 9–12, 16–20, 22, 25, 45–46, 49–62, 67–69, 73–86, 89, 97, 99, 107, 112, 114, 120, 124–25, 132–33, 136–37, 146, 159–60, 162–64

metaxu, 62, 67–68, 74–85, 160, 164

Milbank, John, 1, 97, 105–7, 111–13, 115, 117, 119–26, 128, 132–37, 157, 163–64

monism, 5–6, 11, 15, 19, 67–68, 72–73, 84–85, 99, 147

mystery, 6, 9, 15, 17–20, 37, 40, 60, 63, 70, 73–74, 83, 85–86, 92, 133, 153, 163–64

Mythicization, 4, 151–53, 155

mythos, 53, 102, 155

Nagarjuna, 55, 64

Nancy, Jean-Luc, 1–2, 4, 25–26, 28, 30–31, 34, 39, 97

Nouvelle Theologie, 3, 131, 133, 161

ontological difference, 45, 47, 50, 59, 82, 114

ontological distinction, 2–4, 45–47, 49–51, 55–57, 81–82, 84–85, 101, 114, 131–32, 159–60, 162–64

ontological question, 3, 5, 25–27, 30, 39–40, 45–48, 51, 53–54, 89–90, 93, 96, 101–4, 119, 160–62

ontonomy, 3–4, 11–13, 25–26, 32–40, 101, 123, 129–32, 134, 148, 150–51, 153–55, 163

onto-theology, 4, 45, 49–51, 54, 61, 82, 115, 119, 123–24, 160

Ordinary Life, 4, 29–33, 90, 93, 141, 144, 151–55

pars pro toto, 6, 22, 32, 38, 40, 129

participation, 3–12, 15, 20–22, 29–41, 45–46, 56–61, 73, 79, 83–85, 89–97, 99–101, 103–4, 111–13, 115, 123–34, 144–45, 149–55, 161–63

perichoresis, 10–15, 19, 34, 38, 60, 123, 129–31

phenomenology, 2, 6, 10, 13–14, 37, 49, 52–53, 74, 119, 142, 165

Pickstock, Catherine, 1, 50, 115

pluralism, 1, 5–6, 15–16, 19, 36, 51, 70, 72, 77, 112, 120, 133, 142, 145, 164

Index

plurivocity, 6, 9, 17–19, 21, 31, 49, 51–52, 56, 61, 73–74, 76, 163

postmodern, 1–5, 74, 85–86, 89–91, 93, 95–101, 104–5, 111–14, 117, 119, 123–24, 126, 128–29, 132, 134, 148, 150, 159–65

postsecular, 4, 141–49, 151–55

pratityatsamudpada, 10–12, 15–16, 34, 36–37, 55, 57, 130

Protestant, 125, 146, 151–52, 161, 165

Radical Orthodoxy, 1–2, 4, 86, 91, 105, 111–15, 123–26, 128, 132, 134, 160, 164

Radical Relativity, 6–7, 9–12, 15–17, 20, 36–39, 129–30, 132

relation, 3, 5–7, 9–13, 15–16, 20, 22, 25–41, 45–46, 48–51, 54, 57–60, 67–68, 78–84, 92–93, 95, 97–98, 100–104, 111–12, 116, 120–21, 123–24, 127, 129–34, 142–43, 146–47, 149–51, 153–55, 159–63

relational ontology, 3–4, 9, 15–16, 22, 25–26, 28–34, 39–40, 45, 96, 103, 111, 123, 129–33, 160, 163

representation, 7, 57, 94–96, 112, 115–18, 123, 127, 133–34, 161

resourcement, 1, 111–28, 130–34, 155

ritual, 3, 33, 126, 144, 147, 149, 151–55

Romantic, 74, 111–12, 118–23, 127, 133–34

sacralization, 3–4, 141, 147–48, 151–55, 160

sacred secularity, 3–4, 32–34, 39, 86, 141–55, 159–60

Śaṅkara, 6

secularism, 93, 113–14, 124, 141–42, 145–47, 153

secularization, 2–4, 91–93, 113, 118, 141–47, 151–55, 161

shunyata, 6, 18, 34, 57, 59, 70

Taylor, Charles, 1–2, 4, 25–26, 29–32, 34, 39, 86, 90, 93–94, 105, 111–12, 115–23, 128, 132–33, 141–47, 149, 151–52, 154, 160, 163–64

tempiternity, 4, 45–46, 49, 51, 59–61, 73, 83–86, 148–49, 155, 160, 163

transcendence, 2–4, 7, 13, 19, 32, 35, 46, 48–50, 53, 56, 60, 62, 67–86, 90, 92–93, 98–103, 112–13, 120–21, 123–26, 128, 131–34, 142, 144–45, 147, 150–52, 154–55, 159–64

trinitarian, 3, 5, 9–15, 17, 19–20, 34–35, 38, 72, 86, 99, 123, 154, 159

Trinity, 6, 11–15, 18–19, 34–35, 99, 123, 130, 165

univocity, 18, 25, 45–46, 49–52, 59, 61, 67–68, 72, 74, 76–79, 82, 91–92, 112–17, 123, 134, 152

Vedānta, 6, 16, 21

work, 152–55

worship, 3, 17, 32–33, 111, 125–26, 150, 152–55

About the Author

Andrew D. Thrasher is a part-time professor and instructor of religious studies at George Mason University and in the Virginia Community College System, where he regularly teaches courses on Asian and comparative religions. He is a contributor to Peter Phan and Young-chan Ro's recent festschrift on Raimon Panikkar and regularly writes, publishes, and presents on Raimon Panikkar. His work on Panikkar won honorable mention for the 2022 International Panikkar Prize. He currently resides in Virginia outside of Washington, DC.